THE UNFINISHED TASK

THE
UNFINISHED TASK

by

STEPHEN NEILL

EDINBURGH HOUSE PRESS
2 EATON GATE, LONDON, S.W.1

★ ★ ★

LUTTERWORTH PRESS
4 BOUVERIE STREET, LONDON, E.C.4

First Published 1957
Second Impression 1958

MADE AND PRINTED IN GREAT BRITAIN BY
MORRISON AND GIBB LIMITED, LONDON AND EDINBURGH

CONTENTS

CHAPTER   PAGE

1. THE UNFINISHED CHURCH   7

2. THE COMING GENERATION   35

3. FRONTIER SITUATIONS AND FLEXIBLE MINISTRIES   53

4. THE CHURCH AND CHANGING SOCIETY   69

5. THE PROBLEM OF A CHRISTIAN CULTURE   95

6. THE UNFINISHED TASK IN THE YOUNGER CHURCHES   111

7. DYNAMIC WITNESS   146

8. THE DYNAMIC MINORITY   168

9. WHICH WAY DO WE GO?   200

INDEX   225

CHAPTER I

THE UNFINISHED CHURCH

THE task of the Church is an unfinished task, and always will be. This affirmation is made not on the basis of any theological presupposition, but simply in recognition of the fact that the Church exists in history, and that history is the scene of perpetual change. Some religious systems disregard history or deny its importance. Not so the Bible. The Bible teaches that history is the sphere, the medium, in and through which God has chosen to carry out His purposes for the world, and that therefore He can achieve those purposes only in certain ways and not in others. We are in the Church, and we are in history. We are called to take a hand in the fulfilment of the purposes of God. It will help us, if we can come to a right understanding of the conditions under which those purposes are coming to fruition.

Historians inevitably tend to make history appear simpler than it is. In order to deal with its multiplicity at all, they have to select, to co-ordinate, to work out certain lines of development. From the vantage-point of the historian and his readers, it is easy to see why certain events took place just as they did, why certain decisions were the right ones, and led on to consequences that can now clearly be discerned. The point of view of the actors may have been very different from that of the readers. We tend to forget the element of sheer contingency in events, the ignorance under which those who had to make vital decisions laboured, the chances which nearly came off but just failed to do so, the accidents of death and disease that could not have been foreseen, and yet changed the history of the world. It is with the history of the Church as with any other history. We can now see a continuity across the centuries, and can trace the lines of God's providential guidance, at least in the main lines of the development. We forget too readily that none of these things was obvious to the men of earlier times. The Church too had to meet crises for which it was quite unprepared; it had to answer unexpected questions; it had to make decisions, when the materials on which a sound decision could be based were hardly available. In Church history also the element of contingency is clearly marked.

In history there are few absolute beginnings, and few achievements so permanent that they never need to be repeated. The Church has to its credit certain great accomplishments, which have left their mark on all its subsequent history. For instance, in the second century the Canon of the New Testament was fixed, within certain narrow limits of variation, and since then has never been seriously questioned. But the existence of the Canon would not in itself guarantee the vitality of the Church, if the books remained unread, or, still worse, if they became merely a collection of proof-texts, cited mechanically and without reference to their origin ; in a very real sense each generation is called to a rediscovery of the New Testament for itself. The great Councils defined the faith. It is most unlikely that the work of Nicea and Constantinople will ever have to be done again. But the formulation of that faith did not of itself prevent the spread of heresy within the Church. Nothing remains exactly as it was. Old questions raise their heads in new forms ; and though the ancient formulations of the answers may still be valid, it does not follow that the mere repetition of the old phrases will serve to answer all the questions of later generations. The faith remains the same, but it can be kept in life only by the perpetual renewal of thought and conviction.

Looking back from the twentieth century, we can trace a fairly steady line of advance of the Gospel through the world. But we can do so only by ignoring many aberrations and dead-ends, many reverses and retreats. Professor Latourette has appropriately named one of the volumes of his great *History* " The Thousand Years of Uncertainty." Christianity twice entered China, and was twice thrown out, before the Jesuits succeeded in establishing a more permanent foothold. Advance into central and north-eastern Europe was spasmodic, and accompanied by many withdrawals before advance was secured. In our own time promising beginnings of the Church in certain countries have been totally destroyed. Some formerly Christian areas have been lost to non-Christian faiths. Even in countries nominally Christian, defection from the faith has become so widespread as to make it doubtful whether the term Christian can still be used of these countries. Even where the task appeared to have been finished long ago, it seems that it must be taken up afresh almost from the beginning.

There is a tendency among theologians to speak of the Church as though it were some sacrosanct entity, existing in a realm of its own, and untouched by any of the influences of a very secular and imperfect world. That is not the way in which things work themselves out in history. The Church is undoubtedly a divine society, but it is also a society immersed in history, and must live perpetually in action and reaction with the societies by which it is surrounded. Very few metals can be worked in the pure state. It is the art of the metallurgist to discover just those alloys which make gold or iron most effectively workable for the particular purposes in view. Pure Christian truth exists; but it has in fact been able to incorporate itself in the life of men only in the form of an alloy, through admixture of some of the forms and processes of their ordinary thought. This process is going on to-day. Even in western Europe Christians of the various nations do not think in quite the same way; they express their experiences in varying forms of worship. One of the greatest of the achievements of the early Church was the adoption of Greek thought-forms for the expression of the truth. It is unlikely that we shall ever be able to free ourselves completely from the tradition that was thus established; we have roots in the traditions both of Israel and of Greece. But there is always the danger that the proportions of the various metals may be wrong, and that the alloy may thus lose its effectiveness. In various parts of the theological world to-day there is the feeling that the Greek element has too much predominated, and that we must look much more to the Hebraic approach, with its greater directness and concreteness, if we are to recover the power of the Gospel. As in other fields, so also in the field of theological thought, the task of the Church is not finished, but must be taken up again in the light of the new tasks that God lays upon each generation.

None of these things need depress or alarm us, if we are prepared to take our stand firmly within history, and to recognize the twofold nature of the purpose of God. It is an eternal purpose, and therefore, because God is true, it must come to its destined fulfilment. But at the same time it is a purpose that works itself out in history through many failures and frustrations, and through the sinful and imperfect will of human beings. We stand within that purpose, and at a particular point of the unfinished task of the Church. Like our predecessors, we have to face unforeseen crises, to attempt to answer unexpected questions, to make decisions where the data for such decisions are sadly lacking. We are called to move forward into a future which is as uncertain to us as it will be clear to those who come after us. We can learn much from the past, if we do not make the mistake of supposing that it ever exactly repeats itself in the present. By looking out on the world situation in the present, we can acquire some idea of where we are to-day in the purposes of God. We can look out on the future with confidence, because it is God's future, and He will not let it fall out of His control. But it will help to guard us against undue optimism, and against undue disappointment at the failure of illusions, if we can arrive at a correct understanding of the place of the Church in the providence of God, of what can be expected of the Church and what should not be expected of it, and of how through the Church God can be served in the present generation. The more we can free ourselves from error and from illusion, the better fitted we shall be to take up our appointed post with alertness and with intelligent devotion.

One of the most fruitful sources of misunderstanding has been the identification of the Church with the Kingdom of God. In Scripture the Kingdom of God always means the Sovereignty of God, personally and directly exercised. Since the term is itself ambivalent, and in most languages has other associations and meanings, it is all too easy to begin to think of the Kingdom of God in terms of a geographical or social area within which God is at work, in terms of institutions or organizations through which His work is carried on. The error is most clearly identifiable in its Roman Catholic and its liberal forms.

In Roman Catholic theology there is an almost total identification of the Kingdom with the Church. This leads by natural degrees to the idea of a Vicar, through whom an absent Sovereign visibly exercises His authority ; to the necessity of an independent earthly Kingdom, however small, for the Pope ; and to the combination of royal and priestly authority in a single man. If the premise is false, if, that is to say, the relation between Church and Kingdom is really other than is implied in this theology, these conclusions can hardly be sustained.

After the first world war there was a great renewal of interest in the idea of the Kingdom of God, though without an adequate rediscovery of the biblical theology in the light of which the term has to be understood. Especially in Anglo-Saxon countries it was common to speak of the Kingdom as something which man could bring about by his own efforts, or at least in the bringing in of which he could co-operate with God. Thus preachers spoke of establishing the Kingdom of God, extending it, bringing it in ; and often the Kingdom was thought of in somewhat humanitarian terms, as the extension of earthly justice and the maintenance of peace, rather than as that ultimate criterion by which all man's poor efforts are judged. A reference to the New Testament should have been sufficient to warn such preachers that they were not on the lines of the original Gospel. In the New Testament it is God's will to *give* His little flock the Kingdom. The Kingdom can be proclaimed as good news. Men can receive it, or enter it, or even force their way into it. They can inherit a Kingdom long since prepared for them. But in all these phrases man is, in the modern phrase, on the re-ceiving end. The sovereignty remains with God—the Kingdom is His act, His power. What part man may be called to play in relation to the Kingdom we shall consider later ; but no confusion must be allowed between the role of God and the role of man in relation to it.

A further reference to the New Testament may clear up a number of points on which Christian thought is not always as clear as it should be. It is well known that in the Gospels the message of the Kingdom is central, whereas the word " Church " occurs only twice, both times in the Gospel of Matthew (16 : 18 ; 18 : 17) ; both times in contexts which would be widely recognized as belonging to a late stage in the development of the Gospel tradition. In the visions of the end in the closing chapters of the Book of Revelation, the Church as such does not appear. References to the Kingdom again become frequent, from Rev. 11 : 15 (" The kingdom of the world is become the kingdom of our Lord, and of his Christ ; and he shall reign for ever and ever " [1]) onwards. There is indeed a message in Rev. 22 : 16 to " the churches " ; but in Revelation " the churches " are the struggling, afflicted churches, called to pass through the great tribulation. In the visions of glory the redeemed

---

[1] Note the very important theological difference between this, the R.V. and correct translation, and " the kingdoms of this world ", found in the A.V.

appear not as the Church, but under the similitudes of the bride, of the people of God and of the city.

In the Acts and Epistles, by contrast, references to the Kingdom are few and far between, and the Church and the Churches are in the centre of the stage. The reason perhaps is partly indicated at the beginning of the Acts, when the disciples ask, " Lord, dost thou at this time restore the kingdom to Israel ? " (Acts 1 : 6). Naturally the question as asked cannot receive a direct answer, since it is wrongly framed ; but the answer that is given, with the contrast between the " times or seasons, which the Father hath set within his own authority " and the present gift of the Holy Spirit, seems to indicate that the manifestation of the Kingdom is a secret of the time of the end, whereas the Church is to live in the epoch of the Holy Spirit, during which the sovereignty of God is withdrawn from direct apprehension, but is present as a hidden reality, discernible only by faith and operative within the fellowship of the Holy Spirit.

It is never wise to base an argument too exclusively on words. But words, after all, are the outward signs of things ; and, if we are right in attributing importance to this change of usage in the various books of the New Testament, this change itself may help to clear up many misunderstandings as to the nature of the Church. It would indicate, to use a convenient German term, the nature of the Church as existing *zwischen den Zeiten*, between the epochs. In Jesus of Nazareth the Kingdom of God was visibly present among men. His mighty works were the signs of the presence of the Kingdom, of that authority which God was directly exercising upon earth in the person of His anointed Servant. At the end of the days that Kingdom will again be manifest in power, in a way that at present we are not able even to imagine, in what is commonly called the Second Coming of Christ. In between is the long period which is to be filled in by the ministry of the Church. The Church is provisional and transitory. It takes its origin in the proclamation of the Kingdom ; at the end it will itself be merged into the manifest and triumphant Kingdom. This is not to say that the Church is unimportant ; indeed, in the epoch of its operation, the epoch of the Holy Spirit, it is all-important. It is not itself the Kingdom, but it is the point at which the now hidden Kingdom impinges upon the life of earth. Every proclamation of the word of God by the Church is a testimony to the reality of the Kingdom. Every victory of an individual Christian over sin is a revelation of the power of the Kingdom. Every act of mercy done in the Name of Christ is a manifestation of its nature. And yet the Church is always subject to the judgment of the Kingdom, since it can never more than so very imperfectly represent the majestic perfection of the Sovereignty of God.

If we have rightly understood this transitory nature of the Church and its true relationship to the Kingdom, we are likely to be much less disturbed than otherwise we would be by its all too evident imperfections. The mixed and miscellaneous character of the Church has made it all through the centuries the target for the criticism of its foes, from the pagan critics of the early centuries, Celsus and the Emperor Julian the Apostate, who poured scorn on the queer rag, tag and bobtail that the Church of that day had managed to gather into itself, down to the complacent scorn of the Brahman of to-day for the thousands of oppressed and illiterate outcastes, who in many parts of India constitute the Church. It is not only the critics from outside who can see the weakness of the Church. The Christian himself can hardly read its story with complacency. Bishop Lightfoot did indeed say that the study of history is a cordial for drooping spirits, and this is true if history is taken in large enough quantities and over long enough periods. But much of Christian history is dreadfully depressing. There have been so many great betrayals, so much persecution of Christians by Christians, so many periods of dark corruption ; and, what is worst of all, so much of the terrible and self-complacent mediocrity of the average Christian congregation. If we have been tempted to identify the Church with the Kingdom, or to suppose that it is through its ministry that the Kingdom is to be brought in, we might well despair. If we recognize it in its true character as the witness to the Kingdom, no wiser and no more perfect than were the Apostles in the days after the Resurrection, and yet equally with them the accredited witness to the Resurrection of Jesus Christ, we shall not be unduly disturbed by those manifold imperfections of which we cannot but be painfully aware.

The great controversies about the person of Christ and about the relationship of the divine and the human in Him are curiously illuminating also in relation to the doctrine of the Church.

The Monophysites laid great stress on the unity of the person of Christ, such stress indeed, that they were in danger of slipping over into the error of teaching that in Him the human element was so absorbed by the divine as no longer to have separate existence. Eutyches was condemned as heretical precisely for refusing to admit that on one side Christ was " of one substance " with us as on the other He is " of one substance " with the Father. Clearly there is a Monophysite view of the Church. There are those who see the Church always under its divine and perfect aspect, as the glorious body which directly carries on the work of Christ. Christians may sin and may be divided ; the Church can never sin and can never be divided, because it is the body of the one and sinless Christ. This view, impressive and strongly held as it is, can be maintained only through a certain unwillingness to accept the all-too-human element in the Church, and makes a separation between the Church and the Christian which is hardly justifiable, since the Church on earth can live its life only in the lives of its members. It is true that, within the Church, we are within the sphere in which the Sovereignty of God is at work, and this must never be forgotten. But even within that sphere we are still imperfect, wilful, and only very gradually transformed according to the likeness of Christ. The only Church we know is one which shares in the weakness and imperfections of its members.

The other great heresy was Nestorianism. The Nestorians were accused, perhaps falsely, of teaching that in Christ two Sons, one divine and one human, co-existed, bound together only by the link of moral consent and not substantially. The Church rightly saw that this involved such a separation between the divine and the human as made it virtually impossible to maintain the unity of the one Christ. Clearly there is also a Nestorian view of the Church. Some people make such a distinction between the invisible and the visible Church that it is hard to see that they really have very much to do with one another. The invisible Church, which is known to God alone, is to them all important. It is by faith alone that a man belongs to this invisible Church, and that is a matter between him and God alone. The visible Church is accepted, if it is accepted at all, only as a rather regrettable necessity. It is recognized as being in some sense the body of Christ on earth ; but the visible and the invisible live their lives as it were in parallel, neither in reality having very much to do with the other.

In 451 the Council of Chalcedon settled the question of the doctrine of the Person of Christ, by affirming that " as the reasonable soul and flesh is one man, so God and man is one Christ ". To do justice to the mystery of Christ we must lay equal stress on the divine and on the human sides. The life that He lived was a truly and fully human life ; and yet in that life it was God Himself who was the experiencing subject. How this could be, Chalcedon does not try fully to state, and the mystery remains ; but any other doctrine does less than justice to one side or the other of the Person of Jesus Christ, both God and Man. And here we come near to the true understanding of the Church. It is the body of Christ. It is divine, because it is the instrument of a divine purpose ; but of a purpose which God will not carry out in any other way than through the co-operation of the imperfect and sinful wills of men and women. The Church is made up of human beings in all stages of imperfection ; yet it is of them that God has said, " I will be to them a God, and they shall be to me a people ". It is not that the invisible Church is divine, and the visible is human ; that the invisible Church is perfect, and the visible Church is imperfect. No such division may be made without tearing apart the whole fabric of the Church's life. If Christ is one Christ, very God and very Man, the Church of which He is the Founder and the Life, divine and human as it is, must still be one Church.

Of course we must be careful not to press this parallel too far. What Christ took upon Himself was our nature " apart from sin " ; what we bring to Him is a nature that needs through Him to be cleansed of sin, and in this life is never perfectly cleansed. The expression " the extension of the Incarnation ", as sometimes used of the Church, is misleading, since only a sinless Church could truly continue the sinless life of the Incarnate Lord. The true extension of the Incarnation is the Holy Spirit, through whom the risen Christ lives and reigns in the Church, and through whom with infinite toil and labour He is bringing it to that perfection which from the beginning it was destined according to His will to inherit.

In the light of the Chalcedonian Christology, we shall not expect the Church, as we know it, to be either sinless, or infallible, at any given time or in any one form of its existence. We shall, however, expect it to be *indefectible*. Truth may be menaced, for a time may be held only by a small minority of the faithful ; yet, because it is God's truth, it cannot finally be lost but in the end will reassert itself. Over long periods the Church[1] may grow corrupt and may seem much more dead than alive ; but in the end new life will come, and it is always within the Church itself, though not infrequently only on its margin, that the springs of new life are found. It is this fact that gives the assurance that, though the inner and outer conflicts of the Church will last as long as time itself, at the end of the days the Church will be found still existing as the pillar and ground of the truth.

How, then, to come to more positive formulations, are we to think of the Church ? People never define that which they take for granted. It is only when the accustomed and the familiar is challenged that an attempt has to be made to say what it means and why it is important. The faith of the Church came to be defined only as it was called in question by one heresy after another. And, since from an early period in Christian history, the Church was taken for granted by everybody, it is not altogether surprising that the last area of theology to be seriously studied has been precisely the doctrine of the nature of the Church. In the *Summa* of St. Thomas Aquinas, which deals with almost all things upon earth and a great many in heaven, there is no section *De Ecclesia, On the Church*. Moreover, when the problem of the Church was raised, politically at the end of the Middle Ages, more theologically in the Reformation, the natural tendency was for men to define the Church in terms of that which they knew, that is to say, to rationalize their own experience rather than to ask the fundamental question about the place of the Church in the purposes of God. We may find reason to think that some of the things they said and wrote need to be reconsidered in the light of a deeper understanding of the nature of the Church.

In the first place, it is evident that, when in the Apostles' Creed we say that we believe in the Holy Catholic (i.e. Universal) Church, we are expressing our faith in something which is coming into existence, but does not, as universal, yet exist. In principle the

---

[1] Consideration of space makes it impossible to discuss here the immensely important question of " the Church and the Churches ", the relationship between the one Body of Christ, and the fragmentary societies each of which claim the name of Church. I may perhaps refer to the study of this question in my book *The Christian Society* (Nisbet, 1950).

Church has been universal from the beginning. Christ died for all men ; and therefore the Gospel must be preached to all men, and disciples must be won from every nation. But that is a task which is not yet accomplished ; there is a fulness of universality into which the Church has yet to grow, and in which alone the perfection of its nature can be revealed.

The ground plan of the Church, in its doctrine, its worship, and its organization, is already discernible in the New Testament. To this we must constantly refer, and anything which clearly falls outside that plan must be regarded as false, or at least as unessential to the structure. But to have the ground plan of a cathedral is not to see the building in all the splendour of its completion, and in all the bewildering variety of delights with which successive architects, working in freedom within the limits of the original design, have enriched its growth. It was a serious misfortune that in the third century the word " catholic " changed its meaning, and came to be identified almost wholly with that orthodoxy of the Church's belief, which would better have been included under the term " apostolic ". Other aspects were not wholly lost sight of ; but the emphasis was mainly on the givenness of the Church, on what we have received from the past, and far less on the other aspect of creative development. But creativity, too, has its part to play in the fulness of the Church.

One side of creative development is a willingness on the part of the Church to receive new truth. To-day the scientists are enlarging the frontiers of truth in every direction, and uncovering the strange secrets of the universe in which we live. All such new knowledge may at one point or another present a challenge to the Christian tradition as we have understood it in the past, and all too often in the past the Church has met the scientist with mere hostility and incomprehension. But, in so far as the scientists are studying the handiwork of God, it may be thought that further knowledge of the created thing may in its degree contribute to a deeper understanding of the mind of the Creator. Again, it may well be thought that, as the Gospel is passed through the minds of men of different races and traditions, new facets of the truth will for the first time be lighted up. Long ago Bishop Westcott of Durham, the greatest of English commentators on the Fourth Gospel, gave it as his opinion that the definitive commentary on that Gospel would come only from the mind of India, a prophecy and a hope as yet unfulfilled.

Further, a due understanding of the element of creative experience in the life of the Church deeply affects the attitude of the individual Christian to his own situation in the Church's life. He is pledged to loyalty to the past, since we are all immeasurably indebted to the traditions from which we are sprung. But mere conformity, mere docile acceptance of that which is given by authority, can no longer be regarded as the highest virtue. The Church is an organism, growing into an unknown future, and developing towards an as yet undefined perfection. Within it the individual also is called to the adventure of growing. Without a share in the life of the whole, as a Christian he is nothing. But as a living cell within it, he can make his own individual and irreplaceable contribution to its growth, just as each microscopically insignificant cell in the physical body has its part to play. Such a dynamic concept of membership is the only real answer to the loud question of the young: " Why should I go to Church ? " It has the advantage of coming very near to what St. Paul is talking about in the Epistle to the Colossians.[1]

The contrast between static and dynamic aspects is met with in another area of the Church's life. The Church may be thought of either as an existing worshipping society, or in terms of its possible missionary outreach. When the Reformers had to define their position as against the Church of Rome, they naturally thought in terms of the countries that they knew, where everyone was at least nominally Christian, and they came down on the side of definition in terms of the existing society. Article XIX of the Thirty-nine Articles of the Church of England states that " The visible Church of Christ is a congregation of faithful men, in the which the pure Word of God is preached and the Sacraments be duly ministered." This comes close to the 7th Article of the Augsburg Confession, " The Church is a congregation of saints, in which the Gospel is purely taught and the Sacraments rightly administered ", and to Calvin's affirmation that " wherever we find the Word of God purely preached and heard, and the Sacraments administered according to the institution of Christ, there, it is not to be doubted, is a Church of God."

[1] Col. 2 : 18.

Now all this is perfectly correct as far as it goes, but does it go far enough ? What is the mental picture called up by such definitions ? Is it not that of a respectable Christian congregation, sitting under the instruction of a godly minister, and being trained so to pass through the troubles of this transitory world that they may in the end obtain a celestial inheritance ? And what are the " notes " of such a Church as they are laid down in the best manuals ? They are (1) pure doctrine held in faithfulness to the unchanging deposit received from the past ; (2) valid Sacraments, the necessarily fixed and unchanging elements in the Church's worship ; (3) godly discipline, by which the little Zion of the Church is safeguarded against the rude irruption of either false doctrine or moral obliquity. All the emphasis is on that which is fixed, stable, and unchanging ; and it is these elements which most naturally find their expression in a fixed and unchanging organization. For this reason, controversies between the Churches tend to find their centre in the question of the ministry and the order of the Church, and of the validity of the Sacraments which are dependent on such ministries. It is impossible to overestimate the debt of later generations to the organization through which the treasures of the Church have been kept safe and handed on ; without that stable organization there would be no Church at all to-day. But is that all that the Gospel has to tell us about the nature of the Church ?

The Lord Himself affirmed that His Word was a fire, which He had come to cast upon the earth. It is to be thought of as like a burst of shrapnel, with immense force at the point of impact, and violent projection forwards from that point. The Gospel was given as an explosive force. It was the intention of its Founder that His Church should enter into conflict, never to be ended as long as time shall last, with every system of human thought and conduct that will not surrender to its power. It was His expectation that it would be bitterly persecuted, and would spread only through the power of suffering. He appointed to it a living Word and a living Spirit, and only the minimum of organization. He was Himself a Man who had no place to lay His head ; He appointed His Church to be always a pilgrim Church. The Churches by contrast have always shown a marked tendency to settle down. At times they have not merely appeared unconscious of the missionary outreach, but have gloried in their repudiation of it, maintaining that the Church has nothing to do but attend respectably to its local responsibilities.

It is because of this inveterate tendency of the Church to localize, to stabilize, and to organize itself that some recent thinking on missionary problems has doubted whether the missionary aspect of the Gospel and its world-wide outreach can ever be expressed at all in the categories of the Church and its life.

The earlier World Missionary Conferences had had little to say about the Church as such ; it was widely held that the Tambaram Conference of 1938 had marked an advance on its predecessors in its clear recognition of the Church as the centre and focal point of the whole missionary enterprise. The aim of the missionary must be, under God, to bring the Church into existence ; once the Church exists it becomes the bearer of the Gospel, dependent only on its Master, ideally at least independent of all human control though linked in fellowship with all the scattered members of the body in all the countries of the earth. This view has steadily gained ground—indeed at Tambaram it was not wholly an innovation. The Whitby Conference of 1947 took up the idea where Tambaram left it, and carried it perhaps a stage further :

> The task of world evangelism to-day starts from the vantage ground of a Church which, as never before, is really world-wide. This universal fellowship is in the oft-quoted words of William Temple the great new fact of our era. It is working itself out to-day in a real partnership between older and younger Churches.[1]

No sooner had this new stand been taken than it was exposed to the fire of criticism. The first shots came from America, and largely in the eloquent tones of Dr. Stanley Jones, the eminent evangelist, who feared that the substitution of the idea of the Church for that of the Kingdom of God might minister to human self-satisfaction, and rob the Christian enterprise of the needed fires of imagination, enthusiasm, and self-criticism.

Much more serious, because based on a far deeper theological understanding, were the strictures of Dr. J. C. Hoekendijk, now Professor at the University of Utrecht. Against this new interest in the Church Dr. Hoekendijk wishes to put up a very large red

[1] *Renewal and Advance* : ed. C. W. Ranson (Edinburgh House Press, 1948), p. 214.

ag of warning, since on his view interest in the Church is generally sign of spiritual tiredness or even of decadence :

> In history a keen ecclesiological interest has, almost without exception, been a sign of spiritual decadence ; ecclesiology has been a subject of major concern only in the " *second* generation " ; in the " first generation ", in periods of revival, reformation or missionary advance, our interest was absorbed by Christology, thought-patterns were determined by eschatology, life became a doxology and the Church was spoken of in an unaccented and to some extent rather naïve way, as being something that " thank God a child of seven knows what it is (Luther) ".[1]

We may pause to reflect that experience always comes before ormulation, and that, though these two are not the same, it does ot necessarily follow that the latter is a sign of decadence or of oss of life. It is unlikely that the Apostles on the day of Pentecost ad a clear theological idea of what they were doing when they aptized the first Christian converts. For all that, we are not sorry o have the sixth chapter of the Epistle to the Romans. But we must ass on to Dr. Hoekendijk's application of his thesis to current missionary thinking :

> The Church-centric conception, which since Jerusalem 1928 appears to have been the single, almost uncontested, dogma in the theory of missions, has clasped us so tight, has so spun its web about us that we ourselves hardly realize how far the Churchification of our thought has gone. From this crushing embrace we shall never escape, until we learn to ask again and most seriously what it means when we repeat again and again our beloved missionary text " This Gospel of the Kingdom must be preached in all the world ", and to attempt to find our solution of the problem of the Church in this framework of Kingdom-Gospel-Witness (apostolate)-World.[2]

Such criticisms, coming from such a source, are very serious nd must be treated with the utmost respect. It would be impossible o deal with them fairly in a page or two, and no such attempt will ere be made ; and this is the less necessary in that in a sense the vhole of the rest of this book is a result of the writer's attempt to grapple with the problems that Dr. Hoekendijk has raised. If the Church were true to itself, there would be no problem. Let us

---

[1] *International Review of Missions*, 1952, p. 325.
[2] *I.R.M.*, 1952, p. 332.

look again at Dr. Hoekendijk's four pillars : Kingdom-Gospel
Apostolate-World. The Church is the area within which the King
dom is constantly making contact with the world in judgment and
renewal. To the Church has been committed the proclamation of
the Gospel in all its penetrating and explosive power. When Jesus
said to His Apostles, " As my Father hath sent me, even so send
you ", He was committing to them that apostolate that He had
Himself carried as the Sent One of His Father, and which the
Church was now to carry to the ends of the earth and to the end
of time. The Church is sent out into the world, for the salvation
of the world, if need be to give its life for the salvation of the world

It is clear from history that, as the Church has institutionalized
itself, it has shown a marked tendency to lose its hold on all these
four principles. It has found it possible to turn itself into a very
good likeness of the kingdoms of this world. Its Gospel has been
muted to a mere repetition of edifying formulas. It has tended to
become so introverted as to spend the whole of its strength on the
spiritual up-building of the faithful. It has become either so separated from the world as to have no ready point of communication
with it, or so identified with the world as to be no longer capable of
challenging it. But is this a picture of the Church, or a caricature
of it ? Is this what must always and necessarily follow on the creation
of a Church as Church ? Are we really bound to create a new
sequence, with apostolate at the centre, and to by-pass the Church
or treat it as unessential ? Is there any effective apostolate apart
from the Church ? Can any Church claim the name or nature of
a Church unless apostolate is at the heart of its being ? Is it actually
the fact that the emphasis placed on the Church in missionary thinking in the last twenty years has led to such an arteriosclerosis as
Dr. Hoekendijk's protest would suggest. If so, what is our remedy ?
Is it not evident that apostolate which does not lead to the founding
of a Church tends to vaporize itself, and that a Church which has
not heard the call to apostolate is condemned to sterility ? Is not
the task to-day to bring the two sequences together, to recall the
Church to a rediscovery of its own nature, and to challenge the
missionary movement to become genuinely a Church movement,
without losing its passion, its flexibility and its power ?

To suggest that this is impossible would seem to be a counsel
of despair. This is a theme to which we shall recur frequently in

different sections of this book. For the moment it may be useful to cite one or two contemporary witnesses, who, taking the problem as seriously as Dr. Hoekendijk, arrive at conclusions rather different from his.

One of the most interesting of these testimonies is that of a German layman, Dr. Hans Dombois, who is a lawyer as well as a theologian. He makes a distinction between what he calls the *thetic* and the *eschatological* aspects of the Church. The latter of these is related to the missionary command of our Lord (Matthew 28 : 19), the former to the promise that the living Christ will be perpetually present in the midst of the worshipping believers. In elucidation of this thesis, he writes as follows :

> From this it follows that from the beginning these two aspects have existed together in the Church—the missionary proclamation, with baptism as its goal ; and the actualization of the Church in the Lord's Supper. Otherwise stated, we find both that universal Church, which is to be gathered out from among all peoples, and the single congregation gathered together for the purpose of worship. Any over-emphasis on one of these aspects at the expense of the other, and equally any disregard of either of them, must inevitably lead to a distortion of the picture of the Church.[1]

This is well stated. It recognizes that the concept of the Church as institution and the Church as missionary body are not alternatives, but simply two facets that must be held together in the reality of one Church.

The Willingen Missionary Conference of 1952 was clearly thinking along the same lines, when it affirmed that

> there is no participation in Christ without participation in His mission to the world. That by which the Church receives its existence is that by which also it is given its world mission. . . . God sends forth His Church to carry out His work to the end of the earth, to all nations and to the end of time.[2]

The only defect of this Willingen statement is that it seems to take for granted agreement on some subjects on which it is not certain that agreement will be forthcoming. What do we mean, when we say that " God sends forth the Church to carry out His work " ? Is the Church the only instrument which He uses to

[1] Hans Dombois, in *Credo Ecclesiam* (Kassel, 1955), p. 47.
[2] *Missions Under the Cross*, p. 190.

carry out His work, or are there others ? What is the work that God has constituted His Church to do ? What measure of success has He promised it in the carrying out of its task ?

Some, in reaction against the mistaken identification of the Church with the Kingdom of God, would say that this last question is one which we have no business to ask. The task of the Church is simply to bear witness to the Gospel or to the Kingdom. To it is committed the responsibility of serving as a herald ; all else is the affair of God. Theologically this is unexceptionable ; but still practical questions do arise, and do clamour for an answer, even though no more than a hesitating and provisional answer can be given. Our Lord came as a herald ; but He did collect some disciples, and He did bring into being that organization which later took to calling itself the Church. My father used to say, somewhat cynically, " Preach the Gospel but don't make any converts." But, where the Gospel is faithfully preached, converts have a way of coming in—and that is where all the trouble begins. While the Churches have on the whole been successfully sleeping, a worldwide Church has come into being as a result of the modern missionary enterprise. What is to be the end of all this ? What further measure of expansion may we expect to be prepared for the Church in the providence of God, and to what ends should the activities of the Church be now principally directed ? It is precisely on this subject that there is at present considerable division of opinion, in consequence of a rather rapidly changing climate of theological thought.

Those of us who are past middle age remember the time when the general expectation, among those who cared for missionary work at all, was that of a steady triumphal progress of the Gospel across the world till all the nations were gathered in. " From Greenland's icy mountains " is now rarely sung, which is a pity, because it is a very fine hymn ; [1] and the first four lines of the last verse—

> Waft, waft, ye winds, His story,
> And you, ye waters, roll,
> Till, like a sea of glory,
> It spreads from pole to pole

---

[1] Why anyone should ever have supposed that Bishop Heber intended to imply that the people of Ceylon are particularly vile, I cannot imagine. He would unhesitatingly have said the same about the population of England, or even of Scotland, if it had fitted with his verse. Nevertheless, I have a certain feeling of sympathy for the Ceylonese.

are a noble expression of what must be the aspiration of every Christian heart. The danger is that, in this moving picture of the forward sweep of the Gospel, less than due account may be taken of the frustrations, disappointments, and hindrances which may lie in its way. This is what happened in the earlier years of this century. Success stories abounded ; and there was evident a tendency to regard as a guaranteed concomitant of the modern missionary movement what was in fact no more than a conjunction of favourable political circumstances. And, in fact, almost before these expectations of world-wide triumph had been formed, the political situation had changed. The defeat of Russia by Japan in 1905 sounded the death knell of the colonial era. Thereafter, in two successive suicidal wars the Western nations recklessly threw away their claim to the moral leadership of the world, and wrought prejudice to the Christian cause the full effects of which it is not yet possible accurately to estimate.

Even before all this happened, a slight knowledge of Christian history might have warned the optimistic Christian not to sink down too luxuriously on his bed of optimism. Strange things have happened before now in Christian history. The strangest of all was the coming of Islam. Within two centuries all the ancient heartlands of the Gospel had ceased to be Christian, and Spain had become part of the Muslim Empire. During eight centuries the great Christian Empire of the East was worn to death by standing perpetually on guard against the Muslim invader and finally fell. For the time being the wave has receded, though the Arab countries still remain the storm centre of world politics. But the great and ancient Churches in the Islamic lands have known no second spring ; where they have not been obliterated they have survived as a tolerated but not highly respected minority, not greatly enriched by any living springs of Christian vitality within themselves, and apparently with little sense of responsibility for the evangelization of their Muslim neighbours.

Why did God allow all this to happen ? This is one of the darkest and most inscrutable mysteries of divine Providence, and one with which the dogmatic theologians do not seem to have dealt satisfactorily in that section of their systems marked " Providence ". It is all too easy to give plausible and facile explanations—to speak of the corruptions, weaknesses, and unfaithfulness of the Eastern Churches, and even to see in Islam a kind of cleansing manifestation of God's judgment. This leaves unanswered the question why the Eastern Churches alone were called to undergo this fiery trial, and not to be delivered out of the burning fiery furnace. Were the Western Churches at that time so respectable and full of zeal as to be able to claim of right the protection of God against their enemies ? Were the Western Papacy and Empire such dedicated servants of God that it was right and proper for the great and ancient civilization of Byzantium to be sacrificed on the altar of their preservation ? To the question thus formulated there seems to be no obvious answer.[1]

Reflection on the history of Islam may help to throw some light on the phenomenon of Communism at the present time. The two systems, Islam and Communism, are at certain points basically incompatible. Superficial resemblances in the suddenness of the appearance of each, and in the extraordinary rapidity of their initial successes, are readily observable and are not very important. What is significant, from the Christian point of view, is the character of each as a post-Christian heresy, as a deliberate denial of one or more of the basic truths on which the Christian faith rests, and as a system vowed to the destruction or at least to the paralysis of the Christian Church. In a thousand years of controversy the Gospel has made remarkably little impression on the fortresses of Islam. The recovery of the West has led to the liberation of Christians in a number of areas that had been for centuries under Muslim control, but this has not resulted in the conversion of the Muslims. We cannot say for certain that the course of events in Communist countries will follow the same pattern. Christian recovery may follow different methods, and Communism may prove less resistant to the Gospel than Islam. But both of these great catastrophes ought to warn us that there is for the Church no guarantee of steady and automatic progress. We may be assured that the purpose of God is going forward to its predestined end ; we may be equally sure that it will not follow the simple and straightforward course that we would like to mark out for it, if we could.

---

[1] Cf. Bernard Manning : *Essays in Orthodox Dissent* (Independent Press, 1939, p. 14) : " It would not be difficult indeed to show that the Christian societies of the East stamped out by Mohammedanism had many grievous faults ; it would only be difficult to show that we in the West who escaped had fewer or less grievous faults. Nor had we need of historical research to teach us this ; if we had remembered our Saviour's words about the Galileans whose blood Pilate had mingled with their sacrifices."

Another illusion of the early years of this century was a belief in the coming of the Kingdom of God on earth through inevitable progress and the evolution of the human race. It was recognized that this might take a very long time, but, as was sometimes said, " we are the early Christians " ; and, since God has endless years to work with, we need not be surprised if the working out of His purpose takes what from our point of view is an unimaginably long span of time. In the meantime, our business is to co-operate with Him in His work, not to be in a hurry, and to believe that all things will be well in the end. There was nothing low or stooping about such ideas ; if they were optimistic, it was in many cases with a genuinely Christian optimism, based on belief in the goodness of God, and in His creative power still at work in the world. The only question was as to the basis of fact on which these ideas had been constructed. The experience of the Nazi times in Germany and of war against the Japanese convinced many people that the transference of evolutionary ideas from the biological to the moral sphere was at best a somewhat uncertain process, and that, whereas human nature can certainly be transformed by grace, its transformation by merely natural process is something on which we should do well not to count too confidently.

Optimistic illusions have been swept away. Mere pessimism tends to paralyse the Church in its apostolic mission. Is there any alternative view, which, while avoiding errors in both these directions, will give us some clue as to what it is that God is planning to do through His Church in the present age ?

The renewal of a genuinely biblical theology may give us the help that we need. Recent study of the Bible has drawn our attention to the close parallels between the Old Covenant and the New, between the destiny of the Old Israel as set forth in the Old Testament, and that of the New Israel, the Church, as indicated in the New Testament. We must be careful not to exaggerate, and not to take anything in the Old Covenant as determinative of the interpretation of what is to be found in the New. But, even when due caution has been observed, we can recognize certain similarities within the differences. The vocation of the new people of God is not precisely the same as that of the ancient people ; but there is a real resemblance between the tasks to which each in its own dispensation has been called. What is it that the people of God,

in the old dispensation as in the new, has been called to do ? The
answer can be given in a phrase—*before all else to prepare the way
for the coming of the King*.

The scene of the Jewish ministry and witness was the Mediterranean world—in earlier times the world of the first great Kingdoms,
in later times the world throughout which Greek was the common
language of educated men. Gradually the witness of Israel fell apart
into two rather sharply distinct forms. There was the safeguarding
of a heartland, a home of the Jewish people. There was a scattering
abroad, a Diaspora, in which the Jews lived as aliens in the midst
of a far larger non-Jewish population.

Palestine was the heartland. This did not mean that every Jew
was a faithful Jew, or that the whole nation was penetrated through
and through by a sense of its Messianic destiny. It did mean that
the whole life of the people was touched and affected by the Jewish
law ; that Jewish worship was everywhere honoured and protected ;
that the bad Jew was to some extent at least conscious of his badness.
Within the periphery of the nominal, the half-hearted, the hard-
hearted, was the central group of the faithful, those who looked for
the redemption of Israel ; and among them in due time Jesus of
Nazareth was born.

From the point of view of Christian history the Diaspora may
be regarded as even more important than the heartland. It has
been reckoned that in the time of Christ there were half a million
Jews in Palestine, and four million scattered throughout the Mediterranean world.[1] In the time of St. Paul there was hardly a city in
the Mediterranean world, from the Euphrates to the pillars of
Hercules, which had not its synagogue and its body of Jewish
residents. Some of the communities, such as that of Alexandria,
were large, rich and influential ; others were small and feeble. But
the situation of all of them was alike in one respect—the civilization
by which they were surrounded was based not on Jewish but on
pagan principles. Jews were on the whole disliked by their neighbours as a surly and non-co-operative race, and this dislike was
liable to flame up in such frightful riots as those of which we read
in the pages of St. Paul's contemporary, Philo. Yet these Jewish

---

[1] Reliable data for such calculations are hard to find in ancient sources. The
numbers given may be considerably too high—the proportions are perhaps roughly
correct.

communities were on the whole less bitter, less prejudiced, more open to new ideas than those of Palestine. It was among them that the original Gospel found its readiest and most attentive hearers. These partly Graecized Jews, and those godly people who, without joining the Jewish community through circumcision, had come deeply under the influence of the Jewish law, formed the majority of the earliest groups of Christians, and provided that élite from which the majority of the leaders were drawn. It was the existence of this prepared and already formed élite that in large measure accounts for the astonishingly rapid progress of the Gospel in the ancient world, and that saved the Christian cause from disaster, when the Jewish people as a whole rejected the Messiah.

The purpose of God which was fulfilled in the history of Israel was twofold; first, the provision of a homeland, within which Christ the Son of God could be born and grow and accomplish His work; and secondly, the preparation through the Diaspora of a wider world in which the Gospel could quickly take root, and in which the Church could quickly develop to such maturity as would enable it to survive both the destruction of the Jewish nation and the collapse of the Roman Empire.

Is God doing something of the same kind through the Church to-day? Is the ministry of the Church to prepare the way for the second coming of Christ, as that of the Jewish Church was to prepare the way for His first coming? Is the Church asked to do on a world-wide scale what the Jews were called to do within the Mediterranean area?

Let us bear in mind the warning that we are not entitled to make *inferences* from the Old Covenant to the New, though we may be aware of similarities and correspondences. Let us also remember that we are not endued with the gift of prophecy, and must therefore always speak with much hesitation. Nevertheless, when all this has been allowed for, the parallel between the old Israel and the new does make sense of Christian history so far, and does give both encouragement and direction in what the Church is trying to do to-day.[1]

God has brought into existence a heartland of the Gospel. The

[1] I pass over here a subject which could not be handled without lengthy discussion—the question whether the old Israel is also called to play a part in God's purpose for the time of the end, and whether the miraculous preservation of the Jewish people through all the centuries is an indication that God still has a special plan for it.

ancient heartlands—Palestine, Syria, Asia Minor, Egypt, North Africa—have all been lost to Islam, and there seems no immediate prospect of their recovery for the Church. There has been a westward shift, and the heartland is now to be found mainly in North-Western Europe and in North America, with outliers of the nominally Christian races in other parts of the world. To state this is not to encourage the illusion that there is such a thing as a Christian nation or that the cause of Christ is to be identified with modern Western democracy. That is nonsense. But it is a fact that there are certain nations the culture of which is based on the biblical revelation, and the life of which has been profoundly, though still very imperfectly, penetrated by the principles of the Gospel; in which the profession, the practice, and the teaching of the Christian faith are unimpeded, and in certain cases positively encouraged by the state. We who are so painfully aware of the treacheries and infidelities of our so-called Christian nations may be inclined to doubt whether there is anything in this, or whether the words " a Christian civilization " have any meaning at all. Long residence in a country the life and civilization of which have never been touched by Christian ideas and ideals may tend to make us think otherwise, and to make us at least hesitate before dismissing the idea of a Christian civilization as wholly meaningless.

It would be unwise to attempt to define too exactly the frontiers of the Christian heartland. Are the countries beyond the Iron Curtain, where the Churches have been reduced to heroically struggling minorities, to be regarded as merely temporarily isolated from it; are Christian ideas destined to become again the basis of their civilization ? We do not know. Again, we have to recognize that what is now the heartland may not continue to be so till the end of time. There has been one great shift already; there might be another. Through our unfaithfulness, or through the violence of the enemy, our candlestick could be taken away. If what is now partly pagan and partly Christian Africa became completely Christian, and created a new civilization on the basis of the Gospel, the centre of the Christian world might be found in that zone of tropical Africa which runs south-westwards from Uganda through the Belgian Congo to the Atlantic Ocean. Such secrets are not revealed to us, and it would not greatly profit us to-day to know the answer to such questions.

It seems that in recent centuries God has been calling into existence the Christian Diaspora, not now on a Mediterranean but on a world-wide scale. The net result of Christian missions, especially over the last two centuries of rapid expansion, has been exactly this—that they have brought into being the Christian Diaspora, the scattered people of God living as aliens in the midst of civilizations determined by principles other than those of the Gospel and irreconcilable with it. We shall consider later how far these Christian groups have been unnecessarily alienated from their own people, and how far it is a necessary part of their vocation to live as strangers and pilgrims among them. Of the reality of the separation there can be no doubt. In hardly any region of the " non-Christian " world has the witness of the Church effected any profound change in the attitude of the people as a whole or of its government. The Philippines and Uganda are the only areas of a considerable size in which more than half the population has been even nominally brought within the Church. There have been deep spiritual penetrations in both directions—of the ancient religions by the Gospel, and of the Churches by the spirit of the ancient religions. Yet, in the main, the Churches are still a " Diaspora ", a scattered people, tolerated, partly accepted, but still strangers and pilgrims on the earth.

An accurate map of the Christian mission in the world on a sufficiently large scale would look very much like a map of the starry sky. Across the sky sweeps the Milky Way. There are areas where stars are many and bright, other areas where stars are few and dim ; and those great mysterious spaces over the north where all is dark and no star shines. The parallel with Christian achievement is too close to need to be worked out in detail. There are in the world the countries and areas where the Church has taken root and flourishes, where great Christian communities exist, as in some parts of India and Africa, prosperous and independent, though still a small minority among the people of the country. There are the bright and isolated stars, limited areas in which some special success has been accorded to Christian witness, as in the Batak Church in Sumatra. There are the faint stars of the tiny groups of converts in Islamic countries, precious first-fruits indeed, but still only first-fruits. And there are the still dark areas, the closed countries such as Afghanistan and Tibet, where the light of the Gospel has not yet appeared.

The new factor is that, for the first time in history, the Diaspor
has become very nearly world-wide. This raises in the mind o
the Christian the question whether we may not be at or near on
of the turning-points of the ages. As to the nature of that turning
point it may be well not to enquire too closely. Those who hav
occupied themselves with the question of the Second Coming o
Christ have tended to think in earthly and, it must be admitted
highly improbable terms. By reaction the majority of theologian
do not attempt to give content at all to the idea of the Secon
Coming, and merely affirm in rather vague terms that the end c
history must be beyond history, whatever that may mean. Now i
seems clear that what the New Testament looks forward to is th
triumph of God in time and within history, a triumph to be brough
about solely by His own act, but at the same time dependent on th
preparatory work of the Church, without which God cannot mov
forward to the next step in the accomplishment of His great desigr

The object of this enquiry has not been to unlock the secret
of a future which is kept in His own hand, and within His ow
guardianship ; it has been an attempt to determine the nature c
the Church in relation to its missionary calling. If our interpreta
tion is somewhere near the truth, we may come to understand mor
exactly what was meant when it was said earlier that the Churc
is provisional and preparatory in character. In its own dispensatio
it is all-important, but that importance is derived not from what i
is in itself, but from that for which it prepares the way. The glor
of the old Israel was that it was the cradle in which in due time th
Messiah was born ; it is the glory of the Church to be the fore
runner to prepare the way for the coming again of its exalted an
glorified King. It is only in relation to a future as yet undisclose
that its true nature in the present can be discerned. This under
standing of the Church's situation gives us the right perspective i
Christian missionary work, and enables us to keep the exact middl
line between the activism of ill-founded optimism and the inactivit
which is the result of pessimism. If it were the task of the Churc
to convert the whole world, we might well despair ; in nearly tw
thousand years so very little has been done. If, on the other hand
the task of the Church is world-wide witness, and the preparing c
the way of the Lord by gathering out an elect people in every natior
there is no reason for despair, and at the same time, no excuse fo

anything but the strenuous, intelligent and resolute undertaking of that work of preparation, without which this epoch cannot lead out into that which is to follow it.

All this makes it possible on the one hand to avoid the deification of the Church, and on the other to love it in all its imperfections ; to detect it under all the rags and squalor of its divisions and its sins ; to see it in all its significance in relation to the coming Kingdom of God. For in this epoch of the Holy Spirit the Church is the vehicle of the redeeming grace of God. It is not merely that the Church is building also in eternity, and that by far the greater part of it is already in the eternal world. That is true. But it is also true that everything that happens in the Church, every act of worship, every victory, every achievement in the temporal sphere has its lasting significance, since God is a thrifty worker, and will not allow anything of value to be lost. As a contemporary preacher has finely said:

> The Resurrection of Christ then shows us temporal good as something which can be eternally possessed, earthly experience and achievement as something which can be given permanence in Heaven. . . . This may be comforting. But it is also extremely challenging. For it invests the historical order with an almost terrifying significance. It means that what we are and do here on earth is of supreme importance. For out of this material God is building His eternal city. Not for one moment can we abandon the attempt to make the world a better place, to contribute to its store of beauty and truth and goodness. For however ephemeral our efforts may be, however here and now they may fail or be superseded, it is with them that God has willed to weave a tapestry which will be forever His possession and ours.[1]

To put this a little more theologically, the life of the Church in its passage through time is and always must be sacramental, just because this is the time of the dispensation of the Holy Spirit. It is the work of the Holy Spirit to take the things of Jesus and to make them real to us, to make available to us now the reality of those things which because we are in time we cannot as yet fully enjoy. When the fulness of all things has come in, when we know even as we are known, and are like Him because we see Him as He is, there will be no more need for sign or sacrament, because

---

[1] The Rev. H. A. Williams in a sermon broadcast on Easter Day 1952.

U.T.—2

the full reality will be already possessed. It is for that reason that we observe the Lord's Supper only " until His coming again ". The sign in the Sacrament is outward, poor, visible and physical. But any man who for this reason despises or neglects the Sacrament does so to his own great spiritual impoverishment. There are Sacraments in the life of the Church, because the Church is itself sacramental. It is the outward and visible sign of a greater and more perfect reality. Here too the outward and visible is often tragically unlike the reality that it is called upon to represent. For this reason good men have often despaired of the only visible Church they knew, and have tried to retire into a state of purely inward and individual fellowship with God. If such an attitude is ever justifiable, it can only be in the extreme case of a Church which has entirely forgotten its true nature and vocation. But where this extreme situation has not been reached, the Church is our home, the place of our witness, the instrument that God has chosen to do His work. A clear and unimpassioned consideration of the imperfections of the instrument need be no obstacle to an understanding of the supreme significance of the work. If we are concerned about the work of God, we had better lose no time in coming to terms with the instrument, because there is no other ; and what God is prepared to acknowledge as His own, it ill becomes us to despise.

CHAPTER 2

THE COMING GENERATION

IN thinking about the Church it is easy to slip into the erroneous idea that, because a country or parish has once been Christian, it will remain so until the end of time. A moment's thought will show that this is no more than imagination or wishful thinking. One generation succeeds to another, and that which comes is not naturally and inevitably Christian. In the life of the Church there is a spiritual and supernatural continuity; there is no natural continuity. The task of the Church must always be unfinished, because so much of its energy must go into the endless business of winning the younger generation for Christ.

The possibility of the disappearance of Christian faith from a once Christian community is not in our time, if it ever was, merely a matter of theory. The maintenance of spiritual continuity is always difficult. The natural difficulties can be immensely increased by deliberate interference on the part of the state with the religious instruction of the young, and this is a process that is going on in Russia and other countries before our eyes. There no public instruction of young people under the age of eighteen is permitted in either school or Church. The family becomes all-important as the sphere within which the continuity of the Church's tradition can be assured; if the parents have become alienated from the faith, there is little chance of any Christian influence playing upon the children. If this " safeguarding of the spiritual independence of children and young people " could be carried out to the limit, in thirty years Christian faith would largely have faded out as an effective force in the life of a nation; in sixty years, apart from miracle, it would almost have disappeared. This, too, is not merely theory; there is ample historical evidence to support this view. In the Turkish Empire it was the custom to take the children of Christian families of good position at an early age, to separate them entirely from their parents and to bring them up in the Muslim faith. The Janissaries became the most fanatical of Muslims and the most intrepid defenders of the Muslim cause. Every recollection of their Christian

origin seems to have been obliterated from their minds, and the fac
that as infants they had been baptized made no difference to th
wholeheartedness of their acceptance of Islam.

This is the extreme case. But the problem, in less acute form
is observable under very different and more normal condition
Why in the younger Churches has it proved so difficult to maintai
in the second and third generations the enthusiasm of the firs
beginnings ? No Christian leader has ever worked with great
success in a " mass movement " area than the late Bishop Azaria
of Dornakal ; yet it is well known that towards the end of his episc
pate of thirty years he was growing discouraged by the new problem
that had to be faced as the third generation of Christians began t
grow up. Azariah himself had been born in Tinnevelly just at th
time (1874) when an earlier mass movement had come to the en
of its advance, and he had seen as a boy the terrible things that ca
happen to a Church when stagnation sets in after advance. He ha
hoped that, with his own dynamic and indigenous methods, thi
retrogression could be avoided ; but success was less than he ha
hoped. The reason was not far to seek. In the first generation c
converts from illiterate and underprivileged groups, understandin
may have been dim, knowledge limited and moral achievement im
perfect ; but at least the Gospel had been accepted as a challenge
there had been a call to decision, and not infrequently to the endur
ance of persecution. Even in the second generation, and still mor
in the third, acquiescence could all too easily take the place c
positive choice. The children could accept as normal the limite
knowledge and imperfect achievement of their parents, and suppos
that not much more could reasonably be expected of them. Exactl
the same process has been observed in such African Churches a
that of Uganda. There is genuine loyalty to the faith in which th
Christians have been brought up, but it is marred by the persistenc
of many sub-Christian elements. Where this hardening has set i
recovery and renewal seem to demand an even greater price tha
the original effort which brought the first converts into the Churc

In " younger Churches " the contrasts between the generation
are more startling ; but in principle the problem is no differen
from that which is faced by every Church and by every type c
Church, once it has been long enough in existence to have acquire
the stability of a tradition. Tradition tends to kill spontaneit

he intense conviction of those who had to fight for their faith can
ery soon change into the placid conformity of those who have
ever known anything else, and who accept as a badge of respecta-
lity that form of religious observance in which they have been
rought up.

It was in protest against this spirit of conformity that the
Churches of Believers " were brought into existence. There is a
ear distinction of principle between the " multitudinist " Church
nd the Church based on the individual's own profession of faith.
1 the one case, it is taken for granted that everyone is a Christian,
nless he has specifically contracted out of the obligation of being
ne—and until very recently in some European countries it was im-
ossible to contract out of the national Church (e.g. by becoming a
oman Catholic) without contracting out of citizenship as well. In
ie other case, no one is regarded as a Christian unless he has
eliberately declared himself to be one, and has at least to some
xtent manifested the signs of conversion. That great ecumenical
inker Dr. Nathaniel Micklem once remarked to me that the re-
onciliation of these two concepts of the Church seems to him to
e the hardest of all ecumenical problems ; he could see the justifica-
on and indeed the necessity for the existence of both types, but he
ould not see how they could be brought together in a united
hurch.[1]

In daily existence these two types of Church are not perhaps
uite so far apart as a strict application of their principles would
iggest. In believers' Churches the children of Christians are not
egarded as being in exactly the same position as the children of
eathen. Some of these bodies have even maintained the ceremony
f infant baptism, though with less sacramental content or doctrine
ian would satisfy the adherents of more traditional Churches. In
ome national Churches Confirmation has been reduced almost to
ie level of a social ceremony, somewhat like the puberty rites of
ie primitive African tribe ; as an eminent Swiss theologian has
emarked, to the Swiss boy Confirmation means three things :
Now I shall start to wear long trousers ; now I shall be allowed
) smoke ; and now, like Daddy, I shall be able to stop going to

[1] They have in fact been ingeniously brought together in the union of the
Iethodist Churches and some of the Free Churches with the Reformed Church
f France (1938).

church." Yet even in these Churches Confirmation is usuall
associated to some extent with the idea of decision for Christ an
of the personal acceptance of responsibility ; almost concealed :
it may be by a mainly intellectual preparation, or by a perhaps to
exclusive emphasis on the purely sacramental character of the gi
in Confirmation, the idea of personal decision is seldom wholl
absent.

What brings the various types of Churches even closer togethe
is the manifest and massive failure of all of them, older and younge
to hold their young people. Whether there is to-day less religiou
conviction and a lower standard of morals among young peopl
than in " the good old days " is known to God alone. When societ
was more closely integrated, the weight of social pressure was greate
and conformity more natural. Now that personal action is free an
so many forces are active against Christian faith, all the Churche
are beginning to feel the draught. Ireland is rightly regarded a
the country *par excellence* in which the Roman Catholic Church ha
managed to maintain its hold upon the people ; yet recent offici:
utterances of the hierarchy deplore the fact that so many youn
men emigrating to England cease to practise their religion, and see
immediately and with pleasure to grasp at a freedom that was mor
difficult to exercise in their own country. Statistics of the Churc
of England suggest that, whereas two-thirds of the children bor
in England are baptized in the Church of England, less than ha
of those baptized come forward for Confirmation, and considerabl
less than a quarter become regular communicants. In the younge
Churches the level of conformity tends to be distinctly higher ; bu
here, for reasons that we shall consider later, the tensions betwee
the generations are more acute than anywhere in the olde
Churches.

Clearly, then, the first frontier on which the Church has t
bestir itself is that of the younger generation. How are the youn
people to be kept within the fellowship of the Church ?

The answer that seems to find most favour at the present tim
is the development of Christian nurture. Let the child from th
start feel that it belongs to the Church. Let it be surrounded, i
home and school and elsewhere, with Christian ideas and habits a
a normal part of daily experience. Then it may be expected tha
with the unfolding of the child's natural capacities, there will b

also an unfolding of Christian sentiment and Christian conviction, without crisis and without upheaval, in one single line of almost uninterrupted development.

This idea found one of its first, and one of its most permanently moving, expressions in the writings of the American theologian Horace Bushnell. Thus he writes :

> Let every Christian father and mother understand, when their child is three years old, that they have done more than half of all they will ever do for his character. What can be more wide of all just apprehension than the immense efficacy imputed by most parents to the Christian ministry, compared with what they take to be the almost insignificant power conferred on them in their parental charge and duties ? Why, if all preachers of Christ could have their hearers for whole months and years in their own will as parents do their children . . . if also a little farther on, they had them in authority to command, direct, tell them whither to go, what to learn, what to do, regulate their hours, their books, their pleasures, their company, and call them to prayer on their own knees every night and morning, who could think it impossible, in the use of such a power to produce almost any result ? Should not such a ministry be expected to fashion all who come under it to newness of life ? [1]

It is perhaps a little surprising that Bushnell of all men should have been the author of this passage, with its idealization of the influence of early training, and the excessive hopes it seems to rest on Christian training within the home. For Bushnell himself had gone through the experience of a sensational conversion at an identifiable moment of time. In his college days he was distinguished by great intellectual gifts and powers of leadership, but had been led to take up an agnostic and rather harshly anti-Christian position, in reaction against a premature and emotional " decision for Christ ". It is best to let him tell in his own words, in a sermon which evidently describes his own experience, what happened to him as a young teacher at Yale College during the revival of 1831 :

> He drops on his knees, and then he prays to the dim God, dimly felt, confessing the dimness for honesty's sake, and asking for help that he may begin a right life. He bows himself on it as he prays, choosing it to be henceforth his unalterable eternal endeavour. It is an awfully dark prayer, in the look of it ; but the truest and best

[1] Horace Bushnell : *Christian Nurture* (1847), Part II, Chapter I : quoted in John Baillie : *A Diary of Readings*, p. 320.

he can make, the better and the more true that he puts no orthodox colours on it ; and the prayer and the vow are so profoundly meant that his soul is borne up into God's help, as it were, by some unseen chariot, and permitted to see the opening of heaven even sooner than he opens his eyes.[1]

It cannot be doubted that this is an accurate account of the preacher's own experience of conversion. All Bushnell's actions at the time make this evident, and the whole witness of his life confirms it. And yet he has become one of the prophets of those who deprecate the idea of the necessity of conversion, particularly of conversion at a definite and identifiable moment. Bushnell had reacted rather sharply against the revival methods that were common in the American Churches in the nineteenth century and have not altogether disappeared to-day, with their almost brutal emphasis on sin, the building up of emotional pressures and the bullying and badgering of people to make decisions for which they may not be either intellectually or emotionally ready.

The controversy continues. Many maintain to-day that, in the case of those regularly brought up in the Church, development should be by a gradual and uninterrupted process, and that there should be no moment of crisis or definite decision. Sometimes the upholders of this view seem unable to get beyond the idea of *emotional* conversion, of an exciting and no more than transitory experience ; in this case those who plead for the necessity of conversion and those who deprecate it are not really speaking the same language. To avoid confusion it might be well to avoid the word altogether, though no satisfactory alternative seems as yet to have been suggested. But, whatever word we use, we are dealing with a problem which in the older Churches has reached the dimensions of tragedy, and in the younger Churches presents itself under a form of particular intensity ; young people as a whole are no longer finding their home within the Church of Christ.

Let us throw away at once the unhelpful and inaccurate distinction between " once-born " and " twice-born " Christians, apparently invented by F. W. Newman, brother of the more famous Cardinal, and unfortunately popularized by William James. There

[1] *Life and Letters of Horace Bushnell* (New York, 1880), p. 59. In the following paragraph Bushnell himself speaks of the experience as an experience of conversion.

can be no such thing as a once-born Christian. Our Lord laid that down with crushing simplicity when He said " That which is born of the flesh is flesh, and that which is born of the Spirit is Spirit." There is a real discontinuity between the natural and the spiritual. The recognition both of that discontinuity and of the divine grace by which it is bridged would seem to be part of Christian faith and experience as these are presented to us in the New Testament.

Further, let us yield every possible point to Christian nurture. The accumulation of evidence is unnecessary ; the apostolic succession of the godly family is one of the most certain and easily demonstrable successions in Christian history. But some cautions have to be entered. In the first place, there can be no Christian nurture in the home unless the parents really put Christ at the centre of family life. No one could lay greater stress on this than Bushnell himself : " It is vain, let all parents so understand, to imagine that you can really fulfil the true fatherhood and motherhood, unless you are true Christians yourselves. . . . Be Christians yourselves and then it will not be difficult for you to do your true duties to your children. Until then it is really impossible." [1] This in so many cases is exactly what is lacking. The teaching of a few perfunctory prayers and the sending of the children to Sunday School cannot counteract the general load of indifference under which the inactively Christian family is weighed down.

But, even where the best conditions are fulfilled, things do not always work out as expected. Christian parents are often followed by joyously Christian children. But there are also many cases of rebellious children in godly families. If these cases could be examined with the clinical minuteness of the psychologist, it might be found that in most of them there were cracks in the godliness of the family. Children are dreadfully quick to spot anything that savours of pose or insincerity in the attitude of parents. The yoke of Christ seems delightful only if parents make it clear that they desire their children to accept it because they themselves are wholly subject to it. Even where the parents are wholly sincere, if too great moral or emotional demands are made on the children, the reaction of rebellion, covert or open, is likely to set in.

Our main problem, however, in both older and younger Churches

[1] Quoted in Baillie, *A Diary of Readings*, p. 209. The whole passage should be read.

is that in the majority of cases the conditions of Christian nurture are not being fulfilled. Far too many parents have entirely abdicated their responsibility. Many children are growing up under no Christian influence at all. Some are lost to the Church at the end of childhood. Others who remain grow increasingly restless through-out adolescence. A further group breaks away at the dawn of adult manhood and womanhood ; and what is left is often but a sorry fragment of the company that started out on the way. Many who have grown up in traditionally Christian families have to be won back from a situation of almost total ignorance of the Christian faith. Others have to be reclaimed from the reactions of prejudice and dislike, from rebellion, from self-pleasing and from confusion of spiritual sight and understanding. For all this let the term " the ministry of conversion " for the moment stand. And let it be recalled that we are here still speaking of a ministry within " Christendom ", and not of missionary work outside it. How is the Church to set about the task, on this, the most evident and immediate of its frontiers ?

In the first place, all serious investigators would probably agree that there is no such thing as a specific religious sense. To locate such a sense in any part of man's nature, to attribute to it any special function, is as difficult as to identify the place and function of the soul within the body. Religion is an affair of the whole man or it is nothing at all. On the other hand, it is an activity which is different from any other. In terms that are becoming increasingly popular, religion is one particular language of humanity ; it deals with the same reality as science and art and politics, but it deals with them in its own particular way. The answers we get from reality depend very much on the questions that we put to it. If we ask a scientific question, we shall not get a religious answer, though we may get an answer that can become the raw material of religion. If we never ask a religious question, we shall never get a religious answer ; but, if we do ask a serious religious question, we can never ask it with anything less than the whole of ourselves, since the whole of the reality of our personal being is at stake. Within this framework of wholeness there seems to be a fairly close correlation between different parts of man's complex nature and the various stages of his development towards intellectual and spiritual maturity.

In the pre-adolescent stage the emphasis is naturally on feeling. The religion of a child tends to be imitative. But it can be perfectly sincere, spontaneous and charming, though evidently at that stage of life it can have very little intellectual content. It would not do for an adult to attempt to remain at that level ; but it is not the will of God that any of these earlier stages should be wholly and permanently lost to us, and it may be supposed that a perfectly balanced Christian personality, if such existed, would retain to the end of life much of the spontaneous joyfulness of the child in his approach to religion.

In the next stage, that of adolescence, the appeal of religion must be mainly to the will. Adolescence is usually represented as a stormy period of inner conflict and uncertainty, of loneliness and sentimental longing. All this is, no doubt, true ; but concentration on these rather superficial aspects tends to draw attention away from what is far more important—the fact that this is the period in which the hard, firm lines of the structure of character are being laid down. By the end of the period of adolescence the major structural changes in the body have taken place. Out of a wide range of earlier possibilities, the intellect is beginning to settle down to certain chosen lines of interest. Character to an almost alarming extent has taken on the outlines that will remain permanent, and within which in the majority of cases only a limited growth and modification are likely to take place. It is only to be expected that decisions affecting the whole of a man's approach to religion for the rest of his life will, in a great many cases, be taken in this period. All statistical study of the phenomenon of conversion show that the majority of definite conversions, the result of which is permanent, have taken place between the ages of twelve and seventeen. Even that Church which has less of a doctrine of conversion in this sense of the word than any other, the Roman Catholic Church, expects that in the majority of cases vocations to the priesthood will come to the point of at least initial decision in those years, and that training may suitably start at the age of seventeen.

This will appear disturbing only to those who have not grasped what the question at issue really is. It is the question of the centre around which the personality of the human being is to be developed. The natural centre of man is God ; only when God is the centre, and when the whole of life is related to Him, can man find peace and wholeness. But the mark of original sin upon us all is just that this natural relationship has been disturbed, and that we are all born in the abnormal situation of being each the centre of his own world. Baptism, participation in the death and resurrection of Christ, involves death to self and affirmation of the unchallenged authority of God. Through humble and conscious submission of the will of man to the will of God, this sacramental reality must become experienced reality. Adolescence is the period of the affirmation of human individuality, not infrequently in terms of rebellion proportionate to the real or imagined attempts of other individuals to suppress or thwart the freedom of the newly developing personality. It is clear that ultimately there are only two possibilities— that the personality should continue to develop around the Ego as its centre ; or that the Ego should be displaced from the centre and replaced by the living God. The word " conversion " has no meaning unless it is related to this change in the structure of personality. The change may be extremely gradual or it may in appearance at least be sudden. It may be marked by no crisis, or by a memorable crisis. It may take place at an identifiable moment or not. None of these differences is of any great importance ; what is all-important is that the change should genuinely have taken place.

Confusion is introduced into the subject at this point by the fact that it is possible, indeed easy, to become religious without ever having been converted. Religion can be made use of as an admirable means of inflating the vanity of the Ego. This is only the continuation into more civilized spheres of the primitive tradition of magic ; the difference between magic and religion being that magic aims at dominance of the deity, at power to use the deity for its own ends, whereas religion is self-abandonment to the will of God. The existence of self-centred, and therefore magical, devotion among Christians is too widespread to be doubted. Some of the symptoms of Christianity without conversion are not difficult to identify : scrupulosity, morbid anxiety about one's own salvation, tiresome and fussy religiosity, excessive interest in the externals of religious observance.

At this point it may rightly be objected that the battle against self-will must go on to the end of life, and that Dagon dethroned will continue to the end of time the attempt to set himself up again upon his throne. But no one who has understood the real nature of conversion has ever imagined anything else. Especially when the convert has come in from a wholly non-Christian background, he brings in with him, however sincere he may be, a " heathen " imagination, a non-Christian set of standards that can only very gradually be reduced to order. William Temple with his usual shattering commonsense once remarked that a man's business is to surrender as much of himself as he knows to as much of God as he knows ; and obviously this must be a lifelong business. But this is not to deny that the process must have a beginning ; that in the case of those who have been conscious rebels the process of surrender must have a conscious beginning ; and that the dethronement of the rebellious human will is something categorically different from religious nurture, from moral education, from spiritual emotion, or from the enlightenment of the intellect.

In point of fact, the most striking thing in many records of conversions, the genuineness of which has been evidenced by their permanence, is the extraordinarily small part played in them by emotion. Often the crucial experience has been preceded by a period of struggle and emotional upheaval ; sometimes conversion is accompanied by tumultuous and almost inexpressible joy. But it seems that in many cases the stormy wind must die down before the still small voice can speak. Of course, it is hardly possible that there should be no accompaniment of feeling, but the feelings actually recorded are most diverse, and hardly those which would most naturally be expected. Again and again, the experience at the moment of crisis is recorded as being like that of the mathematician who sees staring at him the solution of a problem that has long perplexed him (or of the crossword addict, before whose eyes an anagram suddenly falls into its proper shape !) ; a feeling of clear release, and of slight astonishment—" It was as simple as all that, and somehow I couldn't see it." Others have left on record a sense of utter tranquillity, " through clear shining after rain ". With yet others, nothing more has been involved than a quiet decision to fulfil some obvious but unattractive duty, and only reflection long afterward has revealed the crucial nature of a decision which was taken at the time without apparent effort, and without any idea that it could be related to anything so grandiose as conversion. Mr. C. S. Lewis has recently provided us with what must be the classic instance of the convert who entered into the Kingdom of Heaven in a state of exasperated irritation :

> In the Trinity Term of 1929 I gave in, and admitted that God was God, and knelt and prayed : perhaps, that night, the most dejected and reluctant convert in all England. . . . But who can duly adore that Love which will open the high gates to a prodigal who is brought in kicking, struggling, resentful, and darting his eyes in every direction for a chance of escape ? . . . The hardness of God is kinder than the softness of men, and His compulsion is our liberation.[1]

The variety of feelings and emotions should not be allowed to obscure that that which is central and essential in any genuine experience of conversion is the surrender of the human will, expressed at once, or very soon after, in an act of obedience : " Lord. what wilt thou have me to do ? "

But the role of the intellect in conversion must not be overlooked. Obviously there must be some intellectual content in every experience of conversion, however simple. This is especially plain in the case of conversion from a non-Christian faith to Christ ; a man must at the least believe that God is and that He is a rewarder of them that diligently seek Him ; he must at least have a fairly clear mental picture of the Christ in whom he is bidden to believe. It is not surprising that, though there are on record cases of non-Christians who have believed in Christ at the very first time of hearing of Him, they are exceedingly few ; faith has in most cases followed only on a prolonged period of confrontation with Christ and the Gospel.

But this initial and rudimentary intellectual content is sufficient only for the beginning of Christian life, and cannot support the later developments that are needed, if maturity is ever to be attained. A fuller knowledge of the faith itself is needed ; that is simply a matter of time, attention and education. But this is not all. The whole of a man's mental processes needs to be worked over in the light of the new knowledge that has come to him in Christ, and his Christian faith needs to be related to every other part of his mental activity. This is where trouble often begins. One reason why so many of those who seem to have made a good beginning in the Christian way go so far and no farther is that Christian belief and mental development have not been kept in step with one another.

[1] C. S. Lewis : *Surprised by Joy* (Geoffrey Bles, 1955), p. 215.

The tendency, between the ages of sixteen and twenty-one, to question everything and to criticize all the well-established ways is so widely in evidence that it may almost be regarded as a part of human nature itself. The strange antipathy that grows up between fathers and sons, mothers and daughters, is perhaps something that God Himself has permitted " lest one good custom should corrupt the world " ; and, without its existence, it is hard to see how much progress could ever be registered in human affairs. The spirit of criticism can be inhibited or crushed by the pressure of social convention, by inner feelings of guilt or disloyalty, by timidity, or by the sheer weight of parental authority. Too ready submission to this repression must inevitably result in willingness to live imitatively without adventure and on second-hand experience derived from the past. Where repression is vigorous but not quite successful, it is likely to provoke violent rebellion and total rejection of everything that is associated with the repressive authority. In these enlightened days we are no longer born as little liberals or little conservatives ; it might, however, be maintained that the experiences of childhood and adolescence make us either revolutionaries or reactionaries. It is extraordinarily difficult, in the training of the young, to find exactly the point of balance, which makes possible both a due regard for the values of the past and an adventurous openness to the future. What is true in other fields is also relevant to the Christian faith.

This problem, acute everywhere, is specially acute in the younger Churches, because the gap in thought and outlook between the generations is larger than elsewhere.

Picture a Christian boy in West Africa going back to his village after his first term at High School, and going to church. The pastor in his village is a worthy man, who, after working for a good many years as a catechist on the basis of a somewhat elementary general education and a sketchy theological training, has later been brought in for further study of theology, and sent out to work as an ordained minister in the villages. Men of this type have done yeoman service, and in many areas have been the real builders of the African Church. Are they to blame, if they find themselves unable to cope with a rapidly changing situation ? The quality of a man's mind is determined not by the number of things that he knows but by the breadth of the gauge ; what that is becomes evident in the kind of questions a man asks, and in the quality of the answers with which he is satisfied. Everyone who has been concerned in the theological education of middle-aged men is aware of the difficulty that only in very exceptional cases is it possible to broaden the gauge ; the width seems to have become unchangeably fixed at a considerably earlier age.

So our schoolboy, coming home brimful of new ideas and listening to the sermons of such a worthy man, will soon become aware of a clash between what he is hearing in church and what he is learning in school. If he is so bold as to express his difficulties to his pastor, it is not likely that he will get what to him is a satisfactory answer. It is not so much that the pastor does not know the answer to the question—that may well happen to anyone—as that his mind is moving on tracks which make it impossible for him to understand what the question is all about, and why it is important. It is not to be wondered at if the younger generation often concludes that religion is out-of-date, and throws itself with enthusiasm into the new fields of political activity which are opening out before it.

We encounter the same problem nearer home. Younger people complain bitterly of the way in which their genuine intellectual difficulties are handled. Doubts may be regarded by older people as in themselves sinful. Intellectual difficulties may be suspected of being really the rationalization of moral obliquity. Sometimes the young are infuriated by the intolerably patronizing attitude, " Oh yes, we've all been through periods like this ; you'll soon grow out of them." Those who do the gravest harm of all are Christians who give to the serious questions of the young trivial and unsatisfying answers on subjects which they have not taken the trouble to master.

It must, of course, be recognized that the faults are not all on one side. The young are impatient. They do not always take the trouble to formulate their questions correctly ; and they do not always recognize that it is much more difficult to answer questions than to ask them. It is often said that the great source of modern difficulties in religion is that so much education to-day is scientific, as though there were some necessary opposition between science and religion. That there is no such opposition is proved by the very large number of eminent scientists in all ages, who have found t possible to remain humble and believing Christians,[1] and have maintained that science is one of the methods that Christian faith must use if it is to attain to the fulness of the knowledge of God. There is a difficulty, but it lies elsewhere. It is that so much of what passes as scientific education teaches the pupil the use of only one kind of language [2] and the significance of only one kind of evidence. Those who received the earlier type of humane educa- tion, if intelligently imparted, had to acquire at least an elementary acquaintance with the languages of history, metaphysics, æsthetics, morals and religion. The student brought up mainly on chemistry and physics, with their emphasis on that which can be described, measured and weighed, may well remain unaware of the existence and relevance of these other languages. If, as may well happen, we ask a question to which the answer can be given only in a language with which we are unfamiliar, we are faced with two alternatives— either to go for ever without the answer, or to take the trouble to learn the rudiments of the language in which alone the answer can be given. This can be made clear by an illustration.

One of the commonest questions asked by students to-day is as to our knowledge of the historical reality of Jesus Christ. Clearly such a question can be answered only in terms of historical evidence (historical evidence will never make any man a Christian, but with- out a real historical Jesus there is no Gospel) ; this is a strange world to a student who has had no training in the handling of historical evidence, and he may be a good deal disturbed by the disparity between what he may wrongly have been taught to regard as the certainties of science and the merely relative probabilities with which history is concerned. What is certain is that he will never get any answer to his question unless he is willing to submit himself at least in a measure to the discipline of historical study.

" How do we know that the Gospels are authentic ? " is another question that is likely to come up in any group of students in any part of the world. With a little knowledge and a blackboard, it is possible to hold almost any group of enquirers enthralled with the story of the Bible, told backwards from the first printed Bible to

[1] On this see Arthur F. Smethurst : *Modern Science and Christian Beliefs* (Nisbet, 1955), especially pp. 32–41.

[2] In the sense, in which this term has been used above, of a particular approach to reality which asks a certain type of question and is therefore accessible to a certain type of answer.

the Chester Beatty papyrus and the still earlier papyrus fragment of St. John's Gospel, with side-glances at the Dead Sea Scrolls and the Tel-el-Amarna letters. But obviously this cannot be done in ten minutes, and it is not worth attempting, unless the original question was asked in such a spirit of earnestness as makes it likely that the questioner will stay the course.

Clearly not every Christian can hope to answer every question on every aspect of the Christian faith. But a special responsibility rests on the ordained minister to be aware of the kind of questions that younger people are likely to ask, and of the significance that they have for the younger generation. In the younger Churches, the disparity in the educational level of the generations makes it more difficult for the older man trained on conservative lines to keep up with the movement of thought, while at the same time the situation becomes daily more urgent, as an increasing proportion of young Christians get their education in secular or even anti-Christian schools. This is one of the reasons for which a raising of the level of theological training is recognized as the top priority in Christian strategy in almost every part of the world ; and, until this is achieved, the rapid production of Christian literature on all levels is only a short head behind in the classification of priorities.

All that has been said in this section is an expansion of the statement that no Christian experience can be fully valid or satisfying unless it touches every part of human nature ; and that, though Christian commitment must necessarily have a beginning, the full development of it is a lifelong task. The same affirmation has recently been made very strikingly from a different point of view. A Hungarian participant in a World Council Conference remarked that every man really needs three conversions—to Christ, to the Church and to the world (i.e. back to the world in witness and devoted service). It is an observable fact that these conversions may come in any order. One man first finds himself challenged to surrender by the recognition of Christ as the supremely lovable and adorable Master. Another first finds the reality of Christian faith in the shared fellowship and mystery of the Church. A third finds himself overwhelmed by the sorrows and sufferings of humanity, and discovers in Jesus of Nazareth the pattern and the inspiration for a life of service.

Probably in all genuine Christian living there is some element

all these three approaches. But it is evident that completeness
experience is possible only if one form of experience leads on to
the other two and all are held together in synthesis. It is not difficult to identify the type of anæmia which is likely to result, if one
of the elements is unduly dominant over the others. If a purely
personal devotion to Christ is central, the result is likely to be
individualism or introversion. If the factor of the Church is over-
emphasized, the characteristic deformation is ecclesiasticism. A too
exclusive stress on service may easily lead to a somewhat superficial
activism, which takes less than due account of the recalcitrance of
human nature, and of the difficulty of producing any extensive
change in society without a deep inner change in a fair proportion
of the individuals of which it is made up.[1]

It is equally clear that these partial emphases correspond, though
only roughly, to the characteristic strength and weakness of different
types of Church. The first is the strength, and also the danger,
of the evangelical Churches ; the second of those Churches which
may, in the broad sense, be called catholic ; the third of Churches
and movements of the liberal pattern. Many of the younger Churches
were brought into being by Churches and missions in which the
stress on individual and personal conversion was extremely strong.
This has resulted in many areas in a high level of commitment and
of interior devotion, whereas other aspects of Christian faith have
tended to lag behind. The importance of the Church as such was
not perhaps fully accepted in missionary thinking until the Tambaram Missionary Conference of 1938. Christian responsibility in
social and political witness, and the immense new opportunities that
political independence has brought to Christian minorities, are even
newer discoveries, which in many areas have not yet been fully
appropriated.

How are we to make sure that the Gospel in its fulness is presented to the rising generation ? Here we encounter the tragedy of
a divided Church. Those Churches and Christian organizations
which are strong in presenting the challenge to personal and whole-
hearted commitment to the service of Christ are in general suspicious
of " the social Gospel ", and those which are strong on the social
witness of Christianity are feeble in presenting the challenge to

[1] To the reader is left the interesting task of working out the other possible
permutations and combinations.

personal surrender. If the message of the Churches is divided,
cannot be wondered at if the faith of the younger generation
divided, distorted and imperfect. It will be our wisdom, if by wide
spread repentance and renewal we qualify ourselves to present the
fulness of the Gospel to those who are to follow us, and by so doing
anticipate the judgment that otherwise they will certainly pronounce
on the parents and teachers from whom they have received the
impressions of the Christian faith.

CHAPTER 3

FRONTIER SITUATIONS AND FLEXIBLE MINISTRIES

THE traditional structures and patterns of the Church's life are being threatened or broken up by the enormous growth in the population of the world, and the new period of migrations and movements of populations that that growth has ushered in. It is probable that, since the first appearance of recognizably human life on this planet, the population has been slowly but steadily increasing. This development has, however, been gradual and retarded by the recurrence over large areas of natural disasters. Epidemic disease and famine have claimed innumerable victims. Of the former, the best known instance in our history is the Black Death of 1349, which carried off about a third of the population of the country, and hastened, if it did not actually cause, the break up of the comparatively stable feudal structure of the Middle Ages. The great famine in Scotland in the reign of Queen Anne seems to have been almost as destructive as the Black Death. The ravages of war, except in such cases as the murderous wars of extermination carried on by the Huns and the Tartars, seem on the whole to have been less severe and more quickly repaired, though in certain parts of Germany two centuries were to pass before the devastations of the Thirty Years' War had been fully made up.

Alongside these sporadic visitations there was one constant and unchanging factor—infant mortality. John Colet, Dean of St. Paul's at the beginning of the sixteenth century, is recorded to have been the only child to survive from a family of twenty. Queen Anne was the mother of five living children (apart from miscarriages and still-births), not one of whom lived to succeed her. In Uganda at the beginning of this century it was reckoned that 80 per cent of the babies died. More than any other single factor, better medical care and the reduction of infant mortality have contributed to the sensational growth of the world's population in the last century and half. At the other end of the scale, better medical care means that men and women live longer, and so the problem is accentuated.

In almost every country in the world, the long familiar situation of an almost stable population has disappeared.

We may take it as probable that, unless checked by unforeseen calamities like the great influenza epidemic of 1918, the population of the world will rather more than double itself in every succeeding century.

Experts disagree as to the maximum population which it possible for our world to support in comfort. Some maintain that numbers are growing faster than the available production of food and that there are not many fertile areas left to be brought into the service of mankind. Others point to the immense surpluses produced by agriculture in America, although this is very far from having reached its maximum possible development. There are certainly vast areas in Central Asia waiting to be opened up. Canada could probably support four times as many people as it has at present and though the optimum population of South America, the continent of the future, is a matter for conjecture rather than precise calculation, it would certainly be far in excess of present numbers.

The Church cannot dissociate itself from these great new problems, as though it had no concern with them. On political developments the Church has in most countries little influence on agricultural economics it has no special word of wisdom to say But there are many problems of a practical nature by which the Church already finds itself faced in the new situation.

In a stable world the Church had developed for itself a largely static form of organization. For a thousand years the Church of Jesus Christ has been in the main a village Church. The unit was the small rural community of from two hundred to four hundred people, in which the pastor was one of the natural leaders and could know every member of his flock by face and by name. There are thousands of villages to-day in which these conditions still obtain The church is perhaps the only stone or brick building amid houses of mud and thatch, the centre of life and the natural meeting-place for the whole community. The festivals of the village are the Christian festivals. The rites of the Church touch the life of every individual at every important turning-point, and all the events of the farmer's year, ploughing and sowing and harvesting, are accompanied by the prayers and blessings of the Church. In hundreds of Indian villages known to me no Christian would lay the foundation of a new house without calling in the pastor or catechist for prayer, and no family would move into a new house until the appropriate ceremony of dedication had been performed. In some areas this simple natural life will continue for very many years, perhaps until the end of the world.

One of the first results of the modern growth of population has been the mushroom development of the enormous city. In eighteenth-century England the towns, with the exception of London, were still much like overgrown villages, living in close contact with the countryside by which they were fed. Cities like Norwich or Cambridge seem to us very much over-supplied with churches ; but, in the days when merchants still lived over their shops and it was taken for granted that everyone went to church, the churches were well filled and were real communities, fulfilling a social as well as a religious function. It was only the Industrial Revolution which let loose upon the world the increasingly menacing phenomenon of *les villes tentaculaires.* At the beginning of this century there were, I believe, only seven cities with over a million inhabitants ; to-day there are fifty-three (including such unexpected places as Seoul in Korea), and twenty-three others are rapidly approaching the million mark.

It has long been evident that industrialized man, the dweller in the great city, represents a new type of humanity. Here are men cut off from birth from contact with nature and with the fixed and slowly revolving order of the seasons, without roots and without traditions, with no ready-made and accepted community, other than the artificial community of the factory in which family, neighbourhood, leisure and religion naturally play little part. All the Churches were caught wholly unprepared by this development. The old structure of Church and parish has in many areas broken down. Where, as in England in the middle of the nineteenth century, the growth of cities was followed by an intensive programme of church building, it was already too late. Industrial man had already lost touch with the Church. He could no longer be fitted into the regular life of the parish ; the rhythm of the Church's life no longer seemed to correspond to the rhythm at which his life was lived, and the Church's message as ordinarily preached awoke no echoes in his mind.

This is a frontier of which the Churches in all lands have become painfully aware in recent years. The problem has been that of breaking through into this largely unknown world, and finding or creating the bridgeheads from which Christian advance can begin again. There have been a number of exciting experiments in flexibility—industrial chaplaincies, new types of ministry in the parish, and so on. The best known experiment of all is that of the worker priests in France, with their moving and in part tragic history of adventure, identification, witness, disapproval from above, reconstruction and determination to persevere. At the same time the French Roman Catholics have done more, and more thorough, study of the basic problems, psychological, sociological and religious, of industrialized man than has been carried out in any other country. Intensive study on the same lines in England and other countries is greatly to be desired.

But the movement of men from the country to the city, though it is the most obvious, is not the only way in which old structures and patterns have been broken up, and in which the Church has been challenged to find a new flexibility of method.

Contemporary with the Industrial Revolution was the diffusion of the white race across America and the subjugation of the American continent. Once again a new frontier was created for the Church, and once again the Church was almost wholly unready to see what was happening and to take in time the necessary action. Here the word " frontier " is particularly appropriate, since " the Frontier " is recognized by the majority of American historians as having been a more important actor in nineteenth-century American history than any human individual. Ever moving forward to the Pacific and from the Pacific, ever ahead of civilization and order, the frontier called out both the good and the bad qualities of the pioneer. This was the epic age of American history, with its fantastic journeys into the unknown, its intolerable hardships and loneliness, its brutality and courage, and its final triumph over all the obstacles that a generous but capricious nature could present. About 1880 the two advancing frontiers met, and the epic age came to an end.

Where in all this was the Church ? For many areas the answer is short and clear—" Nowhere ". The older and more respectable Churches of the East had early settled down into the traditional static forms, which made them ill-adapted for pioneering. The contemporary pattern of American religion has to a large extent been determined by the relative flexibility and inflexibility of the Churches. Usually first in the field was the Methodist circuit-rider, carrying with him no more than could be got into his saddle-bags, hastening from settlement to settlement, content with what hospitality could be had, and preaching a rather rough-and-ready Gospel. With the stage-coach arrived the more orderly Presbyterians and Congregationalists. Solid German and Scandinavian farmers brought their religion with them, and made the Middle West the great stronghold of Lutheranism. It is not quite fair, but not wholly unfair, to say that the Episcopalians waited and followed in the train.

It was the American frontier that produced those peculiarly American forms of religious expression, the camp meeting and the planned revival. And what else could have been expected ? Where there was no Church for a whole group of scattered settlements, the only place to meet was the open air. The visiting preacher must crowd into a week all the instruction that would more normally be extended over a year. Probably nothing would have touched the hardened pioneer but plain preaching about heaven and hell ; and if, for those culturally and emotionally starved dwellers in the wilderness, religion took on a deeply emotional colouring, that can be regarded only as entirely natural to their condition.

Statistics of Church membership in the United States at different dates show that, at the start of the rapid westward development, almost the whole population was lost to the Church. The striking increases in the figure over the last few decades [1] show that the Churches are at last catching up on what they ought to have done a century ago, and the increasing depth and intellectual maturity of American religion is evidence that the frontier period has now at length been outgrown. But it is significant that the largest Protestant groups in the United States are still those which best and most rapidly adapted themselves to a moving situation, the Methodists and the Baptists.

It has been worth while looking at this great nineteenth-century movement of the nations since it seems clear that in our day a similar

---

[1] It is reckoned that at the beginning of the nineteenth century less than 10 per cent of the population in the United States held membership in any Church. By 1910 this had risen to 43 per cent ; the figure is now about 60 per cent.

movement must begin anew. Certain countries are intolerably over-
populated, and must find areas into which some of the surplus
population can be spilled out. In Asia this applies especially to
Japan ; in Europe to Holland and Belgium and Italy. The extreme
limit seems to have been reached in some of the West Indian islands
when the present writer was discussing with a Puerto Rican friend
the possibility of a visit to Puerto Rico, another West Indian friend
standing by remarked, " In that case someone will have to take a
holiday—to make standing room for you on the island ! "

Much attention has been drawn, and rightly, in the Christian
world to services to refugees and displaced persons. Perhaps the
most successful piece of ecumenical service since the war has been
the provision of spiritual ministration in the refugee camps, the
Church being for thousands of these unhappy people the one thing
that still speaks of home, and provides a bulwark against the moral
deterioration that is almost always the consequence of long years
lived under such conditions. The steady movement of some 12,000
refugees a year to new homes beyond the seas is an achievement of
which the World Council of Churches may well be proud.[1] But it
must not be forgotten that this movement of peoples is on a far
smaller scale than the more normal emigration, the tempo of which
is now once again steadily increasing. Not long ago the General
Secretary of the World Council of Churches remarked that, the
farther afield you go in Australia, the more Dutchmen you are
likely to meet ! True, many have gone already ; but it is reckoned
that another million Dutchmen ought to leave Holland in the next
ten years. For Italy the number is perhaps two million, if Italy is
to be set free from the menace of chronic unemployment. When
such movements are in full swing, where is the Church to be found
and what ought it to do ? When the *Mayflower* set sail in 1620
the Pilgrim Fathers carried their minister with them ; is it possible
that such a situation can be reproduced to-day ?

The initial problem is only the introduction to a whole series of
delicate and interesting problems. In the first years of their life
in a new country, emigrants will long for, and should probably be
provided with, religious services in their own language and according to the tradition of their own Church. But should this be

[1] Not forgetting that Lutheran, Roman Catholic and Jewish agencies also have
a noble record of achievement in this field.

regarded as a permanent solution ? Or should the emigrant as far as possible be content to settle down as a member of one of the local churches, provided that there is one, and its order is not too far removed from that to which he is accustomed ? [1] Where, as in Britain, the immigration is largely of coloured people, ought special Churches to be provided to maintain the fellowship in which the immigrants arrive, or is this merely to encourage a dangerous isolation from the people in the midst of whom they have now to take up their life ? Point is given to the question by the experience of some of the Lutheran Churches in the United States. The Augustana Lutheran Church is almost wholly of Swedish origin, the Evangelical Lutheran Church of Norwegian origin. In earlier days services were in the language of the old country, and the Church was, and to some extent still is, a precious link with the old life. But to-day almost all the services are in English, and the younger generation is so thoroughly Americanized as to have no more than a sentimental link with a European country. Yet the two Churches remain distinct and separate in organization. Is this a situation which it is desirable to reproduce elsewhere ? The Churches will need far more flexibility than they now have if they are to follow their wanderers in this new Diaspora. May it not be that they will also need far more flexibility in thinking boldly and constructively along the lines of Church Union, before the lines of denominational division have hardened in the old pattern, or in a pattern even more complicated than the old ?

It is not only the crossing of geographical frontiers by large numbers of people that creates new frontiers for the Churches and challenges them to new adaptability ; the same thing can happen on a smaller scale within a single country.

A vivid contemporary illustration is the situation of Protestantism in France. It was only in 1801 that, through Napoleon's Concordat and the granting of equality to all forms of the Christian religion, the Huguenots obtained tolerable conditions of living. Before that, and especially after the Revocation of the Edict of Nantes in 1685, they had been a persecuted and harassed people. As a result Protestantism had almost died out over the greater part of France,

---

[1] It is unlikely, for instance, that members of the Orthodox Churches, who are emigrating in increasing numbers to Australia, will naturally find a home in any of the existing Churches in that continent.

and maintained itself mainly in its central strongholds in parts of Provence around Nîmes and Arles, in the Cévennes and in the western region around La Rochelle. Centuries of persecution and dogged resistance had produced a dour rocklike character, widely different from the Englishman's traditional idea of what a Frenchman is like, but appearing to grow quite naturally out of the equally dour and unpromising hills of the Ardèche and the Drôme. But in recent years the growth of the population has threatened to break up this old and well-ordered Protestant tradition of life. These rough hills and valleys cannot support more than a limited number of people ; at the same time the hard and exacting conditions of peasant life are proving less attractive to the younger generation, and over the last thirty years a steady drift away from the old scenes to the towns has become manifest. From the Cévennes many go to the manufacturing city of St. Étienne ; and this is less serious, since there the Reformed Church is established in strength, and can hope to care for newcomers. But how many move to areas in which no form of Protestantism exists ? Since it is most unlikely that they will become Roman Catholics, the probability is that they will be entirely lost to the Christian faith. And how can a Church, already hard put to it to pay its ministry, develop appropriate methods adequate to care for such a " dissemination " throughout the nation ?

In India the Church is faced with a similar " dissemination " but for a slightly different reason. Most of the Christians in India are of village origin and of the socially less distinguished castes. But the immense educational effort of the Protestant Churches, especially over the last hundred years, has brought into existence a surprisingly large Christian professional class—teachers, doctors, government servants and so on—who move in search of work, or follow their employment to regions far distant from their homes. Some years ago I visited the capital of a Native State (evidently this was before Indian independence) with a population of two million, in which no Christian propaganda among non-Christians was permitted. I was able to hold what was believed to be the first Christian service for twenty years. In my congregation of four persons was the head of the State medical service, an Indian Christian from the United Provinces ; it was known that there were other Indian Christians in the town, to whom it had not been possible to send notice of the service, or who had been prevented from attending. It is probable that there is now no town of 10,000 inhabitants in India in which no Christians at all are to be found.[1] Many of these lay Christian groups live hundreds of miles from the nearest mission station or ordained minister. What should the Church do to provide spiritual ministrations for its scattered sheep ?

In the last few pages the word " flexibility " has recurred with almost monotonous iteration. The Churches are for the most part familiar with only one form of organization—the Church or parish, with its ordained minister or paid lay catechist in charge, and the faithful under his care. Certainly this must remain the normal and standard form of Christian living ; no one has ever succeeded in suggesting anything that could adequately take its place. But what is the Church to do at times and in areas in which the system has clearly broken down, and no longer corresponds either to the Church's duty to witness or to the needs of those for whom the Church is called to care ?

Clearly the question reduces itself to this—in such situations what use ought the Church to make of its existing ministry, and what other emergency ministries ought it to develop ? Let us take the second question first.

The Churches can meet situations of rapid change only if they are prepared to make far more use of lay people than, with some shining exceptions, they have been accustomed to do. Most Churches have become far too much pastors' Churches ; in many little more is expected of the layman than that he should sit through the sermon with reasonable patience, and take out his cheque-book at the right moment. Some of the Churches which talk most about the priesthood of all believers are in this matter the most to blame. All this needs to be changed. We are not here considering the witness of the Christian layman in the world outside the Church ; that will come before us in another chapter. Here we are dealing with the question of that ministry within the Church for which every Christian is authorized by the fact of his baptism, and, which, when the circumstances demand it, he ought to be able and willing to exercise.

Let us go back to the Central Indian town, of which I was

[1] This is certainly true of South India. I have not been able to check with the Census reports whether it is equally true everywhere.

writing a few pages back. Why had there been no Christian service for twenty years ? Is the accident that apparently no ordained minister had visited it during that period a sufficient reason or excuse ? Surely, if there are only three Christians in a place, it ought to be possible for them to meet regularly for worship, and, even if they are cut off from the sacramental ministrations of the Church, to strengthen one another's hands in God through the fellowship of the Word and of prayer. Not long ago *The Times* informed us that for the first time in history a Protestant minister of religion was to take up residence in Kabul, Afghanistan, one of the countries that has always been most firmly sealed off from every kind of Christian propaganda. When the new minister arrives, he will not have to start from scratch ; he will be taking over a congregation formed ten years ago on the initiative of the British ambassador, and kept in being by the efforts of lay folk at times when the visits of ordained ministers were of very rare occurrence. This is an admirable example of what can be achieved by lay leadership. In such circumstances, Churches which have a fixed and regular liturgy appear to considerable advantage ; three Anglicans gathered around a single prayer book and Bible have everything ready prepared for them, even though there may be a great deal of Anglican timidity to be overcome before any one of them will venture to open his mouth in public. Nothing impresses continental travellers on a British ship more than attendance at a Sunday morning service at which the officiant is the captain of the ship. It may not be very well done ; it is the fact that it is done by a layman, without fuss and as part of his regular job, that makes the profound impression.

It is not only on the extreme frontiers that the problem of the lay ministry presents itself with ever increasing urgency. A good deal of interest has lately been directed to experiments in the Church of South India, where a change in circumstances has drawn attention to the danger of dependence on a paid ministry, and the inadequacy of such a ministry in certain circumstances to meet the needs of a growing Church.

Almost the whole of the life of the Church in the villages of India had been built up on the basis of the village schoolmaster, who was also the catechist in charge of the services in church. This system goes far back into the beginnings of missionary work. But its rapid growth began when, in 1860, the government decided to ay grants-in-aid to non-government schools which would accept a easonable amount of control and supervision by the Education Department. About two-thirds of the cost was met by the government and the remainder by the Church. This made possible an immense development of Christian educational work. In my old diocese of Tinnevelly,[1] there were 700 village schools with more than 50,000 pupils, of whom rather more than half were non-Christians. Over considerable areas every single school was a mission school. This made it possible to provide a resident Christian worker in every centre in which a school could be founded. But or some time it had been evident that this system might not last much longer; there was a movement on foot in favour of a national system of education entirely controlled by the government, and already the government was beginning to place restrictions on the leisure activities of those for so much of whose professional services it was itself paying. But, if this old and well-tried system broke down, what was to take its place? The answer could only be the development of a genuinely lay ministry, in place of the ministry of the paid catechist, who is not a layman in the full sense of the word.

The training of village leaders in the Bible and in the art of leading public worship did not prove to be an easy task. At first the experiment was tried of bringing a number of potential leaders in to one of the theological schools for a month. This did not work well. There are times of year at which there is not much work to be done in the fields, but it is only rarely that the farmer can afford to be away for so long; and a man whose mind is half on his fields and his cattle is not likely to absorb much of what he is being taught. So another method had to be found. The next experiment was that of week-end courses for a group gathered from a much smaller area. This was found to be very promising and practical. But it is going to take a very long time, on this method, to train as leaders in worship men who, however sincere, have not advanced beyond elementary education, and who start with only a limited knowledge of the Bible. Still, a beginning has been made; and these week-end meetings may prove to be of enormous importance in the future development of the Indian Church. Churches in other parts of the world might find themselves well-advised to follow this example.

[1] Now divided into the two dioceses of Tinnevelly and Mathurai of the Church of South India.

Having gone as far as this, the Churches may find themselves reasonably well satisfied with their provision for the ministry of the Word. But is this all that is required ? Traditionally the ministry is a ministry of the Word and Sacraments. How are the Churches on the frontiers faring in the provision of an adequate sacramental life for the faithful of their congregations ?

In many areas ordained ministers are all too few. Each has charge of a large area, with Christian groups in many villages. With the utmost effort it may not be possible for him to pay more than one visit every two or three months to each. Most of my Indian colleagues had to celebrate Holy Communion three times every Sunday, travelling considerable distances between the services. Such a hurried and occasional visit from a pastor who is already tired, and who, as soon as the service is over, must hurry on to his next engagement, hardly gives the congregation a due understanding of the central position of the Holy Communion in the life of the Church. The very rarity of the event ought perhaps to convey a special sense of solemnity ; but this can hardly be achieved unless, as still happens in the Highlands of Scotland, the infrequent Communion Service is preceded by a period of special and elaborate preparation. It is much more likely that the Sacrament will come to be regarded as an ornament on the periphery of the Church's life, a certificate of merit for those who are exceptionally regular in Church attendance.

So the question has inevitably been raised whether many of these lay workers in the villages ought not to be ordained to the ministry of the Sacraments, as well as being commissioned to the ministry of the Word, without being obliged to give up the ordinary avocation by which they earn their daily bread. During a period of rapid expansion in the mass movement area of the Methodist Church in the Nizam's Dominions a number of village workers were licensed annually to administer the Lord's Supper, without being ordained. But this was an emergency measure of a different type. These worthy men were only " half-laymen " in the sense that they were servants of the Church, who earned their living in whole-time Christian service. Furthermore, such a method could not be followed by Churches in which authority to celebrate the Holy Communion on behalf of the whole Church is given only in the solemn rite of the laying on of hands, in which the authority of the whole Church is conveyed in permanence to the one thus solemnly ordained. The question we are now considering is that of the possible ordination of the ordinary farmer or merchant or lawyer, who is prepared to give freely to the Church the time that he can spare from the ordinary occupation in which most of his time must be spent.

The proposal seems to us strange only because, from the point of view of the Early Church, we have got things thoroughly turned upside down. In the early days the essential thing was that every Christian group should have the Eucharist every Lord's Day ; a sermon would be provided when it was possible ; if it was not possible, the worshippers must be content with readings from what Justin Martyr calls the " memoirs of the Apostles " or from an apostolic letter. It is hardly too much to say that in those days almost anyone could celebrate the Holy Communion, and hardly anyone except the bishop could preach ; whereas now almost anyone can preach (or, rather, is allowed to preach !) and hardly anyone can celebrate Holy Communion. Lack of balance in either direction is to be deplored. In the Middle Ages the village priest said Mass every day, but hardly ever preached, preaching being left to the visiting friar or evangelist. To-day in thousands of villages a lay or half-lay leader preaches every Sunday, but is never able to celebrate the Holy Communion. Ought we to aim at a system in which the balance is better preserved ?

These experiments in South Indian villages have been recounted at some length not only because they are interesting in themselves, but because they raise so clearly the kind of questions that the Churches ought to be asking themselves in every frontier situation, where the traditional forms of the Churches' ministries have proved inadequate to meet the needs of growing or of moving populations, and not least on that most tragic of all frontiers, where the Church finds itself on the fringe of great city populations now almost wholly alienated from the Christian faith.

It has come to be increasingly recognized that it is useless to talk about bringing these people back to the Church. They have moved away from the Church, or perhaps have never been seriously conscious of its existence. It is for the Church to follow them, and to make their acquaintance in the places where they live and work. In some cities in Britain most interesting experiments have been made in the way of bringing the Church out of the Church, and back into the neighbourhood and the street. Holy Communion has been celebrated in private houses specially for the people of a particular street or area. No doubt such a form of worship lacks the splendour and dignity of traditional worship in the setting of the Church; but those who have been present have borne witness that in such services they have felt something of the atmosphere of the primitive Eucharist, as celebrated in a city of the Roman Empire in the days of the persecutions. There is no doubt that members of " the working-class " feel more at home in the intimacy of the small fellowship than in the more impersonal atmosphere of the great Church. Is there here a line of approach that might profitably be followed in a great many other similar situations ?

At once a question arises like that posed by the Indian village. To make the fellowship real there ought to be a centre of worship in almost every street. To maintain the fellowship there should be regular acts of worship. But one or two overworked ministers, nominally caring for fifteen or twenty thousand souls, cannot themselves create so many centres or pay regular visits to them. Are we not once again driven towards the conclusion that each of these centres should have its own minister or ministers, drawn from the neighbourhood and from those who earn their living in lay avocations ? Dare we go further, and venture to affirm that, if the local fellowship, still related to the large Church for common acts of worship, is to centre locally, as it ought to do, on the Table of the Lord, all these local ministers should receive such ordination as would enable them to minister the Lord's Supper in their neighbourhood and for the people of their fellowship ? This would be in marked contrast to current practice in most of the Churches; it would perhaps bring us back nearer to the primitive presbyterate as we can dimly apprehend it in the Epistles of the New Testament and other early Christian writings.

Some notable experiments have been made in the ordination to the ministry of men engaged in some other career, which they have not surrendered in order to give themselves wholly to the work of the Church. Perhaps the best known example is that of the outstanding nuclear physicist, Dr. William Pollard, who as a fully ordained presbyter of the Episcopal Church in the United States, continues to serve as the Executive Director of the Oak Ridge stitute of Nuclear Studies.[1] The consideration of such experiments at once brings us face to face with certain difficulties. Many professional men, by the nature of their employment, are liable to transfer from one place to another; in consequence a Christian group might lose its minister just at the moment when it most needed him, or when he was beginning to attain to his highest usefulness. There is the contrary situation in which a man cannot move, when on Christian grounds it might be highly desirable that he should! Most Churches have some provision for the transfer to another sphere of a minister who has fallen out with the faithful of his congregation. But a farmer cannot leave his lands, a doctor cannot leave his practice, when circumstances outside his professional responsibilities might suggest that a move would be a good thing. Undoubtedly there would be difficulties; but these difficulties ought not to stand in the way of courageous experiment on a large scale and in many directions. God has faced the Churches to-day with rapidly changing situations. In the past it has been largely the inflexibility of the Church's organization that has hindered it in keeping in step with the demands of the times. Everything to-day suggests that the risks involved in experiment are less than those of trying to maintain inflexibly the traditions that have come down from the past.

These various suggestions for lay ministries and part-time ministries must not, however, be taken to imply that the Churches could contemplate a reduction in either the numbers or the quality of their whole-time paid ministry. The development of new ministries could be only a supplement to, and not a substitute for, existing ministries. Indeed the development of such new types of ministry would actually impose new duties and new demands on the whole-time minister. The part-time minister cannot in the nature of the case have received a very thorough training; he will need careful guidance and help in all that he undertakes. If the local centre of worship within the larger parish were developed, the minister of the large church might find himself at the head of a college of a dozen presbyters, all looking to him for pastoral care, for instruction, and for guidance in their work. His position would be, in fact, very much like that of the primitive bishop. The Indian and African

[1] For his personal testimony, see *Modern Canterbury Pilgrims* (Mowbrays, 1956).

ministers of many Churches already find themselves placed in charge of anything up to fifty villages, with a team of perhaps a dozen partly-trained and paid catechists. If new schemes are worked out by which the paid catechist is replaced by a voluntary ministry, the pastor may find himself at the head of a much larger, though perhaps less well-qualified, team of workers. He will find himself literally *pastor pastorum* ; it will be his task to do as little as possible himself, and to attempt to do everything through those colleagues into whom it is his task to breathe something of his own spirit, or, as we should rather say, something of the spirit that he has himself received from Christ.

There is no reason whatever to suppose that the Church will ever be able to dispense with a whole-time ministry, though in times of necessity it may have to learn temporarily to do without it. But, for as long a period as we can in any manner foresee, better training for the full-time ministry of the Church will, as has been already remarked in the previous chapter, remain a first priority in the lands both of the older and of the younger Churches.

CHAPTER 4

THE CHURCH AND CHANGING SOCIETY

THE problem of the Church and society is not the same as the problem of Church and State; but a brief consideration of the latter may well serve as an introduction to the former, which is the special subject of this chapter.

Almost every possible form of the relationship between Church and State has been tried. Each has been found for a period tolerable; each in the end has been found to be in some way unsatisfactory.

At one extreme is complete " theocracy ".[1] The classic example of this in history is the Jesuit mission in Paraguay in the seventeenth and eighteenth centuries, where the Church controlled equally men's bodies and their souls. This system had the advantage of creating order and a measure of economic prosperity. It failed to produce liberty or initiative; it is noteworthy that in two centuries not a single Indian was elevated to the priesthood.

At the other extreme is the attempt to deny any relationship between Church and State, as though each moved in its wholly separate world without point of contact with the other. Through a misapplication of Luther's doctrine of the Two Realms, the Lutheran Churches in Germany have at times tended to this position.[2] The inevitable result of this doctrine is on the one hand the demonization of the State, and on the other the emasculation of the Church.

The Middle Ages made the noble attempt to relate Church and State in the person of the Pope and Emperor, considered as the twin lights of the world. There have been State Churches, as in Scandinavia and in Spain, with the minimum of toleration for those outside the State Church. There are countries like England and

---

[1] The term, of course, is not exact. It is used of the uncontrolled rule of those who claim to be acting in the name of God.

[2] It cannot be too often or too emphatically stated that Luther's doctrine is not that there is one Realm of God and another of the devil. The two Realms are those of Law and Grace. The Law is the Law of God, just as Grace is the Grace of God. In both Realms it is God who is drawing near to man. The ruler in the Realm of Law is directly responsible to God, just as the Christian in the Realm of Grace is directly responsible to God. Luther held that it was the task of the Church constantly to recall the ruler to this responsibility.

Scotland, in which there is an established Church which is not State Church in the full sense of the term. Another possibility i that of the " free Church in the free State ", in which the way i open for extensive co-operation between the two powers, withou infringement of the independence of the one by the other. And i many areas over long periods the Church has existed as a minorit community in a State the general outlook of which is determine by religious principles incompatible with those of Christianity. Thi was the situation in the early days of the Roman Empire ; it i still the situation in many parts of the world, particularly in Muslir lands, where the most that the Church can hope for is a somewha grudging toleration, with little possibility of influencing the life c the nation as a whole or of contributing to the formulation of th policies of the State.

In all these situations the Church has been able to settle dow and to live, though evidently some are much more favourable t its freedom and growth than others. But there is no inevitable an final form of the relation between the two entities, since neithe " Church " nor " State " is a term to which one definite and un changing meaning can be assigned. The relationships between ther must necessarily be like that between two moving bodies, perpetuall changing, especially as the Church is preoccupied with dimension of being which do not rightly fall within the purview of the State This has been so well expressed by Dr. T. M. Parker in his recen study of *Christianity and the State in the Light of History* that i would be hard to improve upon his statement :

> As I have tried to study a subject of undoubted fascination an complexity, it has been borne in upon me more and more that th real problem of Church and State arises from one fact. Christianit is a religion not easily fitted into the categories of natural huma: life. . . . May it not be that the many minds which have sought i vain a tidy formula for the ideal relations of Church and State i a sinful world have failed because their task was like that of mixin; oil and water or yoking together incompatible animals of the plough Certainly no attempt here explained seems to be perfectly self consistent or stands up fully to the logic of facts. Is it possible tha men have sought a synthesis where they could expect to find onl a *modus vivendi* ? [1]

[1] T. M. Parker : *Christianity and the State in the Light of History* (A. & C Black, 1955), pp. 171–2.

If this is true of the relations between the State and the Church, *a fortiori* must it be true of the relations between the Church and society. For the State as such has at least an identifiable outline and a measure of continuity, whereas the term " society ", in the sense of the forms of organization which men have produced in order to live together, covers an almost infinite variety of possibilities perpetually in kaleidoscopic change and modification. In order to live and bear witness, the Church must enter into relations with society ; the moment it does so, it undergoes modification and itself contributes to the modification of society within which it dwells ; and this is a ceaseless and never-ending process.

In theory it ought to be possible to produce a completely and unchangeably Christian society. If all the members are Christian, why should this not be attainable ? Christians believe that there is nothing sacred in itself and nothing profane in itself, that all things come from God, and that the power of the Gospel is destined to penetrate to every part of man's being and to every area of his life. Yet history shows that this vision can never be more than transitorily translated into reality. Christian realism must take account of the ever-present fact of human sinfulness ; and it is the unvarying character of sin that, unlike righteousness, it never abideth in one stay. Even in the Trappist monastery human egoism and ambition and sloth continue to do their devastating work. But, even apart from this activity of sin, there are other factors in the human situation that make the stable Christian society an ever receding dream. We are related to God in different ways on different levels of our being. On the specifically religious level, we are, or should be, in direct personal fellowship with God through the Holy Spirit. All our life in society with our fellowmen, all our use of the good gifts of nature around us, should be determined by the Christian sense of this fellowship with God in Christ ; yet in these " secular " spheres of life the relationship with God is indirect, and each has a relative autonomy of its own. In these partly autonomous realms changes may take place so rapidly that the Christian conscience lags behind in its attempt to understand them and to bring the changed situation once more under the dominion of the law of Christ.

The Marxist interpretation of history is narrow and incomplete. But, since Marx wrote and thought, it has been impossible for serious students to disregard the enormous significance for human life of a change in the methods of economic production. Ideas are not mere epiphenomena of economic changes ; they have legs, and are far more effective and independent than Marx was prepared to recognize. But it is just the fact that economic changes do affect social order, and that this in its turn has profound influence on thought and outlook. All of us in the West, and even in the United States, are far more Marxist in our general outlook than we imagine. Now methods of production belong to one of the autonomous spheres, and changes can take place in them rapidly and almost unobserved. To say that there is no connection between economic laws and Christian principles, or that Christian judgments have no relevance to economic laws, is almost blasphemy. But such changes may already have taken place long before their significance for any Christian concern can be perceived, and still longer before a Christian interpretation or judgment can be arrived at. At such times there is great danger that the Church may fall out of step with the movement of the time, and may lose its power to bear relevant and effective witness. It is at such times that the relationship between Church and society becomes problematical and uncertain.

To live at all, the Church must arrive at some kind of a *modus vivendi* with the society in which it dwells. Since the Church, both by its divine calling and by its own inner coherence, is more stable than any human society, it tends to be conservative ; there is always the danger that it may attribute to the *modus vivendi* a permanence greater than belongs to what is in essence only a provisional arrangement. If the Church attaches itself too closely to one ordering of human society, it runs the risk of perishing in the dissolution of that order. At times of rapid change, what might at first appear as the disaster of schism has sometimes in the end been beneficial, since within the schismatic body the Church has found new resources for adapting itself to a situation in which otherwise it might entirely have failed to find a foothold.

The first great revolution in the Church's relationship with society was brought about by Constantine's conversion and his acceptance of Christianity as the religion of the State. Almost overnight the Church emerged from a situation of persecution and obscurity into one of safety and privilege. It settled down very comfortably in these new green pastures, not without grave peril

its soul. There was always the danger that the Church might
nk back from a Christian to a pagan concept of its nature, being
ntent to be no more than the spiritual counterpart and consecration
f the activities of the State, instead of standing firm in its own
ndependent nature as critic, judge and, when necessary, prophet of
oom. And, in its conflict both with heretics and with pagans, the
hurch learned that dreadful habit of relying on the secular arm to
chieve supposedly spiritual purposes, from which it has never
nanaged wholly to free itself.

In Constantinople this system lasted for more than a thousand
ears. In the West, providentially, the barbarian invasions brought
to an end much sooner, and the Church was set free to follow a
r more diversified course of development.

Most Christians in the West had so far identified the Church
ith the Roman Empire as to believe that the fall of the Empire
ould only usher in the Kingdom of Antichrist. When the Goths
cked Rome in A.D. 410 it seemed to many that the end of the
orld had come. As years passed, the Church woke up almost
ith surprise to the discovery that often human ends are divine
eginnings ; and that, so far from the fall of the Roman Empire
aving marked the end of the Church's influence, it was a call to
he Church to a new career of service as the most formative influence
n those barbarian kingdoms, from which all the nations of modern
urope are sprung. The period which began with the baptism of
lovis may be thought to have ended only with the Europeanization
f Russia under Peter the Great. In those barbarous times the
hurch of the Romans alone could supply the kings of the new
ingdom with that administrative experience of which they stood
n need. The bargain was struck, and the Church settled down
o the somewhat stormy amenities of the Feudal Age.

The word " feudal " has come to be almost a term of abuse, as
hough it stood for nothing but the exploitation of the poor and
elpless by the wicked and unscrupulous rich. It cannot be denied
hat this was a hard and cruel age, and that there was a great deal
f oppression. But feudalism was an improvement on the epoch
f pure chaos that had preceded it ; and, so far from being primarily
n instrument of exploitation, it had its basis in a strong feeling of
nutual dependence and obligation. The men of that time did not
hink of themselves as " feudal men ". Custom was much more

flexible than the history books sometimes make it appear. Para doxically, the only area in which feudalism was systematically worke out in any complete form was the artificial Crusader Kingdoms the Levant, and even there it may be thought doubtful whether th elaborate customs recorded in the text-books were ever fully p into effect. But, by and large, there was a certain uniformity organization, a certain sense that the strong were bound to prote the weak, and that those whom they defended were bound to serv their protectors. And everything depended on the land.

On what else could it depend, when the good old Roman coinag had practically disappeared, and commerce was almost at an end The bishop had to live if he was to be of service to the king. Th king must supply him with lands for his support, and for them I must do homage to the king like any lay baron. The priest mu live, and therefore the lord of the manor must give him land. Bu by accepting land at his lord's hand, the village priest became muc more his lord's man than the bishop's man. To us, accustomed a money economy, this system seems very cumbrous and secular but at the time all these things seemed perfectly normal, and trac of the system are with us yet. The Church had certainly succeede in finding a *modus vivendi*, in becoming integrated with the surroun ing society ; perhaps too successfully, and once again to the per of its soul. There was grave danger that the unity of the Chur might be finally broken up through its subjection to contendir feudatory princes ; there was equal danger that, through too clo alliance with the powers of the world, the Church might lose i power to teach and to protest against injustice.

The Feudal Age lasted a long time, though with many inn modifications, and with outlying bastions highly resistant to chang But signs of change were there many years before the beginnir of the next epoch of history. Already in the fourteenth century th great growth of the Free Cities (in north Italy, in the Low Countrie in the German Hanse league), the renewal of commerce, the econom changes set on foot by the Black Death, the beginnings of scepticisr in philosophy and of anti-clericalism in religion, all portended change. Power was about to pass from the great nobles to th landed gentry, and to the vigorous, thrusting, adventurous, intelliger merchant class of the cities. What was to be the future of th Church in the new world that was about to come to birth ?

The period of the Reformation has been described in a great many different ways. It is not always noticed that it is the beginning of the period of the layman. Up to the end of the fifteenth century authority had everywhere been concentrated to an astonishing extent in the hands of ecclesiastics. The turning-point in England is the reign of Henry VIII. The last great ecclesiastical statesman is Cardinal Wolsey ; the first great lay statesman is Sir Thomas More. It is perhaps indicative of the greatness of More that he seems to belong equally to the medieval and the modern worlds, being on the one side the intellectual ancestor of the Cecils and Bacons of a later age, and on the other the begetter of the saints of the Roman Catholic tradition in England. For a short time under Charles I the virtuous Bishop Juxon of London was Treasurer of the realm, but this was only an exception. The sixteenth century permanently limited the field of the churchman, and opened out new pastures to the vigour and enterprise of the layman.

It was perhaps fortunate that just at that moment Protestantism was there to head the new layman off from the violent anti-clericalism which was beginning to develop just before the Reformation, and to offer him a form of religion compatible with that sense of individual liberty, freedom of judgment and personal responsibility, which he was beginning to claim as his birthright.

It is interesting to note certain contrasts between northern Europe and the countries in which Protestantism never took root, or was suppressed. In France the ecclesiastical statesman continued long after he had disappeared in England, and the seventeenth century was the century of Richelieu and Mazarin. The Papal States continued till 1870 to be governed by churchmen and to be far the worst governed country in Europe. Is it fortuitous that Christian statesmen such as Mr. Gladstone and Lord Shaftesbury were English, whereas the creator of modern political Italy was the liberal agnostic Cavour, and that a succession of anti-clerical ministries in France led up to the separation of Church and State under Combes in 1905 ?

The next great revolution in society was the emergence of the proletariat as the major force in the political world. The first sign of this change came when the Paris mob transformed the bourgeois French Revolution into a reign of terror. For more than a century statesmen in Europe lived in fear, and not altogether unjustified fear, of the same thing happening again and happening elsewhere.

It has often been asserted that Methodism saved England from revolution. On some lips this is the highest praise, on others a rueful condemnation of a movement that ought to have been democratic and was not. In neither case is the real nature of the Methodist contribution very accurately understood. At the time of John Wesley's death Methodists in England were too few and too scattered to exercise any great influence. It was only after Waterloo that Methodism showed its capacity to serve as the proletarian Church, and to offer a new and rising class a Christian home such as it had not succeeded in finding in the established Church. The Methodist chapel, small and perhaps unnecessarily ugly, sprang up everywhere.[1] Readers of *Shirley* will remember Charlotte Bronte's description of the services of the Ranters, and can well understand how uncongenial they must have seemed to persons of culture and refinement. But to the crushed and underpaid workers Methodism offered light and warmth and hope. Here a man was personally and individually valued. The money that others spent on beer the Methodist saved, penny by penny, out of his hard-won earnings to build himself up a modest competence. The leisure that others spent in the public-house he devoted to educating himself, laboriously learning with a dictionary the language of Shakespeare and the Bible as though it had been a foreign tongue. The class meeting gave him the idea of disciplined organization. The temperance crusade gave him a platform and that experience in public speaking which ultimately was to lead him into public life and to the House of Commons. It must not be forgotten that William Booth in early life was a Methodist evangelist ; and that, at a time when the older Methodist Churches were engaged in becoming respectable, the Salvation Army carried on the original proletarian tradition.

It was this Christian leaven in the working class, together with the Christian Socialist movement of F. D. Maurice, Charles Kingsley and their friends, that gave to the British Labour movement up to the end of the nineteenth century a character so different from that of similar movements in other countries. Throughout the nineteenth century all over the continent of Europe it was taken for granted that the Church would always be on the side of power

---

[1] All dissenting bodies seem to have acquired new life in the first half of the nineteenth century ; but in the main it was to the Methodists that the poorest classes turned.

against the oppressed, and that it would resolutely oppose any change in the *status quo*. It is only in this century that Christians on the continent have found it possible to take their place naturally within the parties of the left; and the separation between Church and working class became far more radical than it ever was in Britain.

It will have been noted that, in each of the two cases cited from British history, the price of division had to be paid for the ability of one part of the Christian fellowship to adapt itself to rapidly changing conditions and to find itself at home in a new and emerging society. The question of whether this was inevitable must engage us a little more closely.

It is natural that the Church should be conservative. It is an anvil that has worn out many hammers. It has seen the Roman and Byzantine Empires pass away; it has outlived the Feudal Age, the squirearchy and the rule of the merchant princes. The Archbishop of Canterbury is the heir of a longer uninterrupted line of predecessors than the Queen of England. The Church knows that it will long outlive all existing systems and forms of government. In all those long years of experience, it has learned that almost any form of order is to be preferred to violence, since in the days of violent revolution the weak and innocent are likely to suffer more than others.

And the Church knows well that change can be accompanied by loss as well as gain. Its message is and always must be revolutionary in principle—" He hath put down the mighty from their seat "; but no one could have been less revolutionary in His immediate acts than Jesus Christ; indeed it was His failure to take the path of the popular revolutionary that led Him to the Cross. This is often overlooked by those who claim to be the friends of progress; sometimes they give the impression of taking it for granted that all change must necessarily be for the better, and that no price is too high to pay for a new and better world. But evidently this is not so. No one who is old enough to remember what the life of the poor was like in Britain in the early years of this century is likely to question that the social revolution of the last fifty years has been a very good thing. But need the losses have been so heavy and the price so high ? It is possible both to appreciate the changes, and at the same time to deplore the savage and wanton destruction of the beauty of Britain by which they have been accompanied. A little more patience, a little more reverence for the past, and much of the spoliation of our treasures could perhaps have been avoided.

Yet, when all possible defences have been put forward, it remains true that the greatest temptation to which the Church is exposed is that of seeking rest, of ascribing permanence to some state that cannot be other than transitory, of failing to discern the signs of the times, and so of identifying itself with an order of society that is already passing away.

When that has happened, it is most urgent that the voice of the Christian prophet should once again be heard. It was prophetic vision that made F. D. Maurice in some ways the most significant Christian thinker in the England of the nineteenth century. The Evangelicals had an incomparable record in the righting of social wrong, in England as well as in the British Empire overseas. But they dealt with evils one by one, and within the framework " of the duty of a Christian nation ". It was given to Maurice to look deeper, and to see that the very existence of the Christian nation was being threatened by a false philosophy and a false doctrine of society. The erroneous belief in the natural harmony of interests and of the self-acting character of economic laws led many Christians, while regretting poverty and suffering, to believe that they were inevitable, and that to " interfere with economic laws " would be contrary to the ultimate interests even of the poor. It was this false doctrine that Maurice challenged in the name of Christ. He saw that, in the changed conditions of the time, the whole basis of society had to be thought out afresh, and that the domain of economics must be claimed as a part of the Kingdom of Christ, that, like any other part of that Kingdom, is subject to His laws. If the Church failed to take the lead in this re-thinking, it might find itself wholly excluded from influence in the new society that was coming into being.

Never could the prophetic gift have been more urgently needed than to-day, when the Church lives everywhere under conditions of rapid change, where it has to learn to adapt itself to the life of new societies, and where the conditions for its effective witness are by no means clear.

The first, and most obvious, area of rapid change is that of the Communist-controlled countries. What is to be the attitude of

Christians to the revolution that has swept over them ? To the majority of Christians, no doubt, the events of these years have presented themselves as nothing but a series of disasters ; and there has been a real danger that the Church, almost the only institution that has survived the deluge, should become the centre of nostalgic regrets for a past that can never come again. To accept this position would indeed be to condemn the Church to live irrelevantly in the past. Some leaders, in lands in which the Communists are now in control, have taken a very different view. In the West it is still possible to speak theoretically about the revolution. Over more than a third of the world it has already happened. The task laid upon the Church in such areas is not to discuss theories, but to find out the will of Christ in a situation that has already arrived. Some leaders are prepared frankly to accept the Communist revolution as a judgment of God on Churches which had failed to realize or to preach the social implications of the Gospel. The Protestant Churches in Hungary had been closely associated with an organization of society which till the revolution had still been largely feudal and patriarchal, and had lived mainly on extensive endowments in landed property. Now all is changed. In this revolution the Churches were deprived of their lands ; they found it necessary to accept temporarily a measure of support from the government to carry them through the interim period, until they could depend for support only on the generosity of the faithful. The Hungarian Churches learned to accept these losses as a just judgment of God, and to express their sense of guilt for the failure of the Churches in the past to attend to the cry of the poor. The spiritual revival, which apparently these Churches are experiencing, is attributed by many to their ability to read prophetically the signs of the times, and so to find principles by which to live in a world of revolution.[1]

This process of adaptation raises in its acutest form the dilemma of the Church in its relation to society. If it is to be a witness and a power in the life of a society, it must in a measure accept that society and identify itself with it. If the identification is carried too far, the necessary distinction between the Kingdom of God and the kingdoms of the world is blurred. How can the middle line

---

[1] These lines were written before the tragedies of late 1956. Historically they are correct. How far they correspond to the present situation it is impossible to say.

be found between these two dangers, in the midst of a society that
is professedly anti-religious and has never repudiated its purpose
to bring all religions to destruction ?

It is this that causes the Churches on one side and the other of
the Iron Curtain to look at one another with a considerable measure
of anxiety, amounting sometimes to distrust. Those in the West
are inclined to think that the Churches in Communist countries are
in danger of yielding themselves up as docile instruments of an anti
Christian ideology. The partners on the other side of the line reply
that the Western Churches have long since made a similar surrender
and are now not so much the voice of God as faint echoes of the
capitalist system. The West refuses to follow Russia in support
of the Stockholm Peace appeal on the ground that this is merely a
political move. Russia replies that the Western Churches are now
merely pawns in the game of American dollar imperialism and
America's will to war ; their unawareness of their situation is taken
as clear evidence of the completeness of the surrender that they
have made.

" At last we are free ", say the Churches in Hungary. " At last
we are free to be ourselves ", say many of the Christian leaders in
China. It is impossible to doubt that the revolution has brought
to these Churches a real sense of liberation. But what is the nature
of that freedom ? It is a great thing that the Churches survive and
have liberty to worship. But the price that has to be paid for this
freedom would seem to be the withdrawal of the Christian into the
purely " religious " realm, and silence on every other subject, especially if to speak would seem to involve any criticism of the existing
régime. Where, then, is the prophetic liberty to express the judgment of God upon the nations and upon society ? The problem of
the Church's freedom was recently discussed by the well-known
Czech theologian, Professor J. L. Hromadka, and his words deserve
close attention :

> As theologians we are aware that the Church in the true sense
> must always be shaped by forces which come from above and which
> liberate us internally—or are we not aware of this ? The crisis of
> the Church throughout the world consists in Churches not realizing
> this, in that they constantly seek support where they should not, and
> do not have the courage of inner freedom which her true substance
> gives the Church. The question of freedom is a difficult theological

problem, for true freedom is not something served up to us on a platter : " Help yourself ! " On the contrary, it is something which must always be fought for and won in spiritual courage against our own human self and everything to which we are accustomed. What joy it is when we realize that the Church is actually living by this freedom and that it cannot be taken from her by anyone. What breadth is necessary here, what inner liberation and what love for those who are around us.[1]

Certainly there is a liberty which can never be taken from the Church—the liberty of a man's own conscience in his inner fellow-ship with God ; the liberty of the desert, into which some good men at all times have found it necessary to retire rather than com-promise with what they judged to be evil ; the liberty of martyrdom, when this is the only form in which witness can be rendered. Dr. Hromadka may be right in thinking that these are the only forms of liberty that matter to the Church. But this is not the ordinary use of the term " liberty ", and some may feel that there is something still to be said for the liberty of life, worship, testimony and influence, which is one of the precious gains of centuries in the very partially Christianized countries of the West.

The Churches of the West have not yet had to face a situation in which all the landmarks of the past have been removed ; yet they too have had a considerable labour of adaptation to undertake. Their problem can be summed up in the single phrase " the Welfare State ". In earlier days the tasks of government were considered to be the maintenance of public order and the administration of justice between man and man. Even at the end of the nineteenth century Lord Salisbury held the view that the best government was that which interfered with people as little as possible. The Constitution of the United States seems to be based on the principle that govern-ment is a bad thing, and that therefore the main purpose of a con-stitution should be to be beforehand with the government, and to see to it that it can do as few as possible of the things that govern-ments ordinarily do. It is for this reason that the progress of the Welfare State, except in the field of public education, has been less rapid in America than in some other countries. But even there, how immense is the change that the last thirty years have brought !

[1] Quoted from an address given on the occasion of the tenth anniversary of " the liberation of Czechoslovakia ".

Simultaneously all the newly independent nations of Asia and Africa seem to have accepted uncritically the ideal of the Welfare State, and to be pressing towards it as fast as they are able. It is possible for the Churches to approve, with greater or less enthusiasm, the changes brought about by this silent but extremely effective revolution, and at the same time to recognize that the Church has been brought through these changes into uncharted and unfamiliar waters.

In the first place, the State has now taken on responsibility for a great many things that the Church used to do. In Britain up till 1870 education was almost a monopoly of the Churches. To-day State schools are very much in the majority ; and, though the Butler Act of 1944 recognized the place of religion in education, the Church cannot play more than an indirect part in seeing that religious education is everywhere provided and everywhere adequate. With the rapid disappearance of poverty many of the charitable activities of the Church are no longer needed, and it has become almost impossible to administer many of the ancient charitable trusts. The same transformation has already begun in the younger nations of the East. In India, where the Churches were the pioneers in almost every field of education, before many years have passed the whole of education may be absorbed into a national and secular system. Hospitals, leper colonies and so forth have been a wonderful field for the demonstration of Christian love in action, and there has been little competition. To-day at every point the State is stepping in, not always with equal efficiency, but with immensely greater resources at its command.

The Churches should waste no time in shedding tears over these limitations of their activity. These other things, excellent as they are, are never more than subsidiary to the real vocation of the Church. In many parts of the world Christian education has threatened to become a substitute for the preaching of the Gospel. The extreme preoccupation of missionaries and African clergy with the work of the schools has been identified in certain areas as one of the main causes of the spiritual poverty of the Churches. To be deprived of their schools might not be in all ways a disaster to the Churches. Nor is it likely that the Churches will ever lack for activities and interests outside the walls of the Church building and its worship. One need passes but another comes. All Western countries are faced by the growing and agonizing problem of the old, with their oneliness and the sense of futility that old age often brings. Here more human and gentle touch is needed than can readily be supplied by the noble army of civil servants. Switzerland is one of the most splendidly organized of Welfare States. Frenchmen crossing the border from their own country, where mercifully it is still permitted to be a little dirty and untidy, are at first lost in admiration of the precision and order by which the Swiss way of life is marked ; before long they are perturbed by a sense of the boredom which seems to have descended on the country as a whole. Perhaps in such areas the Church is specially called to bring back into life that eternal perspective, without which no genuinely human life is possible.

But the problems with which the new situation confronts the Church are far deeper than those of practical activities and possible fields of service. What the Welfare State has raised again in an acute form is the question of the nature of the good life for man, and of the value of human liberty. In the life of simple tribes and peoples, everything is controlled, and the liberty of the individual counts for very little. Such a system has many advantages, and it may be doubted whether without it human life under primitive conditions would be possible at all. At a more complex level of civilization, the Indian caste system creates a great brotherhood over a wide area. The widow and the orphan are fitted into the system, and cared for, albeit sometimes harshly. But, where the system has remained unmodified by outside influences, there is little place for individual initiative or for the creative development of personality. The long travail of European civilization has been the liberation of the individual, first the man, and then much later the woman, to be a real person. The caricature of this process is individualism. The fulfilment of it is the society of free persons who live together, not of constraint but of their own choice and decision, in a complex of creative relationships. To-day the swing seems to be away from individual responsibility and towards a highly developed State collectivism. The immense weight of social pressure is exercised in the direction of conformity. The State takes over many responsibilities that till lately were regarded as belonging to the family. Where will this end ? And are there not moral and spiritual problems in this evolution, of which the Churches would do well to be aware ?

Let us take as a single and pertinent example the question of thrift. Until lately it was widely taught, and widely taken for granted, that it was a good and Christian thing for a man to spend less than he earned, and to put something by. This would protect him from being completely dependent upon others in old age. It might make it possible for him to leave a little to his children, and so to make their struggle less harassing than his own had been. Such economy was regarded as a sign of a virile independence, and as a virtue worthy of a free man and a Christian. Now the validity of all these assumptions is being questioned from many sides. The weight of taxation makes it almost impossible for anyone to save at all. The rapid progress of inflation makes it doubtful whether it is worth while to save, since at the time when the savings are needed they may have lost all but a fraction of their value. A serious impulse to save could be given, only if a government were to provide a savings unit the value of which would be kept constant in relation to the actual purchasing power of money at any given time, and this is a burden with which it is most unlikely that any contemporary government will saddle itself. Not only so ; now we are told by some of our guides that the idea of thrift itself has nothing Christian about it ; it is merely a relic of bourgeois morality. A man ought to be willing to forfeit the possibility of saving for himself, in order that the State may be able to provide adequately and equally for all. To desire to save for the family is only a refined form of selfishness, and tends to make inequality permanent. The truly Christian principle is that those of each generation should start equal, without advantages artificially inherited by some from a past which they themselves had no share in creating.

Clearly there are a great many questions here for the moralist and the theologian, as well as for the politician and the economist. Is it self-evident that reward should be equal for all, regardless of what each has contributed in the way of diligence and the bearing of responsibility ? The sense of the family has been a tremendous power in human history. Can its continuity be so easily dissolved. Is the willingness of parents to sacrifice themselves for the advantage of their children no more than a form of bourgeois selfishness. Such are some of the questions with which the Churches in the West must wrestle, as they seek to find a satisfactory relationship to the new society that is growing up around them.

The younger Churches are all caught up in the social and political changes resulting from the passing away of the colonial era.

" Colonialism " is everywhere a term of abuse to-day.   Clear
thought on the subject is not helped either by Russia's failure to
recognize its own sin in producing in the Baltic states a colonialism
as wicked and oppressive as anything ever perpetrated by the West,
or by the American illusion that " colonialism " can mean only one
thing, and that King George III is still as important in the minds
of people in England as he is in the minds of the Americans.   When
the smoke has cleared away, and when full allowance has been made
for the crimes, the short-sightedness and the vacillations of the
colonial powers, it may yet come to be seen that the colonial epoch
made certain positive contributions to the well-being of the peoples
of Asia and Africa, and to the unification of the interests of all the
peoples of the world.

From the beginning of the nineteenth century onwards, the alternative before many primitive peoples was not between liberty and
subjection, but between extinction and protection by a stronger
power.   The statistics of population in hundreds of Pacific islands
make this clear beyond the possibility of doubt.   In Africa it was
the colonial powers that brought slavery and inter-tribal warfare to
an end.   The visitor to the bright and cheerful town of Benin to-day
would hardly believe what a scene of misery and carnage it was
when British troops reached it only sixty years ago.   The great
achievement of Britain in India was the unification, for the first
time in history, of the whole sub-continent.   Asoka in the third
century B.C. penetrated as far as Mysore.   The Moguls from the
fourteenth to the seventeenth centuries controlled the greater part
of the peninsula but not the whole.   It was only in the nineteenth
century that the unity of India was achieved—a unity which in
certain matters persists in spite of the political division of the sub-
continent that has followed the ending of British rule.

The extent to which the Churches and missions were identified
with the colonial powers has been greatly exaggerated.   The history
is far from having been one of harmonious co-operation on both
sides.   Certainly in many cases missionaries have welcomed the
advance of colonial power, but this has not been always from bad
or unenlightened motives.   The missionaries in East Africa who
rejoiced when Britain assumed a protectorate over the region were
not moved, as has been suggested in a recent well-informed study
of the missionary factor in East Africa, by imperialistic aims, but

rather by the consideration that those territories could never b
delivered from the curse of the slave trade, unless the Europea
powers extended to the interior that measure of control which the
had already established over Zanzibar and the coast. On the whol
however, it must be admitted that the Churches settled down com
fortably under the colonial régimes. Yet in most countries the
have experienced remarkably little difficulty in accepting the anti
colonial revolution—a revolution more gigantic than that achieve
by the Communists in Russia, and ultimately affecting a far large
number of people—and in settling down as Churches of the ne
independent nations. Most national Christian leaders were com
mitted in advance to the cause of national independence. Mission
aries may have had their own inner regrets and reservations, bu
they cheerfully accepted the new conditions of work. I have no
heard of a single case in any country of a missionary giving up hi
work and leaving, because of unwillingness to accept the politica
changes of our time ; and those who have been driven out, as man
Dutch missionaries were driven out of Indonesia, seem to spend the
time in longing to return. The transition from one political situatio
to the other was in many cases rendered easier because the Churche
had moved so much more rapidly towards independence than th
states, and were in a position to give rather than to receive lesson
in the gentle art of democracy.

It is impossible, however, not to regret that in some areas th
connection between the Church and the colonial power had becom
so close as to make it difficult for the Church to render an unmistak
ably independent testimony in a time of tension and conflict. Thi
was, perhaps, particularly the situation in West Africa. Govern
ments, for the development of their educational projects, were willin
to use the services of the missions, partly on purely pragmati
grounds—that that was the cheapest and most effective way c
getting the job done—partly from a dim perception that educatio
would create a dangerous vacuum in the mind of the African unles
the sanction of a new religion could take the place of the old primitiv
sanctions that were inevitably being destroyed. It was only too eas
for missionary societies, always hard pressed for funds, to jump a
the opportunity this afforded them of a rapid extension of the
work. Even the Southern Baptists, in America the staunche
champions of the total separation of Church and State, found

possible in West Africa to accept government aid for their educational work. This was always a dangerous policy for the missions, but no great harm was done as long as the colonial situation was accepted contentedly, or at least without violent protest, by the majority of the African population. But, if the colonial power comes to be regarded as the enemy, it is hardly possible for the churchman whose salary is being paid by the government to pretend that his is a completely independent position ; and, in such a situation, the politically-minded African can all too easily come to regard the Church as being on the side of the enemy.

There is no reason why the change from colonial status to independence should not take place peacefully, through intelligent co-operation between all the interested parties. Actually Ceylon is the only country so far that has achieved its independence without bitterness and the shedding of blood.[1] In all other countries there have been violent tensions, and a deliberate attempt on the part of some nationalist leaders to inflame contention and to build up artificially a revolutionary situation. In such a revolutionary situation the first casualty is truth. Words change their meanings ; terms such as " slavery " and " liberty " are used in senses far different from the dictionary definition of them. Moral values become uncertain ; and a dastardly assassination, carried out in " the good cause ", may be applauded as an act of the highest heroism. Concern for immediate political advantage blots out the longer views of statesmanship. It is too often forgotten that violence breeds violence, and that Ireland more than a generation after the Treaty of 1922 is still suffering from the hidden and pestilent evil of the Irish Republican Army. In such a situation it is natural that younger Christians, carried away by a simple and ingenuous patriotism, should demand that the Church should put itself at the head of " the forces of liberation ". It is inevitable that older Christians should want longer time for thought, and that this hesitation should be condemned by the young as pusillanimity or even as treachery.

The recent history of the Gold Coast may provide a clear and not too controversial illustration. Here the period of violence was happily very brief. With the help of the wisdom of a genuinely

---

[1] Many Indians would maintain that this was merely because the more lethargic Ceylonese left the fighting to be done by the Indians, and then profited by their victories.

progressive Governor, of recent British experience in India and else-where, and of the influence of the more stable among the African leaders, critical situations were constructively handled and order restored.   But the atmosphere remained tense.   The party of Dr. Nkrumah, the present Prime Minister, was demanding immediate independence, and there was a real danger of further violent out-breaks.   The majority of younger Christians were supporters of Mr. Nkrumah and were openly critical of the Churches for their failure to come out wholeheartedly " on the side of freedom ".   At this juncture the Christian Council of the Gold Coast issued a wise and carefully-worded statement on the political situation, defending the right both of Churches and of individual Christians to independ-ent judgment and to diversity of opinion ; pointing out the dangers of violence, and deprecating everything that could encourage hatred or ill-will.   The document was not too well received by those who could think only in terms of political struggle.

Not long after Dr. Nkrumah came to power, and the Christian Council's statement is now only a matter of history.   But the events of only a few years have shown how wise was the caution of the older Christians in refusing to identify themselves too closely with the policies of a single party, and in taking into account many factors in the situation which the younger politicians were inclined entirely to overlook.   The Gold Coast derives its unity purely from the accident of British control.   It consists of three clearly distinct and different regions.   There is the coast, which has had long connec-tions with Europe and has a large educated and partly westernized population.   There is the old Kingdom of Ashanti, now extremely rich and prosperous with its cocoa and its gold, and still paying great respect to the Asantahene, the successor of the old kings of Kumasi. There are the northern territories, bordering on the Sahara, and in the Western sense of the term almost completely undeveloped.   Such disparate regions can easily be held together, as the old Austro-Hungarian Empire was, by a centralized and somewhat autocratic government.   It is not at all evident whether unity can be main-tained by Western democratic methods, suddenly introduced and not yet perfectly understood.   Demands for considerable local free-dom for the two northern regions, within a federal form of govern-ment, have been emphatically presented to the British authorities. But federation is an expensive form of government, and it is by no means certain that the finances of a territory of only five million people will support it. And there is the deeper and persistent problem that the real conflict in many parts of Africa to-day is not, as is generally supposed, between black and white, but between the old Africa of the chiefs and of sacral authority, and the new Africa that has learned its lessons in Europe and America and thinks in terms of democratic freedom.

Similar and fascinating problems present themselves in Nigeria and Togoland and Uganda. But enough has already been said to make plain the necessarily ambivalent position of the Church, in that it can wholeheartedly accept great social changes in principle, yet cannot identify itself with the advocates of such changes to the point at which it loses its independence, and its right to suspend judgment or to criticize in the light of longer views and profounder principles than those which may be currently acceptable.

The Eastern revolution has brought to the fore once again the problem of the Church and nationalism. New independent nations have come into existence; independence has very properly been accompanied by a new and proud sense of national dignity. This is a situation to which the Churches must adapt themselves, and within which they must learn to find themselves at home. In two directions it is possible to see at once that such adaptation is both justifiable and necessary.

In the past it has been a disadvantage to the Churches in Asia and Africa that circumstances had brought them into specially close contact with representatives of the Western peoples. This could not but give the impression that Churches in these countries were colonies of the West, and that Christians were to some extent at least aliens from the life and interests of their fellow-countrymen. On the whole, until a very recent date, Christians of the younger Churches did not take much interest in political affairs, and remained aloof from national movements. In part they were repelled by the exaggerations of nationalist propaganda, and by the danger of widespread violence which these movements evidently brought with them. In part they honestly believed that the interest of their countries could best be served by continuing in close association with the West. Now that independence has come, this cross-bench situation can no longer continue; Christians must either accept in permanence the status of second-class and unreliable citizens, or

they must take up wholeheartedly the new responsibilities of in
dependent citizenship.

We shall consider later the difficulties arising for Christians from
the tendency in many countries to identify nationalism with the
ancient religions. Here we are concerned only to note that Christian
in the newly independent countries have accepted the change, ar
determined to assert their equality, and are making a notable con
tribution to the political as well as to other aspects of their countries
life. To the Christians in India opportunity to demonstrate their
worth was given immediately upon the arrival of independence. In
the dreadful days of carnage and violence in 1947, relations between
Hindus and Muslims were so strained that it was almost impossible
for men of goodwill on one side to help those in need upon the
other. The Christians, unattached to either side, could and did
render magnificent and selfless service, wherever doors were opened
to them. When the supply of doctors and nurses ran out, it was
Mr. Gandhi himself who advised the Minister of Health to cable
to the National Christian Council of India, in the assurance that
the Churches would be both able and willing to help.

In a deeper sense than that of merely political loyalty the Churches
need to take root in the life of their own countries. Inevitably at
the start Christianity is a foreign religion ; but if it is to survive in
any country a process of naturalization must take place. Without
yielding to any exaggerated ideas of race or nation, it may yet be
held that race, language and nation are a part of God's providential
ordering of the world ; and that, just as diversities of language and
culture have been the means of drawing out to expression the varied
riches and potentialities of the human spirit, so contact between the
Gospel and varied national and cultural traditions is needed for the
full explication of its treasures. History gives evidence of what this
means. It is customary to speak of Western Christianity as though
it were a unit, and such in origin it is. Yet such a bald statement
is as misleading as the common use of the term " the West " in the
political sense, as though there were no differences in the political
and economic spheres between Portugal, Sweden and the Republic
of Ireland. We can see clearly the difference that language and a
national tradition impress upon the forms of Christian life and
expression even within so closely organized a doctrinal scheme as
that of the Lutheran Churches. When, therefore, the Anglican

Church in India, Burma and Ceylon, on obtaining in 1930 a new
status as an independent province of the Anglican Communion,
declared it to be its intention to work for an Indian expression of
Christianity,[1] it was stating something that not merely corresponds
to the reality of the world as God has made it but is also in itself
highly desirable. Only a Church which is the natural expression
of India's experience of Christ can be at home in India ; and such
a truly Indian expression of Christianity can contribute to the
enrichment of the world-wide Church.

So far adaptation is good and a duty laid upon the Churches.
But, once again, we are faced with the question whether there is
not an ultimate incompatibility between the nature of the Church's
life and every secular principle about which peoples and societies
have chosen to organize their lives. Are nationalism and Christianity
reconcilable ? Can there be such a thing as a national Church ?

That great Orthodox leader in the Ecumenical Movement, Fr.
George Florovsky, once expressed in my hearing the view that the
great sin of the Churches was nationalism—a sin of which they have
never really repented. This is a saying that is worthy of the deepest
attention. In the Orthodox world, as each of the new nations—
Serbia, Bulgaria and the rest—came into existence, it claimed and
eventually obtained the status of an autocephalous Church, with its
own Patriarch, and only a somewhat loose relationship to the Œcu-
menical Patriarch in Constantinople. Natural as this development
appeared to be in the heyday of nineteenth-century nationalism, it
has nevertheless rendered almost impossible any united action on
the part of the Orthodox Churches. At the time of the Reformation,
nationalism was accepted almost as a sacred principle of the life of
the Churches. *Cuius regio, eius religio.* Protestants in Germany are
still divided up among twenty-eight *Landeskirchen*, regional Churches,
each fully independent of all the rest, though with common membership in the Federation of German Evangelical Churches. The
Church of Geneva still lives without contact with the Church of

[1] " This Church aims at accomplishing for India, Burma and Ceylon what
the Church of England has accomplished for England. As the Church of England,
receiving Catholic Christianity from the undivided Church, has given a characteristically English interpretation of it, so the Church of India, Burma and Ceylon
aspires to give a characteristically national interpretation of that same common
faith and life."
Quoted in *The Anglican Communion*, edited by J. W. C. Wand (Oxford, 1948),
p. 83.

the Canton of Vaud, except that both are members of the Swiss Federation of Protestant Churches. Only a set of quite unforeseen circumstances has delivered the Church of England out of the isolation that that name implies into the comparative liberty of the Anglican Communion. The Roman Catholic Church is the most international Church in the world; yet even here it is perhaps unfortunate that four hundred and thirty-four years have elapsed since the death of the last non-Italian Pope.

Is there not a danger that the younger Churches may fall into the pit of ecclesiastical nationalism, just at the time when the Western Churches are beginning laboriously to climb out of it?

It is on this ground that some critics, not all of them unfriendly, have found fault with the idea and the formation of the Church of South India. Is geography (with its possible nationalistic implications) the principle on which a real Church can come into being? Do we not face the danger of a new crop of regional Churches, self-contained, without organic links to other Churches, unrelated unless through artificial connections that will gradually have to be developed? Those who brought the Church of South India into being were well aware of this danger. In the Basis of Union they stated that

> it is the intention and hope of the uniting Churches that all the actions of the united Church will be regulated by the principle that it should maintain fellowship with all those branches of the Churches of Christ with which the uniting Churches now severally enjoy such fellowship, and that it should continually seek to widen and strengthen this fellowship and to work toward the goal of the full union in one body of all parts of the Church of Christ.[1]

Progress since 1947 indicates that this hope of the Church of South India has in a measure been fulfilled. But it is not altogether surprising that the Lutheran Churches in South India find themselves distracted between the rival pulls of closer union with the Church of South India on their doorstep, and closer integration with the other Lutheran Churches in more distant parts of India, and so with the wider fellowship of Lutheran Churches throughout the world.

In spite of the new and intense national loyalties, the tendency

---

[1] *Proposed Scheme of Church Union in South India* (7th edition, Madras, 1943), p. 3.

n almost all the Churches to-day is towards wider fellowships and
keener sense of mutual loyalty across the barriers of national
rontiers. This may be illustrated from many spheres. One vivid
xample is the contrast between Christian experiences in the first
nd second world wars. In the first, Christian fellowship was
lmost completely broken ; and after 1918 in all the international
Christian organizations, such as the Y.M.C.A. and the International
Missionary Council, many years of painful effort were required
before free and confident co-operation could be restored between
those whom the war had turned into enemies. During the second
war, Christian relationships were far better maintained.[1] As soon
as hostilities were over, Germans were welcomed back into the international Christian groupings ; and, as one of them remarked, " It
is only here that one feels oneself to be treated otherwise than as a
member of an inferior race ".

All the major denominations of the Christian world now have
their world-wide fellowships and organizations, the closest-knit and
best organized being the Lutheran World Federation. But, evidently, the most striking manifestation of this new spirit has been
the foundation of the World Council of Churches. It is important
not to exaggerate what has been achieved ; the Council still represents far less than half the Christian world ; a fellowship in which
Rome, Moscow and the Southern Baptists of the United States alike
refuse to share is very far short of a universal Christian fellowship.
But its existence, and its existence in almost all countries and on
both sides of the Iron Curtain, is one of the great new facts of our
time. The enthusiasm of the younger Churches to join the World
Council is an indication that their new national pride and sense
of independence is tempered by a sense of the world-wide fellowship to which a Christian as such belongs, and of responsibility
towards it.

For Christianity can never be anything but an international
religion. A Christian, in so far as he is sunk in local and national
preoccupations, ceases to be a Christian. That is why in the end
all totalitarian systems must make war to the death on the Churches.
Such systems make demands for a total and unconditional loyalty

[1] German missionaries still speak of the visits which the present writer was
able to pay them during their internment in India, when it was found that Christian
fellowship remained unimpaired by the tragedies and sorrows of the war period.

to the exclusion of all others ; and this is a demand to which th
Christian and the Church can never accede.

Recent events in China may serve as an excellent illustration o
this thesis. For a time no personal contact between Christians insid
China and outside it was possible. Chinese Christians, with n
sources of information other than the press of their own country
seem to have wondered whether Christians in the West had simpl
written them off as a lost province. Western Christians, while con
tinuing to pray for their Chinese brethren and to be deeply concerne
about them, wondered whether those same brethren wished to b
regarded as maintaining any associations with Churches outside thei
own borders. The happy renewal of personal contacts in recen
months has made necessary a complete rewriting of the first draf
of the conclusion of this chapter. It is now clear that the Chines
Christians, while aware of certain political tensions and highl
critical of the West, do desire to regard themselves as standin
within the universal family of Christians, and to maintain a loyalt
to the international fellowship which seems difficult to reconcil
with the totalitarian claims of the régime under which they live.

This particular situation draws together all the threads of th
argument of this chapter. Neither Church nor Christian can eve
be perfectly at home in any human order of society. The Christia
moves between the two poles of loyalty and independence, of activ
service and constructive criticism. The Christian can never b
totally absorbed by a national loyalty. Even in time of war he mus
be mindful of the unbroken fellowship with those whom huma
politics have made his enemies. The Christian cannot be committe
unconditionally to any earthly régime, since he is aware of an eterna
dimension incommensurable with the perspectives of the earthl
state. This simply means that Church and Christian alike ar
pledged in perpetuity to a pilgrim condition. Situations change
and men with them. In constantly reconsidering their relationship
to the society around them, and in finding new adjustments as cir
cumstances change or as fresh light is given, Christian and Churcl
alike are engaged in an unfinished task.

CHAPTER 5

THE PROBLEM OF A CHRISTIAN CULTURE

A DISTINCTION can be drawn between civilization and culture, though clearly the two are very closely connected. Civilization denotes the various outward forms and rules, which have been devised to make possible the life of a large number of men in a coherent society. Culture moves on two parallel lines, above and below civilization. On one level it is the expression of the inner meaning of a civilization under the aspect of beauty. On a deeper level, it is concerned with the total instinctive attitude of a people to life, with the deep, agreed, often unspoken wisdom, which underlies conscious judgments and affects reactions to particular situations. Often the shortest way to the understanding of the deeper life of a people is the study of its proverbs.

In all primitive societies different aspects of life are held together in an almost undisturbed synthesis. There is no distinction between the sacred and the profane. The idea of Church and State as distinct entities has not yet dawned. The king is generally priest and law-giver as well as ruler. The whole of life is shot through with religion, and often an astonishingly large part of the time of a people is taken up with the performance of religious or, at lowest, magical cere-monies. Not every primitive society produces art. It is one of the mysteries of nature that some races should be so highly endowed with the artistic impulse and artistic capacity, and others should apparently be wholly or almost wholly deficient in them.[1] But where primitive art is produced, it may be taken as almost certain that it will be religious in origin, and closely related to the deepest levels of a people's life.

Clearly no people can be regarded as genuinely Christian until the Gospel has penetrated below the level of conscious conviction and has become part of the unspoken and accepted wisdom of the people. Without the strong conviction of individuals the Christian

[1] The contrast between East Africa, where indigenous art is almost wholly lacking, and West Africa, with such outstanding centres of artistic production as Benin, is very curious.

tradition will quickly die ; yet there is a Christian tradition whi
is more than the sum-total of individual conviction, and by whi
the continuity of the life of the Church is maintained. But Christ
anity has never found it easy to attain anywhere to such a perfe
synthesis of life, feeling and expression as is found in so ma
primitive societies. This is partly because in the course of its journ
through the centuries so much of its time and effort has been spe
in assimilating peoples whose life had been determined by earli
and non-Christian cultures (we shall return later to the problem
the conflict of cultures in the world to-day) ; partly because t
Gospel challenges and condemns some of the natural instincts
man, to the free exercise of which other religious systems offer
barrier ; partly because any Christian society, which has not becom
static, is bound to be always pressing forward to a more perfe
realization of itself as a Christian society than it has already attaine

In the West there have been perhaps only two moments of con
plete, or almost complete, synthesis of faith and culture ; and ea
was marked by the appearance of one of the supreme masterpiec
of Christian literature.

Augustine *On the City of God* is the last great utterance of t
classical and formative period of the Church's life. For four ce
turies the Church had been at grips with the ancient culture of t
Greek and Roman world. It had made itself at home in that wor
It had mastered its culture. It had passed the sentence of dea
on many of its beliefs and habits. It had domesticated the Gre
and Latin languages to the expression of originally Semitic ide
In all this long process it had not itself remained unmodified, thou
in all essentials faithful to the original deposit of the faith. A
now at the end of the period comes the great genius, who will su
up and transmit to the future all the lessons that have been learne

Augustine was himself an epitome of all that history. Althou
his mother was a Christian, he had lived many years in pagan socie
and as a pagan. As a teacher of rhetoric, it had been his busine
to master the whole of classical Latin literature. As a philosoph
he had been both a Neoplatonist and a Manichean, and some

---

[1] The other manifestation of this synthesis is to be found in the classi
liturgies of the Church, all of them anonymous, all giving shape and form to t
devotion of thousands of unnamed worshippers. The significance of *liturgy*
often overlooked in histories of the Church.

ose who know his writings best doubt whether he ever quite freed
mself from these radically unchristian ways of thinking. As a
aristian he had steeped himself profoundly in the Scriptures, and
ust have known the New Testament almost by heart. And so
the end of his life he sits down to write his philosophy of history,
s understanding of the nature of " the most glorious City of
od ".[1]

Augustine's influence was immense. To the Middle Ages he
as " the Doctor ". The Reform of the sixteenth century in all
s major forms, Roman, Lutheran, Calvinist, Anglican, stood well
ithin the Augustinian tradition. It was only at the end of the
venteenth century, with Locke and Newton, that what we recog-
ze as modern thought had its beginnings, and Augustine became
b more than one authority among many.

Such was Augustine's power as the master of thought in the
:er Christian world. Historically, the *City of God* is the greatest
pression of the classical Christian synthesis just at the moment
its dissolution. The aim of the book was to encourage frightened
aristians by making clear to them that the Church was not de-
ndent on the Roman Empire, and could continue to exist even
the Empire disappeared. In that Augustine was a true prophet ;
e Church did continue to exist, but under conditions completely
fferent from any that he had known. It had to live through the
ng agony and chaos of the Dark Ages. Once again the Gospel
as faced with a new task, that of penetrating the soul of young,
gorous, untamed and undisciplined peoples, and of creating a new
d different type of Christian culture. Superficial conversion was
many cases rapid. Centuries were to pass before men's ways
thinking were Christianized ; and, even then, as always happens
the Christian world, conduct lagged far behind conviction. At
e end of this period came the first and wonderful Renaissance of
e twelfth and thirteenth centuries ; and at the end of that came
ante, to provide another of the supreme classics of the Christian
th.

The great artist is always a mystery. However dependent on
e traditions of the past, he is always to some extent like Mel-
izedek, " without father, without mother, without genealogy ".
the creative instinct is strong enough, it will find its way to

[1] *Gloriosissimæ* is the first word of the book.

U.T.—4

expression even under the most unfavourable circumstances, an
though there be no one to listen. But it may be doubted wheth
the very greatest artistic creation is possible except where the arti
is closely related to a public which shares his interests, which accep
some of his values, and is concerned about the matters in which I
is interested. Could Dante have written as he did, if he had no
lived in an age of faith ? It is easy to criticize the faith of tho
days, and to contrast the brutality and coarseness of even Dante
own Italy with the demands of the Gospel. That it was a real fait
is shown by the Churches of the period ; not only by the gre
masterpieces such as the Angel Choir at Lincoln, but in the hundred
of village churches where architectural skill was unmistakably .
the service of spiritual aspiration. " In the diocese of Exeter the
was a positive craze for the building or rebuilding of parish churche
Bishop Walter Branscombe, 1257–80, rededicated eighty-eig
churches that had been rebuilt or enlarged in a period of nin
years." [1] Those were the years when Dante was young.

Dante, too, was an epitome of his age. He seems to have rea
almost every book which was available in Latin in the thirteent
century. Not only so ; every major interest of his times—th
politics of Pope and Emperor, the scholastic philosophy, predestin
tion and free will, elementary scientific experiment, and many othe
—finds its place somewhere in his poem. But, more important tha
anything else, the whole Christian understanding of man's natur
and of his redemption is set forth in massive architectonic structure
medieval, of course, in form but of the high Middle Age, befor
the idea of Purgatory had been corrupted by the traffic in indulgence
and before Christ had been displaced from His centrality in th
Christian scheme of things.

But Dante, like Augustine, stands just at the point where th
synthesis so long a-building begins to break up. New currents i
philosophy were soon to bring in a mood of scepticism, with a ne
emphasis on God as inscrutable Will rather than as the fount an
light of Reason. Efforts to reform the Church and the papacy wer
to prove unavailing. Nationalism in its modern form was alread
beginning to appear in England and in France. It is indeed signifi
cant that Dante chose to write his greatest work in Italian and no

[1] G. H. Cook : *The English Medieval Parish Church* (Phœnix Press, 1954
p. 45.

Latin. That in itself was symptomatic of the breaking up of a
d-won unity. We are beginning to-day to be more aware of
at we have lost with the disappearance of Latin as the universal
guage of educated men. Latin, indeed, was long in going ; John
sley was still able to use it to converse with his German pietist
nds before he had himself learnt German. But it has now finally
e, and we have no common language. Dante's *Divina Commedia*
the first work of transcendent merit to be written in any modern
ropean language ; and, as such, it is in a way a symbol of that
integration of the West in which we still live.

In English history, subsequent to the break-up of the medieval
ty, there have been two periods in which a partial synthesis of
h and culture has been achieved.

The first was in the second half of the reign of Queen Elizabeth I,
l was closely associated with the general diffusion of the Bible
ong the people. The evidence now available concerning the
nerous editions of the Bible published after 1580, and of the
raordinarily rapid sales, affords the strongest possible confirmation
che saying of John Richard Green that in this period the people
England became the people of a book and that book the Bible.[1]
nost all that was most vital and vigorous in England—Sir Philip
ney, Shakespeare, Hooker—was drawn into the ways of the re-
med Religion. Roman Catholics are heard only in a few subdued
l plaintive notes. On its literary side, the synthesis is continued
ough the seventeenth century in Donne and Herbert and Henry
ughan the Silurist, and finds its final and splendid expression in
Samson Agonistes of John Milton. That was indeed a profoundly
gious age.[2] But the bitter contentions between Christians, with
ir unhappy fruit in civil war, explain why it cannot be called
re than a partial synthesis.[3]

---

[1] Details are to be found in Philip Hughes : *The Reformation in England*,
. III (Hollis and Carter, 1954).
[2] Canon Charles Smyth in *Church and Parish* (S.P.C.K., 1955), pp. 6–21,
s most interesting and moving details of the corporate attendance of the
ise of Commons at Holy Communion in St. Margaret's Church between 1614
1661—notable independents like Oliver Cromwell no less than good high
rchmen such as Wentworth and Hyde.
[3] It should be noted that, towards the end of this period, France was also
eriencing a period of partial synthesis—the age of Pascal, of Racine, of Bossuet
Fénelon. But the Revocation of the Edict of Nantes took place in 1685—
also was a period of only partial synthesis.

Our second period is the Victorian Age. The synthesis betw
culture and religion in this period was mainly due to the Evangel
Revival, and the extraordinarily wide diffusion of biblical knowle
to which it led. Many readers of Hardy's *Tess of the Durbervi*
must have been surprised by the remark that Tess, like all the po
knew the Bible well. But so it was in those days. Until the
of the nineteenth century almost all village schools were Chu
schools, and the Bible was the foundation of education. Peo
went regularly to Church and heard the Bible read. In count
families the Bible was read aloud at family prayers. In many hou
the Bible was the only book.

Once again, we may take literature as a measure of the per
tration of culture by Christian ideas. To an extraordinary ext
almost all the great English writers of the nineteenth century rev
acquaintance with the Christian Gospel, and an acceptance
many of its principles, even though the faith of some of them
liberal and reduced rather than full and supernatural. For the per
of the romantic revival, the atheism of Shelley and the rebellion
Byron are offset by Coleridge, Wordsworth and Scott. Dickens a
Trollope make fun of the less admirable aspects of Evangelicalis
but there can be little doubt as to the source of the profound co
passion of Dickens for the unfortunate, and Trollope in *Orley Fa*
can use quite unaffectedly the expression " her Saviour ". Tennys
and Browning, each in his own way and Browning more emphat
ally than Tennyson, come down on the side of faith. Matth
Arnold and Dante Gabriel Rossetti no longer have faith, but g
poignant evidence of the unhealed wound that its disappearance
left behind. The Victorian tradition in music and painting was l
distinguished than in literature ; but here, too, certain evidences
spiritual aspiration can readily be recognized.

George Meredith seems to me to have been one of the first no
Christian writers in the literature of modern England, and it is
be remembered that *The Ordeal of Richard Feverel* was publish
as long ago as 1859. Hardy would perhaps be more ordinarily cit
But is not Lord David Cecil right in affirming that in many essent
things Hardy is to be reckoned on the side of the Christians ? Aft
all, the " President of the Immortals " against whom Hardy inveig
is not the Christian God, but merely the projection on to the sk
of Hardy's in some ways deeply Christian compassion for the myste

d the tragedy of human suffering. It is in the writers most widely
ad in the early years of this century that the change is most plainly
ident. H. G. Wells, Arnold Bennett and John Galsworthy not
erely show few signs of acquaintance with the Christian faith ;
ey give the impression of never having met an intelligent Christian.
ernard Shaw made acquaintance with the Christian faith only in
der to misunderstand and to misrepresent it. In part these men,
d others like them, were products of their age ; they were drawn
om sections of society which had become lost to the Church or
hich the Church had never touched. In part they helped to
roduce the modern age, with its touching belief in science, its
verestimation of material values, its scepticism, its apparent
nawareness of dimensions of existence other than those which
  acknowledges. No doubt the departure of belief has been
astened by the Logical Positivists, with their affirmation that
ich a statement as " God is love " is a mere meaningless noise, to
hich it is impossible to attach any real or rational significance ;
d by those many psychologists who refuse to treat religion as
ything more than the survival of an illusion. But these men, too,
e perhaps symptoms rather than causes of our present spiritual
tuation.
    We have taken our illustrations so far from England. But it is
idely recognized that this schism in the soul is a phenomenon
hich is universal in the West. In predominantly Roman Catholic
ountries the schism began earlier and became deeper than else-
here. The eighteenth century in France was the century of
oltaire and Rousseau. Though the nineteenth century produced
ome Christian writers of the second class, such as Chateaubriand,
tendhal and Flaubert are much more typical of the age and of
s spiritual disillusionment. The French schools of painting, for
ll the brilliance of their achievement, are not, on the whole, the
xpression of a spiritual understanding of the world. In more recent
ears there has been a renewal of faith, and an attempt at a re-
arriage of faith and culture in the writings of such distinguished
en as Charles Péguy, Paul Claudel and the novelist François
Mauriac ; but the dominant intellectual influence in France seems
till to be that of the existentialists, who cannot make room for
God within a scheme which seems to start from the presupposition
hat God is dead. We must not exaggerate. In Roman Catholic,

as in Protestant, countries, there is a recognition of the cultur:
significance of the Christian classics of the past, even though the
religious message is held to be irrelevant. But here we encounte
that attitude of simultaneous affirmation and denial, which in itse
is a symptom of the spiritual sickness from which we suffer.

Europe and America have spread their own sickness far and wid
throughout the world. We tend to think of our civilization primaril
as a spiritual phenomenon. In spite of the labours of missionarie
and of high-minded college teachers, it is not as such that it ha
presented itself to the non-European world. What has dazzled th
poorer countries has been material achievement leading to unimagir
able wealth. After all, the great majority of those who have repre
sented our civilization in these countries have been mainly concerne
with trade, the exploitation of natural resources and the extensio
of markets. The purveyors of spiritual wares have always been i
the minority. Western education has proved a powerful solvent (
inherited beliefs and ideas, but it has been anything but the prepar:
tion of a favourable soil for the reception of the Gospel. As earl
as 1850 missionaries in India began to note the existence of a clas
of cultivated Indian gentlemen, emancipated from all the prejudice
of Hinduism, but also emancipated from all understanding of th
significance of the spiritual in the life of man. It is in Africa tha
the mischief has gone farthest, just because Africa had no intelle(
tually developed culture of its own capable of withstanding the assau
of European ideas.[1] Earlier in this century there was a great de:
of talk about the Muslim menace in Africa. To-day politicians a:
concerned about the possible spread of Communism in tropic.
Africa. Both of these are, from the Christian point of view, peri
which have constantly to be borne in mind. But the majority (
Christian observers seem to be in agreement that the greatest dang(
of all is that of the dominance of a secularized materialism. Th
need for material progress is so great that concentration on it :
in a sense justified, but that only makes the danger greater. Th
values of genuine material progress may conceal the sickness of a
allegedly scientific scepticism, which denies the relevance of othe
than material values.

[1] Note the word " intellectually ". Observers are more and more coming (
appreciate the values of the primitive African cultures ; but naturally these hav
not been intellectually developed.

For this is far more than a question simply of belief or unbelief. That very pair of opposites " belief and unbelief " implies that there is still a common universe of discourse, in which discussion is still possible and there can be at least a hope of ultimate agreement. What we have to recognize to-day is that between Christians and an immense segment of their contemporaries that common universe of discourse no longer exists. The common Christian and religious terms are no longer in the vocabulary of the ordinary man ; or, if the words are still familiar, the sense in which they are used is so distorted as to be rather a barrier than a highway to communication.

Here we encounter the central problem of evangelism to-day. As has often been noticed, the great evangelists of an earlier day, Torrey, Moody and the rest, could count on a certain acquaintance with the Christian faith in their audiences, and a certain recognition of Christian obligations, even when in practice these were being repudiated. It is impossible to count on any of these to-day.

It is for this reason that Billy Graham cannot be the answer to our major problem in evangelism. I cannot imagine any churchman being anything but immensely grateful for what Billy Graham has done ; indeed, refusal to recognize the greatness of his contribution would seem to me to come very near to blasphemy against the Holy Ghost. But that achievement is limited. The vast majority of those who have professed conversion in Billy Graham's campaigns had already some connection with a Church and some acquaintance with the Gospel. Now to say that Billy Graham's influence is likely to be greatest on the 40 per cent or so of the population which is not yet wholly secularized is in no way to deny its value or importance ; rather the contrary, since in these days when the Church is threatened from all sides, our wisest strategy would seem to be to strengthen those bridge-heads which remain to us in the direction of the unknown and menacing world of secularism. Yet we must recognize that this kind of evangelism is primarily defensive. It may help us to retain the territory that we still hold, but hardly to advance to the recovery of that which we seem to have lost.

Much study has been made in recent years of experiments in evangelism beyond the frontier or the perimeter of the Church, in what we have come to call the " post-Christian " world. What emerges from these enquiries is the conclusion that nowhere in the world has the Church broken through on a wide front into any of the territories from which it has come to be excluded. There are partial and encouraging successes but these are of the nature of forays rather than invasions. In Christian circles there has been a tendency to identify the alienated world with the world of the " working man ". This is a limited and misleading perspective. " Suburbia " seems to present itself as a no less impenetrable fortress. It is hard to imagine any class less readily accessible to spiritual ideas than the successful Swiss bourgeois with commercial interests. Among the intellectual élite there have been a number of striking conversions to Christian faith in middle life, and the rising tide of religious interest in the Universities suggests that a widespread change may be on the way. Certain books with a Christian emphasis have become best sellers. But what has been seen so far is no more than the beginning of a change. In most European countries there is little aggressive hostility to religion ; religion has ceased to be of sufficient importance to be the object of the violent antipathies of the Victorian era. An interest in culture does not imply any interest in religion, and religion has difficulty in relating itself to the prevailing culture.

It is, of course, otherwise in the Communist-controlled countries. There a steady, deliberate and persistent effort is being made in all the schools to eliminate the religious consciousness. Until recently reports of visitors on the religious situation in Russia were rather encouraging ; far more religious belief and feeling had survived than anyone had dared to expect. The latest reports begin to strike a note of deeper anxiety. We forget how short a period has elapsed since the beginning of the Russian revolution. Many of those who are now at the head of affairs in Russia were already grown men when the Revolution broke out in 1917. Millions of people have retained the faith which they learned in the days of the Tsars, and family life, always an immensely strong factor of continuity in a peasant society, seems to have maintained the religious tradition intact through the period in which the Church was hardly able to maintain any public ministry. But now the grandparents who had learned to believe in the days of faith are dying out ; there appears to be a diminution of faith from generation to generation, and it would be well not to be too confident about the future of the Russian Church. In Eastern Germany churchmen are already

eeply troubled by the effect on the minds of the young of the total
ontradiction which exists between what they learn at school and
the traditions of the Christian home and the Church. Will the young
eople be able to endure the schizophrenia resulting from Marxist
ducational policies in a partly Christian country ? The danger
rises not so much from direct attacks on religion as from the
eady effort to create an intellectual and emotional structure to
hich religion, faith and spiritual conviction appear supremely
relevant.

To return to the West. No Christian, looking calmly at the
eligious situation in Britain, is likely to be complacent. Yet there
re equally good reasons for not yielding to an unqualified pessimism.
Ve have already referred to certain exceptions to the depressing
icture of the alienated worlds, and to the signs, small as yet, that
change of climate may be in the early stages of development. No
ne who has had much to do with young people to-day is likely to
oubt the fundamental seriousness of many of them. There is even
new readiness to consider the possibility that religion may have
mething to say. Two whole generations have been brought up
n the doctrine that materialism has all the answers, and that science
an of itself bring about the needed changes in human society.
oung people to-day are beginning to recognize that materialism
as none of the answers ; they are as yet very uncertain whether
ny answers are anywhere to be found, but there is at least the
eginnings of a willingness to look elsewhere. The popularity of
e poetry of Mr. T. S. Eliot and the success of the plays of Mr.
hristopher Fry may be indications of new stirrings of a popular
hristian culture. But it is the attitude of young people to music
at fills me with the greatest hope. To look round the Festival
all during a performance of Handel's *Messiah* or of Bach's *Passion*
ccording to St. Matthew is to me a moving experience. An astonish-
gly large number of young people are apparently prepared to spend
r more than they can really afford in order to sit and listen to
reat religious music. Doubtless they are at present quite incapable
f giving any intellectual formulation to their experiences. What is
ignificant is their openness to profound inner experiences in relation
o great art. Religion on its intellectual side is more closely akin
o science, in its inner aspect as personal relationship it is more
losely akin to the experience of art. To be moved by great music

is not a religious experience. But one who can be moved by gre
music is not incapable of entering into the realities of religio
experience.[1]

What can the Church do to help forward a change in the clima
of feeling, if such is really on the way ? Such changes seem, lik
the changes in social order which we were earlier considering,
come about almost unobserved, and indeed to spring from caus
which are hardly susceptible of observation. This makes difficu
any direct action on the part of the Church. But it would be fat
that it should remain insensitive and aloof. It is not here a que
tion of trying to influence or to modify intellectual conviction. Th
is also a great and necessary task. The works of Canon C. E. Rave
Canon A. F. Smethurst, and Professor C. A. Coulson, and th
publication in English of some of the writings of Professor Ka
Heim, are welcome signs of the seriousness with which Christiar
are taking up the task of meeting the scientists on their own grour
in a spirit of friendly encounter. Here we are concerned not wi
the intellectual level (though we must be careful not to make to
rigid a distinction between the different levels of human experience
but with the attempt to renew an inner structure of thought ar
feeling, within which religion can again become a natural ar
necessary activity of the human spirit. The major task is to g
the Bible back into the consciousness of the ordinary man ar
woman ; for, more than any other single instrument, the Bib
rightly used is able to recreate the climate of faith, throug
opening up to the human spirit consciousness of depths withi
itself of which neither science nor psychology is aware, ar
extending its purview beyond the finitude of time and space to th
eternal world.

In England the Butler Act of 1944 gives a golden opportuni
to the Churches. But are the Churches in any position to tak
advantage of the opportunity ? What concerns us as Christians
not mere instruction in the contents of the Bible ; that is a du
subject, and is likely to be at least as much disliked as any oth
subject in the school curriculum. Nor is it a question of any dire
attempt to convert the pupils ; that is not what the classroom

---

[1] Those who know Karl Barth only as the austere Calvinistic theologian mig
be astonished to see his immense collection of gramophone records of the mus
of Mozart.

or.[1] The aim must be such an imaginative presentation of the Bible as can stir imaginative response, as can create the sense of moving in worlds unrealized.

This has always been a difficult task. There is no doubt that it has been made more difficult by the modern historical approach to the study of the Bible. This will be realized by anyone who imagines himself presenting to a class of intelligent sixteen-year-olds the story of the manna in the wilderness. To the fundamentalist, of course, all is easy. Everything is to be taken literally, and any stirrings of incredulity are to be suppressed by reference to the omnipotence of God. Equally to the liberal there is no great difficulty. Probably he will explain the manna in terms of that particular secretion from the tamarisk, which has been reported by scientists as resembling in some respects the biblical account of the manna. The neo-orthodox may insist that the only important thing is the challenge to faith ; but this will not silence the question which the sixteen-year-olds are almost certain to ask—" But what really happened ? " It takes no small gifts as an expositor to show how the poetic imagination of the prophetic writer took hold of a real and remarkable experience, glorified by distance, and enriched it until it became a profound, permanent and valid symbol of the protecting care of God for His people.

As a young man, I had the privilege of knowing three fellows of Jesus College, Cambridge, the College of Thomas Cranmer, each of whom was in his own way a master of the imaginative handling of the records of the Bible. Alexander Nairne's Exposition of the Epistle to the Hebrews, in the Introduction to his commentary, though a little dated and a little tinged by his particular type of Tractarianism, still seems to me one of the finest pieces of imaginative biblical exposition ever written. Sir Arthur Quiller-Couch's lectures on the reading of the Bible are too famous to need any further commendation. Bernard Manning's lay sermons (*A Layman in the Pulpit*) are perhaps less well known, but in their imaginative insight and restrained expression seem to me perfect of their kind. Who else would have thought of preaching a Harvest Festival sermon

---

[1] But an article entitled " Classroom Conversions " by David Winter, reproduced in *World Christian Digest*, September 1956, suggests that even honest classroom teaching can be surprisingly effective in producing religious enquiry, conversion and Church membership.

on the men of Beersheba who looked into the ark of the covenant (1 Sam. 6 : 19.) These men's love for the Bible lay behind the first Cambridgeshire Syllabus of Religious Instruction, universally recognized to be one of the best of its type ever produced. Have we their like to-day ? And can the Churches produce enough teachers, fired with the same prophetic zeal, who will go into the schools, understanding their work in terms of the mission of the Baptist—to prepare the way of the Lord ?

But it would be unfair to lay the whole burden on the teachers. Must not the Church as a whole rediscover the value of its biblical heritage ? And must not the start be given by the clergy ? One who has grown accustomed to continental habits of preaching cannot but be astonished at the almost complete lack of biblical expository preaching in England to-day. Everything else seems to be treated —morals, current problems, liturgy, psychology and all the rest. It is rare to hear clear exposition of a Bible passage, based on careful and patient study of the text, and lighted up by such flashes of insight as can make a congregation feel that they themselves are standing with Elijah on Mount Carmel or with St. Paul on Mars Hill at Athens. To preach such sermons demands hard work, but it is much less exhausting than the attempt to find a new idea twice a Sunday ; and many of those who will never become great preachers can become in course of time highly competent expositors. There is no doubt at all that a congregation will respond favourably to a sermon which sends it back to the Bible with a sense of old treasures refurbished, or of new treasures yet to be found.

If this is true of England, it is far more true of the younger Churches. Most preachers in these Churches have few qualifications and fewer books. Demands for sermons and addresses are very heavy. The faithfulness of the majority of ministers and catechists is beyond all praise. Yet there is an almost irresistible tendency for preaching to sink down into the dreariest kind of exhortation. A congregation can endure good advice up to a certain limit ; but beyond that limit it ceases to have any effect and results only in weariness. Nothing in the world is easier to produce than conventional exhortations along the well-worn lines of the Christian tradition. But in the younger Churches more than anywhere else the task of the preacher is to be a teacher of the Bible—a task the significance of which will come before us in another connection.

The task of the Churches is not the same in all the various areas of the world. In the West the Churches are called to recover a sense of their cultural mission, to enter into a secularized civilization and to recall it to a sense of spiritual values and of the relevance of religious faith. In the countries which have never been Christian the vocation of the Churches is to develop within themselves a Christian culture, which in course of time will be able to absorb into itself the achievements and the values of the great non-Christian civilizations, and so to produce new and as yet unimagined combinations and syntheses. But basically the problem is the same for all, and God has put the same weapons into the hands of all.

It must not be supposed that an increase of biblical knowledge and understanding would necessarily lead to a renewal of Christian culture. It might result merely in a new pietism, uninterested in culture, and inclined to regard it with puritan suspicion as distracting man from concentration on specifically religious objects. It can, however, be maintained that the West can recover its spiritual health only through a renewal of Christian culture, and that the recovery of the Bible is the indispensable instrument of this renewal. On what grounds can this be maintained ? What is the contribution that the Bible can make to culture ? The Christian answer would be, I think, that the Bible gives to man as thinker, as artist and as creator, increased sensitiveness, deeper seriousness, and more confident hope. In the first place, it restores the dimension of eternity ; it is the lack of this dimension that makes so much modern art seem to the Christian airless and confined. Secondly, it restores a meaning to history ; here there is no mere meaningless recurrence of events, there are real victories to be won, real achievements within the reach of man. Thirdly, it affirms the essential value of every individual. A man may be sternly judged, but he is never to be despised. Respect and compassion are the bases of all good art. Fourthly, it insists on the absolute validity of certain ethical standards. The relativistic attitude towards morals and ethics has a disintegrating effect on culture as on society. Men's motives are undoubtedly mixed, but goodness is a reality, and nobility in thought and action more than an imagination. Finally, the Bible asserts the positive value of self-sacrifice. In a world where nothing really matters, why should any man ever throw away his life for anything ? In a world where everything matters, there are things that matter more than life—and this even the Marxist is prepared at certain moments to recognize.

Culture without a religious (and that must mean in the West a Christian) basis is like an unanimated body. Religion, unincorporated in the life and culture of a people, tends to resemble a disembodied spirit. It is only through the coming together of body and spirit that man can really become again a living soul. In this field the task of the Churches is not so much unfinished as hardly yet begun.

CHAPTER 6

THE UNFINISHED TASK IN THE YOUNGER CHURCHES

FOR forty years it has been difficult for any missionary to tell the truth and nothing but the truth about the younger Churches. Even in earlier times, missionaries, under the influence both of their own loyalty to fellow-Christians whom they loved and of the inveterate desire of the readers of missionary magazines for success stories, tended to cast a somewhat rosy glow upon the field of their endeavours. Plain truth is not always as welcome as truth slightly adorned. But over the last generation the situation has been complicated by the inflamed national sensitiveness of the younger Church leaders and their resentment at anything like criticism from a Western source. The East, Christians included, in a not unnatural reaction against Western dominance, has claimed the right to pour forth a steady stream of vitriolic criticism against the West and all its works. Any come-back from the West in the way of counter-criticism has been regarded simply as a sign of Western arrogance, and of concealed and perhaps unconscious motives of imperialism and racial superiority. In the face of all this most missionaries have found it more prudent to keep silence, or to give at least a non-committal picture of the developing situation in the younger Churches.

Younger Church leaders visiting the West have contributed their share to the development of the contemporary mythology. In justifiable reaction against the appeal to pity, which did too much underlie missionary appeals of earlier days, they have tended to give the best possible account of their own countries and their inherited cultures. Such weaknesses as could not be denied might be attributed to the corrupting influence of the West. Moved by the desire to claim and to establish equality in every respect with the Western Churches, such leaders sometimes gave rather too encouraging impressions of the progress that had actually been made. Many listeners in the West received the impression that the evangelization of non-Christian lands had practically been completed, that though missionaries had done splendid service in the past their day was really done, and that now acceptance of missionaries by the younger Churches was rather the expression of their open-hearted internationalism than of any inner defects such as would make desirable the continuance of foreign help. Such presentations were naturally not very helpful to the cause of missionary recruiting in the Western Churches.

It is an immense relief that, with the easing of political tensions in so many areas, the period of mythology has come to an end and an epoch of realism can begin. The new nations have been accepted in the United Nations and elsewhere on a footing of perfect equality. It has at times been disturbing to the representatives of these peoples to discover that equality involves perfect mutuality of criticism, and a willingness to get as good as you give. It has, for instance, been difficult for Indians to accept the fact that the complete virtuousness and disinterestedness of India's policies is not so evident to all other countries as it is to India herself, and that many in other nations regard India's actions in relation to Kashmir from start to finish with the profoundest disapproval. But these are lessons that have to be learned, by Churches as well as nations that wish to play an adult part in world affairs. Younger Church leaders also are discovering in international assemblies that they must be prepared to meet their colleagues from other Churches on genuinely equal terms, must expect to have their statements challenged, and can no longer count on sympathy and forbearance greater than would be accorded to representatives from any other Church.

All this means that at last we can look realistically at the younger Churches, and ask ourselves, " Where are we really now ? "

Such a dispassionate survey involves recognition of certain weaknesses in the younger Churches, and it is only fair to start with a positive and generous recognition of all that has been achieved in and by the younger Churches, and of their status in the Christian world to-day.

In the first place, the existence of the younger Churches as they are to-day is a standing miracle. When one considers the still undisturbed lethargy of the great majority of Christians in the Western Churches as regards " foreign missions ", the niggardliness of financial support, the numerical inadequacy of the missionary personnel, the generally low average of intellectual and other qualifications possessed by missionaries, the undermining influences of ill-health, olation, loneliness and weariness, the fearful obstacles presented y the constant hostility of the non-Christian environment, not to nention the continuous and combined operations of the world, he flesh and the devil, the marvel is not that the younger Churches re not larger and better than they are, but that there are any younger Churches at all. After all my years of missionary experience, it :ill seems to me totally inexplicable that any Muslim or high-caste Iindu should ever be converted. But most readers of this book re likely to have had the privilege of listening to the testimony of ich converts, and have therefore first-hand evidence of the reality f this astounding miracle.

Secondly, many of the defects that can be seen in the younger Churches are also glaringly evident in the older Churches, and with ery much less excuse. It would be possible to go through this hapter point by point, and to adduce parallels in the life of the Ider Churches to every defect, every weakness, every problem in he life of the younger Churches to which attention is being drawn. ut there is a limit to the size of this book, and certain things must e taken as read. All Churches alike stand under the judgment of fod ; all alike need to learn a new humility, and a more perfect ependence on the grace of God. All need to learn from one another. : attention is mainly directed in this chapter to the younger Churches, uat is simply because such a selection of materials has been deter- uined by the general theme of this book.

To return, then, to the younger Churches. The first fact about hem that must strike any observer is that they are very small. Let s take some samples.

In Japan not more than one person in two hundred is a Christian.

For Siam the proportion is about the same, or rather less.

In India Christians are probably rather more than 2 per cent f the population ; but in Pakistan they are considerably less than per cent.

In Uganda nearly half the population is already Christian ; rogress is still rapid, and there is hope that this may become the rst Christian country in " Africa and the East ".[1]

---

[1] The Philippine Republic has a Roman Catholic majority ; but there are rge Muslim and pagan minorities. It must be noted also that there is a tendency all younger Churches for spiritual vitality to vary inversely with numerical uccess.

Similarly in the Belgian Congo progress has been astonishing rapid, and the Christian population, mainly Roman Catholic, probably nearly a quarter of the whole.

But in Nigeria, the most populous of all African countries Christians amount to not more than 3 per cent of the population. This is in part due to the predominant Muslim influenc in the north, where the British authorities were steadily oppose to Christian infiltration. But even in many pagan areas, where n such hindrances arise, the work of evangelization has hardly bee begun.

In many of the Pacific islands the work of evangelization ha been completed ; and throughout that whole vast area, without an startling mass movements, there has been a steady and impressiv increase in the number of Christians.

When we turn, however, to the Muslim countries, the succes of the Christian mission has been in inverse ratio to the devotio and self-sacrifice with which it has been carried on. In Indonesi where the Muslim world has proved less difficult of penetration tha elsewhere, there are perhaps 60,000 Christians of Muslim origin. Bu in the whole of Iran there are less than 5,000 evangelical Christians and numbers are far less in Iraq, Jordan and Arabia.

On a closer examination of the various countries, the pictur presents itself as even less favourable than the general survey woul suggest. In most countries Christians are grouped in comparativel small areas, leaving wide gaps in which the Christian cause ha hardly even begun to take root.

In Japan the great majority of the Christians live in the citie It is only within the last few years that the evangelization of rur Japan has been seriously undertaken.[1]

In Burma the majority of the Christians are Karens. Th Burmese people as a whole remains untouched by the Gospel.

In India most of the great Churches are in the south. It i still possible to point to many areas the size of an English count or a Swiss canton, and with a population larger than that of the les populous states in America, in which the Churches are represente

[1] The most recent figures known to me are those given on p. 262 of *Christianit and the Asian Revolution.* There are Churches in :
> 229 out of 245 cities (93 per cent) ;
> 487 out of 1,815 towns (27 per cent) ;
> 193 out of 8,381 villages (2·3 per cent).

most by one or two individual Christians who have drifted in in
earch of work, but in which there is no regular Christian witness
f any kind whatever.

In Indonesia, there are great Churches in the Batak area of
umatra, in parts of Celebes and in Timor, but many islands of
hat immense archipelago still remain to be reached.

So far from the evangelization of the world having been nearly
accomplished, it may rather be said that the pioneer stage has at
ngth been passed through, and that this is the moment at which
rious and constructive evangelization ought to begin.

Furthermore, in many areas the Christians are drawn from the
poorest section of the population, and the educational level is still
ery low. This is not anything of which the Churches should com-
ain. In the days of St. Paul those who were given to the Church
ere not the wise or the mighty or the influential; the poor, the
mple and the disinherited were the instruments whom God was
eased to use for the accomplishment of His great work. It is not
be wondered at if history has repeated itself. In India all the
issions began by approaching the higher castes, with some striking
sults but on the whole with a discouraging lack of response. If
-day most of the work is being carried on among the depressde
asses, that is not so much by any deliberate choice as in response
circumstances that would not be denied. Few movements among
the outcastes " have been sought or planned for; [1] they seem to
ave sprung into being almost spontaneously through some deep
ovement of the Spirit; and they have not always been welcome
ther to missionaries or to leaders in the Indian Church.

Even those who most joyfully recognize in such movements
Christ's way to India's heart " [2] must admit that they have brought
ith them immense problems. These poor and disinherited people
ve lived in a state of almost complete illiteracy. It is no doubt
ossible to be both illiterate and a very good Christian; but no one
ho has not personally engaged in the task of instructing illiterate
ults can have any idea of the difficulty of making even the simplest
ligious truth intelligible to them. And the raising up of intelligent

[1] The idea that missionaries started with the depressed classes because there
e going was easier is a part of younger Church mythology that rests on no
storical foundation.
[2] The title of a well-known book by Bishop J. W. Pickett of the Methodist
urch in Southern Asia.

leadership among them is not a task that can be accomplished ove
night. The Churches have wrestled valiantly with this problen
but over the last sixty years the increase in members has been s
great that illiteracy has held its own against the regular education
work of the Church, and against special literacy campaigns on th
Laubach method. Throughout the world the educational level c
the Christian communities is probably far above that of the con
munities in the midst of which they live ; but in some parts c
India illiteracy among Christians is said to be still as high as ç
per cent.

The spiritual and ethical achievement of the younger Churche
is disappointingly poor.

We must be fair to these Churches. Both the current mytholog
and a particular use of language combine to lead the Wester
Christian, and the missionary candidate, unless he has been care
fully warned and prepared, to form expectations of the younge
Churches which a moment's reflection would show to be ill-founde
When we speak of Christians in England, we generally mean co
vinced and committed Christians, among whom it would hardly b
safe to reckon more than one in ten of the nominal Christians.
is all too easy to transfer this usage to other fields, and unconsciousl
to assume that every Christian in India or Africa is a saint in th
making. It is true that in the life of many younger Churches the
is a spontaneity and vigour which is lacking in the rather tire
Churches of the West, and that the Christians in Africa and Ind
and elsewhere are far more regular in their attention to such dutie
as churchgoing than their comrades elsewhere. But, when all tha
has been accepted, it remains the fact that the word " Christian
overseas covers the whole range of possible degrees of adherenc
to the Christian community, from the saint and the ardent Christia
down through the regular churchgoer to the occasional performe
and so to the non-worshipping, the irregular, the excommunicat
and the near-apostate. If there really were ten million apostol
Christians in India, that would be an impressive striking force. Th
reality is glorious ; but it is none the less glorious for bein
realistically viewed.

Every outside observer, and even the experienced missionary
tends to underestimate the gravity of the conflict in which a younge
Church is engaged. There are certain large Christian grouping

or instance in Batakland, in which Christians can live to a large extent isolated from pagan surroundings and a pagan past ; but these are few. Most Christians live and breathe in an atmosphere impregnated with non-Christian ideas, principles and prejudices. They are, as it were, carrying all the time upon their shoulders the weight of an immemorial past. Unless the Christian conflict is maintained at its highest pitch, unless there is constant and vigilant recourse to the Word of God, there is an inevitable tendency for the Church to be drawn down to the level of the life that surrounds it, and to accept standards of conduct which are incompatible with the principles of its own life.

In Africa the perpetual problem is that of polygamy. To the African this does not immediately present itself as a moral problem ; it is much more a matter of social prestige and economic necessity. Among younger African Christians there are not wanting voices to maintain that polygamy is the natural form of the African family, to which the Churches ought to adapt themselves instead of trying to impose the Western and European tradition of monogamy. There are areas in which almost all the leading chiefs are nominally Christian, and almost all are in bad standing in the Church for the open practice of polygamy.

In India one of the main problems of conduct is that of false witness in the law courts. Football leagues not having been introduced on a large scale in Indian villages, litigation takes front rank in the field of recreation and public interest. Both sides tend to regard the lawsuit as a game ; the more serious the charge, the more exciting is the game, and the less scrupulous the methods employed to secure a victory. The man who limits himself to the strict truth is clearly putting himself at a grave disadvantage. It is extraordinarily difficult for Christians to recognize that the ninth commandment is as relevant and as binding in this situation as in any other. The hard doctrine that it is better to tell the truth and see your friends go to gaol than to tell lies and see them acquitted did not in my experience arouse the enthusiasm of the simple and hard-pressed village Christians.

On a deeper level than conduct, and in the end more menacing, is the persistence underground of non-Christian structures and patterns of thought. These patterns are far more instinctive than rational. They persist in all of us, racially as well as individually, and are liable to find emotional expression, as when the Southern Christian in the United States settles the question of segregation with the words, " My daughter isn't going out with a Negro ".

It is best to illustrate the problem by an actual example. A theological teacher in Africa fell to discussing with his students their idea of the Resurrection. It became clear that, in the deeper levels of their mind, they all held the old African conviction that the spirit in man is a temporary loan from the common spirit of the tribe. At death this fragmentary spirit is joined to the central spirit of the tribe, and will be born again in some other individual ; for which reason babies are often named for someone who had died at the moment of their birth. Clearly such a view excludes the recognition of personal immortality, of final responsibility in the presence of God, and of individual judgment. All these students no doubt held intellectually the orthodox Christian view of the Resurrection. That is what they would preach from the pulpit. But, mysteriously, what a preacher really conveys to his hearers is his own deepest conviction, even when the words that he utters are inconsistent with those inner beliefs ; and what touches us on those deeper emotional levels is in the end a far more powerful lever than that which reaches only the conscious and reflective levels of the mind.

Such deeper conviction can long remain unspoken, and can apparently, in Europe no less than in Africa, be transmitted from generation to generation. This explains the distressing emergence in the third and fourth generation of Christians of old evil practices such as one would imagine to have long since disappeared from the Christian consciousness. Examples are the cases of ritual murder in which Christians have been involved in recent years in Basutoland and in the Gold Coast. At a certain point of inner pressure the Christian ceases to feel that these things are wrong ; he may come to regard them as right, and even as obligatory. This inner schism cannot be dealt with by the multiplication of Christian practices and ceremonies. All outward, and even inward, Christian life is built on an insecure foundation, until the inner schism is radically healed.

Why are we where we are, and why, having done so much, have we failed to do more ? Why is it necessary ruefully to admit that, with all the marvellous manifestations of the power of God in the non-Christian world, the net result of so much missionary devotion over two centuries seems to have been the calling into existence in many parts of the world of large and very imperfectly converted Churches? Various explanations are being contemporaneously given, some more valid than others, and all deserving of careful scrutiny.

The first point, on which most critics in the younger Churches themselves insist, is the foreignness of the Church. For this there is at least a measure of justification; there are a number of cases on record in which missionaries have insisted on pupils in their schools wearing unnecessary and unsuitable Western clothes. But has sufficient care always been taken by these critics to distinguish between *foreignness* and *difference*? In Travancore, where the Syrian Church has existed for at least fifteen hundred years,[1] it is not felt by anyone to be *foreign*, in spite of the continued dependence of sections of the Church on Rome and on Antioch. But it is quite *different* from anything else; a Christian church does not look in the least like a Hindu temple or a Muslim mosque, it is just a church ! The same is true in a village in other parts of India, in which the Church has existed for a century or more. No one can remember a time when it did not exist; it may not have been visited by any foreigner for a whole generation. Christians may be disliked and at times even persecuted by their neighbours for such anti-social habits as refusal to pay money into village funds deposited in the local temple; but no one thinks of them as in any way *foreign* to the life of the village. After all, are we not all cousins and second cousins together? In cities foreign connections and foreign ways may be more evident. In most village churches in India the congregation sits cross-legged on the floor; in most city churches there are pews or benches; the appearance of the church is in consequence extraordinarily different from that of the Hindu temple. But to the suggestion that it might be well to return to the simple and more Indian habits of the village, the educated city Christian will reply, " We sit on chairs in our houses and in our clubs; to sit on the floor in church will be for us something like play-acting ". And, as there is no congregational worship in Hinduism, is it surprising that a Christian church cannot really be made to look anything like a Hindu temple ?

[1] All members of this ancient Church would emend this to " nineteen hundred years ", believing firmly that their Church was founded by the Apostle Thomas and by no one else.

Similar questions arise over the attempt to domesticate within the Christian Church traditions of art that have grown up outside it. A study of such attempts raises once again the question of *difference* as opposed to foreignness. To use Hindu motifs in a Christian church, on the ground that these are Indian, will at once alienate every Christian whose background is Muslim ; such a structure will appear to him purely idolatrous. In some of the pictures of Mr. A. D. Thomas our Lord appears as a young Hindu ascetic. Is such adaptation the wisest method to follow ? The Buddhist would, I think, answer No. The Buddha should never look like anything but the Buddha. There may be almost unlimited variations within the type ; but the type was fixed long ago under Greek influence in the north-western kingdom of India, and it is within that tradition that the Buddhist artist must still work to-day. Every experiment in the direction of indigenous art is to be encouraged ; but the honest critic may be compelled to admit that in most areas we have not yet progressed beyond a somewhat superficial syncretism ; we have hardly begun as yet to discover the styles or the idioms in which the Christian soul of Asia and Africa will find its true artistic expression.

Where the missionaries have been foreigners, the first Christians have often too readily accepted the foreignness with the Gospel, and the Church has become more alienated from its surroundings than is necessary. But it does not necessarily follow that foreignness is the main source of the weakness of the Christian Churches. Several recent studies of missionary strategy have concentrated on other sources of weakness, which they have found to lie mainly in faulty approaches to the problem of the growth and independence of the Church.

One such study is Dr. D. A. McGavran's *The Bridges of God*.[1] This deeply moving book deserves the close attention of all who care for the cause of Christ in the world, even if they are not able confidently to accept all its conclusions. Dr. McGavran draws a sharp distinction between the " Mission Station Approach " and " the People's Movement ". The mission station approach involves drawing the Christian converts out of their natural surroundings, settling them in the mission compound, and so developing a well-instructed and orderly Christian group, but one without natural

[1] London : World Dominion Press, 1955.

ohesion. It is doubtful whether any missionaries ever started by planning the creation of such artificial communities. In many parts of the world hostility to the new religion and its adherents has been so intense that the only way in which they could exist at all was by leaving everything to place themselves under the care of their missionary friends. Almost every single one of the converts brought in by the Christian Colleges in India a century ago became a Christian at the peril of his life, and was simply cast out by his family. What course could the missionaries follow other than that of adopting these young men as their sons, and doing everything for them until they could stand on their own feet ? What begins as a necessary practical adjustment may later come to be developed into a theory ; it may be that later missionaries took the view that it was better for would-be Christians to enter the mission compound community rather than risk the spiritual perils of living as Christians in their own non-Christian world. If so, time has shown the weakness of this argument, since in no case has such a mission compound community proved itself an effective instrument for witness among the non-Christians.

With this type of development Dr. McGavran rightly contrasts the " People's Movement ", which begins within a group, and in which the decision to follow Christ is usually made by the group rather than by individuals as such. Here the Christians remain in their own environment, and are free to operate along all the natural channels of kinship and association in bearing witness to the name of Christ. Such movements have proved far more fruitful than any others, and have avoided many of the dangers resulting from excessive dependence on the foreign missionary and his care.

The distinction is a valid one. The weakness of Dr. McGavran's book is in its generalizations. At the end of his chapter called " Pattern of the Great Century " he writes : " So has run the characteristic pattern of the Great Century ".[1] This is far too sweeping. The mission station approach may have ruled in certain cases, but from the beginning both types of movement have existed and have shown their characteristic developments. The first " people's movement " in modern missionary history was the conversion of the Fisher Folk of South India by the Roman Catholics in 1534. This was a true people's movement, very wisely and

[1] P. 67.

skilfully developed by the missionaries. But it revealed from the
start the gravest weakness of " people's movements " ; it affected
only one caste ; when the whole of that caste had been Christianized
the movement as movement ceased. The second movement took
place 250 years later in the same area. In 1796 crowds of people
at the extreme tip of India began to ask for baptism in circumstance
that remain highly mysterious. In six months the Lutheran missionaries from Tanjore baptized more than 5,000 people. The
missionaries were so few that the new Christians were almost wholly
neglected for twenty years. Then began new missionary activity
under the guidance of the Anglican societies. The long neglected
Churches were once again cared for ; conversions began again, and
continued in a steady stream till 1870. But, in spite of the number
of missionaries, the mission station approach was almost wholly
avoided. Almost all Tinnevelly Christians remained in their villages
and, with the natural and delightful vigour of the Tamil race, were
as often engaged in fighting with their missionaries as in submitting
to them ! But once again the fatal defect appeared ; the movement
was almost wholly among the people of one caste ; in that area
converts have been won from all the other castes, but in very small
numbers, and never under the form of anything that could be called
a people's movement.

We are warned to be on our guard. In politics it is wise to
have a few theories and no principles. In missionary strategy it
is well to have one or two principles and no theories. For the
realities are very complicated, as complicated as human life itself
The weakness of Dr. McGavran's book is in its simplification of
the issues ; he safeguards himself at certain points, but those qualifications are not sufficient to guard against the one-sided impression
which the book is likely to leave in the mind of the reader.

Dr. McGavran seems to assume that there is no part of the world
in which a people's movement could not be produced, if the right
techniques were followed. He asks the question, " How are people's
movements brought into being ? " But he himself admits that
" the movements are the outcome of the mysterious movement
of the Spirit of God ".[1] My own judgment is that the origin of
such movements will always remain a mystery. We can see the
predisposing historical causes which lie behind Methodism in

[1] P. 65.

Britain ; but does John Wesley for that reason become any less of a mystery ? Do we imagine that by research and deeper knowledge of spiritual causes we could produce another John Wesley in a test-tube ?

For, in fact, the progress of people's movements as they have so far occurred presents a strangely varied picture, not to be reduced to any single formula. Missions which have striven with prayers and tears to produce a people's movement have not seen the answer to their prayers. Other missions, which greatly disliked the idea of mass conversion and feared its consequences, have been driven by the pressure of the Spirit into courses that theoretically they deplored. When God's appointed time came for the great people's movements among the outcastes of the Telugu area, Anglicans, Lutherans, Methodists, Congregationalists and Baptists were all drawn into the stream. All, in spite of their different conceptions of the Church, were led to follow much the same methods of work, and to produce much the same kind of Churches.[1] Conversely a single mission, working in two areas along exactly similar lines, has been privileged in one area to see the rapid development of a people's movement, and in the other, where similar results might have been expected, seems to have been condemned to plough the barren sands.

No " people's movement " has ever taken place among high caste Hindus (except on a small scale in some areas, as a result of great Christian movements among the lower castes), among Muslims (with a partial exception in Indonesia), or among Buddhists. No " people's movement " has ever taken place among city dwellers. This is not to say that such movements can never take place ; it warns us against considering them as a phenomenon that must necessarily follow, if certain principles of missionary strategy are adopted.

The dangers of theory are even more strikingly manifest when we come to look at some of Dr. McGavran's practical proposals. He writes, in effect, that the whole missionary enterprise should be concentrated on the growing edge of people's movements ; and that

[1] Though still with the problem of movements following the lines of a single caste. In many villages there were two separate caste Churches, the Anglican missionary being known to the people as the Mala missionary and the Baptist as the Madiga missionary !

support in missionary personnel and money should be geared to the
rate of numerical progress in the various areas. I must confess
myself horrified by the application of such mathematical methods
to spiritual situations. It is certainly true that support of people's
movements has on the whole been grievously inadequate, and that
those who have had the responsibility of building them up have
generally had to proceed by a series of desperate improvisations
rather than according to any settled plan of advance. One promising
movement after another has slowed down, or collapsed, or come to
a dead end, just because at the crucial moment support from the
older Churches was suddenly reduced ; and, when such a movement has come to a standstill, it is almost impossible ever to get it
moving again. But it does not follow that support should immediately be withdrawn from areas in which at present the Church
situation is almost static, since we never know where or at what
moment the Spirit of God may work, and a static situation blaze
up into a movement. If Dr. McGavran's methods had been applied
in the nineteenth century, there would have been very few people's
movements ; again and again such movements have started un-
expectedly just at the moment when the missionaries because of
long frustration were on the point of pulling up their stakes and
moving elsewhere.

There has never been a people's movement in Islamic countries
On Dr. McGavran's principles, missions in Muslim lands would
either be abandoned or reduced to the shadow of a shade. An
earlier statement of his views in an article in the *International Review
of Missions* called forth an eloquent and moving rejoinder from
Dr. W. McE. Miller, for many years a missionary of the American
Presbyterian Church in Iran. It is well known that missions to
Muslims are unfruitful ; the baptism of a single convert is a great
event. What, then, is the justification for maintaining these expensive
and numerically unprofitable missions ? A valid answer can be found
only in the command of our Lord that the Gospel must be preached
to all nations, and that therefore the Muslim nations cannot be
excluded. The Churches have to do long penance for their sin
and crimes against the Muslim in the past ; the terrible hatred
generated by the Crusades is still a living power. It may be that
God's time for the Muslim has not yet come ; but is it not arrant
faithlessness to imagine that God is less present with those who

sow in tears than with those who bring back their sheaves with rejoicing ?

> God sees the end from the beginning, He knows that the long winter will pass and the snows will melt and the springtime will come at last, and then will follow the joy of harvest. And He wants us, His children, to sow in hope, to wait in patience and to be stead-fast and unmovable, knowing that the harvest will come and that our labour will not be in vain. We labourers in Muslim lands are not discouraged, for though we have little of the joy of reaping we have much of the joy of hoping and believing.[1]

One of the points stressed by Dr. McGavran is the need for mobility, and here perhaps every thinker on missionary problems will be in agreement with him. It is all too easy for missions to grow conservative, and to believe that the old and well-tried methods are the best. This is even easier for younger Churches, since they have never known any methods other than those practised by loved and honoured missionaries. Many missions have immobilized them-selves by putting up great buildings far too soon, before there was any evidence which way the wind of the Spirit was blowing. It is essential that in every generation there should be a thorough stock-taking and a clearing out of lumber. It may be that some salients in the Christian enterprise should now be abandoned, and that a regrouping of forces is overdue. But woe betide the Church that confuses the mechanical application of a theory with obedience to the authentic voice of the Lord of Hosts !

There has lately been renewed interest in the writings of Roland Allen, and especially in his two books, *Missionary Methods—St. Paul's or Ours ?* and *The Spontaneous Expansion of the Church.* The title of the first book in itself warns us to be on our guard. St. Paul's missionary methods were determined by the presence in his world of precisely that factor which is lacking everywhere in the world to-day—the liberal Jews of the dispersion, and those Gentiles who had come under the influence of the synagogue, and were particularly responsive to the preaching of the Gospel. Serious account has to be taken of this difference ; to set up " the imitation of St. Paul " as a principle of missionary strategy is as grave an error as to set up " the imitation of Christ " as a principle of the

---

[1] William McElwee Miller : " New Methods for a New Age," *International Review of Missions,* April 1956, p. 209.

spiritual life. But once this has been allowed for, there is much in Allen's thought that is of permanent value. He was in violent reaction against those Western traditions which seemed to him to be stifling the free development of indigenous Churches—elaborate buildings, a highly trained ministry paid by foreign money, the imposition of Western theology and ways of thinking. His ideal was the small but expanding group, expanding through the personal witness of its members, autonomous, independent of foreign money and foreign control, with its own simple ministry entrusted with the full authority of the Church, including authority to minister the Sacraments. This is an admirable ideal, and one that the younger Churches may well keep before themselves, provided that it is not imagined that one formula can cover every case, and that it is not forgotten that in certain areas the too rigid application of Allen's principles has led to spiritual disaster.

Nothing has led in recent years to so much heart-searching and re-thinking of missionary problems as the Communist victory in China, the expulsion of missionaries and the apparent turning of so many Chinese Christian leaders against their former missionary friends. One of the most striking attempts to evaluate this situation is Mr. D. M. Paton's book, *Christian Missions and the Judgment of God*. Mr. Paton's standpoint is largely that of Roland Allen. The burden of his criticism of the missions and Churches is along the lines of their failure to adopt genuinely indigenous principles—too much dependence on foreign money ; too little trust in Chinese leadership, and in the work of the Holy Spirit in raising up new forms of leadership ; too limited a ministry, and too little adaptation of the ministry to the real situation of the Church ; too little acceptance of the local worshipping group as the heart of the Church's life, through the work and witness of which the Church must grow and make itself at home in the society which surrounds it. In Mr. Paton's pungent remarks there is much which strikes home. The Churches had been on the whole unadventurous. The majority of Chinese leaders were weighed down by a sense of guilt that their membership in " foreign Churches " had constituted a kind of treachery to the cause of Chinese independence and national dignity. But, when all this has been readily accepted, it may be questioned whether these are the deepest lessons that the missionary world has to learn from the Chinese situation. It is, perhaps, ot so much a question of missionary methods as a question of ιeology.

The rise of the Chinese Churches was contemporary with the eyday of liberalism in America. An enormous amount of American ιoney was poured into China, largely through the Y.M.C.A., and ιis type of Christian teaching all too readily amalgamated itself with ertain tendencies that were characteristic of the Chinese outlook. 'o an outside observer, the following seemed to be the defects of ιe Chinese Churches as a whole :

1. Christianity presented much more as a programme of social and political reform than as a religion of redemption. But the concepts of liberal Christianity proved in the end less dynamic than those of Marxist Communism.

2. A widespread lack of interest in theology, theology being regarded as no more than the perpetuation from the pulpit of old-world terms and phrases, which no longer had any relevance to present-day life.

3. A liberal interpretation of the Bible, from which both the prophetic and eschatological dimensions were almost wholly absent.

4. An almost total lack of the sense of worship. " We Chinese are not mystical " said a great Chinese leader to a missionary friend of mine ; this was his reason for lack of interest in attempts to improve the quality of worship in the University where both worked.

5. An almost total lack of understanding of the nature of the Church. To many leading Chinese Christians, who had come to Christ through a Christian college or through the Y.M.C.A., the Church was not so much the nurse and mother of their faith as an inconvenient though perhaps necessary appendage to it.

6. An almost total lack of understanding of the significance of the universal Church, transcended in the case of the great Chinese leaders through vigorous participation in the ecumenical movement.

We must return to our consideration of the principles of Roland ιllen, and the measure of their applicability in different areas and ιtuations. Can an autonomous, self-maintaining, self-propagating

group, such as he imagined, come quickly into existence among
depressed class community in India, or in a primitive people i
Africa where every single person is at the start illiterate ?

It may be interesting not to treat the problem theoretically, bu
to consider how it was handled by the greatest leader as yet produce
by any of the younger Churches, Bishop Azariah of Dornakal, wh
was familiar with the books of Roland Allen and had deeply pondere
them, though without surrendering any of his own independenc
of thought and action. Here are the principles on which he acted

1. Strong centralized control. The Churches in his area wer
   not to be a heap of iron-filings, but a closely-knit organism
   related at every point to the bishop as the representative c
   the common life of the Church.

2. A numerous and exceptionally able missionary staff. Azaria
   was strong enough not to be afraid of Europeans ; he wa
   able to use them, and to give them greater authority tha
   was being exercised by missionaries in most other areas a
   the time. The missionaries responded by devoted, but no
   uncritical, loyalty to the bishop.

3. Generous and liberal support in foreign money. An elab
   orate organization was built up through which parishes i
   England were linked to villages in Dornakal. The mone
   was mainly used to build schools and churches in villages
   and to supply them with teacher-catechists paid in part b
   the government and in part by the Church.

4. Training from the start in the principles of Christian givin
   (not of " self-support ") on biblical lines.[1] Azariah taugh
   his people that even the poorest family could set aside dail
   a handful of grain ; it would not be missed at the time, bu
   the amount raised would cumulatively be very great. Fo
   the ideas of self-support and independence, so easily mis
   interpreted in a sub-Christian sense, was substituted th
   principle of co-operation in the work of the Lord.

5. As early as possible trustworthy village workers were ordaine
   to the ministry. Many of them were men of very slende

---

[1] See V. S. Azariah : *Christian Giving* (World Christian Books No. 2, Lutter
worth Press). A young American missionary, working in Hokkaido, Japan, wrot
to me recently that, having read *Christian Giving*, he had introduced the idea c
the rice collection in his Japanese congregation with excellent results.

qualifications, who would not have been accepted for ordination elsewhere. Azariah, remembering that his own father had been a village minister of this type, was determined to trust them, and gradually to raise the standard with the development of the Church. By the end of his episcopate (1945) graduates in arts and theology were being ordained.

6. Immense insistence on the principle, " Every Christian a witness ". Each year the great campaign of village preaching by lay Christians brought in requests from many new villages for instruction in the faith. Contrary to the opinion of almost all missionaries, Azariah believed (and his faith was justified) that the converted outcaste would be an effective witness even to the high-caste man.

The work in Dornakal was very far from perfect. As we have already seen, at the end of his life Bishop Azariah was distressed to find in the second and third generations of Christians so much less zeal and devotion than he had hoped for. Nevertheless his work has stood the test. At the end of his life he left behind a church which was still growing in numbers, in knowledge and in capacity to take responsibility for its own affairs. All this was achieved not on the basis of any rigid theory of what a mission should be, but on constant reference to the Bible as the authority, and on the flexible application of a few simple, biblical principles. Missionaries were not foreigners but colleagues. The missionary societies were not directors but partners. Christians, however simple, were to be treated as responsible beings. The Holy Spirit was to be trusted to use the poorest testimony, if humbly and sincerely given.

There are great differences between Church and Church, and between the situation in one country and that in others. But there are certain common weaknesses that recur in many widely separated areas ; and, provided that the many exceptions to each statement are borne in mind, it may be useful to list these weaknesses, as a preparation for our study of what needs to be done at the present time to make the situation better.

1. In many areas, especially those of rapid progress, there has been a tendency to make conditions for baptism too easy. How low the standard can fall is shown by the quite serious remark of a

theological student to me years ago: " These families have bee
attending church for three Sundays; shall I arrange for the
baptism next Sunday ? " To fix the moment of baptism is a mo
delicate operation. If enquirers are kept waiting too long, the
may become discouraged, depart, and be seen no more. On the othe
hand, if baptism is given too quickly, the new Christians are likel
to think that they have done all that is required of them, and t
fail to see why they should continue in the very toilsome pursu
of Christian knowledge.[1] Experience shows that Christian worke
are likely to under-estimate rather than to over-estimate the amour
that can be learned by simple people.

2. Almost everywhere there has been grave failure in the givin
of systematic instruction to the members of the Christian fellowship
There has been plenty of preaching—almost all simple people
especially perhaps those in Africa, seem to have a natural gift
eloquence—but the intellectual content has been small, and the air
is all too often moralistic edification rather than serious instruction
The Bible is a much more difficult book than is often realized b
those who have been brought up on it. Experience shows that
new Christian group needs thirty years of patient, steady building
up in Christian knowledge and character, before it can be regarde
as stable and well-settled in the faith. In many cases sheer weigl
of numbers has made such special care and nurture impossible
but in others neglect of this duty has arisen rather from failure
realize its importance than from the impossibility of attending
it. For it is all-important. Competent knowledge of the Bible
the only basis for effective Christian witness. Some of the Churche
such as those in Korea, which have concentrated most on Bibl
teaching, have been most remarkably blessed with increase in nun
bers. And if missionary support and contact with other Church
are to be withdrawn through the isolating power of Nationalis
or Communism, how much will depend on the presence of tl
Bible in the home, and on an intelligent use of it by the ordina
Christian !

3. In many areas there has been a grave lack of deep, persona
pastoral care for the individual. For this the circumstances of rapi
growth may have been responsible. The missionaries have mo

[1] Insistence on further instruction in preparation for Confirmation is only
partial safeguard against this danger.

id more become administrators, remote from direct pastoral con-
ct with their people ; the national leaders, to whom in so many
ises they have handed on their tasks, have tended to follow in the
ack thus already marked out for them. The only way in which
iyone can learn what it means to be a pastor is through being
imself the object of the pastoral care of someone else. If those
ho are called to serve as pastors and teachers in the younger
hurches have themselves never passed through this experience, it
innot be expected that, apart from some special inspiration of the
oly Spirit, they will know how to exercise it in relation to their
eople. This perhaps more than any other is the point at which
ie life of the younger Churches needs strengthening to-day.

4. In far too many cases Christians have been encouraged to
elieve that the Gospel is a matter of receiving help, without a
irresponding emphasis on the joy of giving. A joyful heart always
iontaneously wishes to share its joy, and the gift to God is always
ie natural expression of Christian joy ; " What reward shall I give
nto the Lord for all the benefits that he hath done unto me ? " [1]

5. All too rarely have Christians been encouraged to exploit to
ie full the natural channels of witness—the family, the wider ties
f relationship, the group, the clan, the tribe. It must not be
nagined that witness along these lines will always be successful—
ie hardness of man's heart can defy the most winning tones of the
race of God ; yet experience in every area of rapid movement
iows that simple witness along these natural lines is far more
fective in keeping the movement moving than the preaching of
iissionary or catechist ; and, if such a movement dies down, the
eason seems almost to be that the majority of Christians have
ecome casual in using their opportunities of witness, or that the
iediocrity of their Christian life is such as to deprive their witness
f any bite or force. Again, the limitations of these lines of action
iust be borne in mind ; a whole caste in India, a whole tribe in
frica, could be brought to Christ by this method, and all the
her castes and tribes remain wholly unaffected. But to say that
method is imperfect is no excuse for failing to use it as far as it
ill go.

6. New Christians have not always been taught from the start
ie nature of the universal Church and the privilege of belonging

[1] Psalm 116 : 11 (P.B.V.).

to it. Here the Roman Catholic missions are probably ahead of an
others ; the most ignorant Roman Catholic in the world know
about the Pope, and knows that he is directly linked to " the universa
pastor of the faithful ". In most Protestant missions the disastrou
separation between Church and mission has done its evil work
the younger Church Christian of early days thought of himself firs
as linked to the mission which had brought him the Gospel, an
learned only gradually, if he learned at all, of that Church whicl
is the greater reality behind the missionary society. The enthusiasn
of almost all younger Churches for membership in the Worl
Council of Churches as a world-wide and universal body show
a healthy reaction against the mission-centred outlook of far to
many missionaries.

Every one of the major problems in the younger Churches
though it may present itself in the guise of finance or organization
is in reality a spiritual problem, such as can be solved only throug
spiritual methods by spiritual men. It is from such consideration
that we can infer the nature of the leadership needed by the younge
Churches at the present time. As missionaries withdraw, or retir
more and more into the background, the initiative must increasingl
and rightly be in the hands of the younger Churches themselves
and humanly speaking everything depends on the spiritual calibr
of the men and women called to positions of great responsibilit
in these Churches in the coming years.

There has been a great deal of talk in recent years about th
development of leadership in the younger Churches. But is th
idea of " leadership " biblical and Christian, and can we make us
of it without doing grave injury to the very cause that we wish t
serve ? It may be well at this point to quote the opinion of on
whose authority to speak in this matter is beyond question :

1. How far is the conception of " leadership " really one which w
ought to encourage ? It is so hard to use it without being misle
by the non-Christian conception of leadership. It has been trul
said that our need is not for leaders, but for saints and servants
Unless this fact is held steadily in the foreground, the whol
idea of leadership-training becomes dangerous.

2. In our training we need to approximate more to the old idea o
apprenticeship than to the pattern so often set in academic courses
Learning the art of Christian service must largely be by doing.

3. This apprenticeship must be served in the atmosphere of companionship. . . . Here numbers are a real danger. The pattern of training in Christian leadership must still be that given in the Gospels—the training of the Twelve.[1]

Each of Bishop Newbigin's three points demands careful consideration.

If we set out to produce a race of leaders, what we shall succeed in doing will probably be to produce a race of restless, ambitious and discontented intellectuals ; to a considerable extent this is what we have done. To tell a man that he is called to be a leader, or that he is being trained to be a leader, is the best way of ensuring his spiritual ruin, since in the Christian world ambition is more deadly than any other sin, and, if it is yielded to, makes a man unprofitable in the ministry.

It has come to be generally assumed that the right way to produce leaders is to bring as many younger Church students as possible to the West, and to enable them to take higher theological or technical degrees. Certainly this is in principle very much to be encouraged ; until educational opportunity in Asia and Africa and Latin America is in every respect equal to that which the older Churches can offer, the doors must be opened as widely as possible to welcome the student from the younger Churches. But let us be under no illusions as to what this can accomplish ; it can provide us with a number of technicians and moderately competent college professors ; it cannot of itself produce one of those men and women of outstanding spiritual power whom the younger Churches so desperately need to-day. The more fully the student identifies himself with the thought patterns of the West, the more difficult will he find it to re-adapt himself to the ways of his own people and his own Church. Already voices are being raised within the younger Churches themselves to ask whether this method of long training abroad is really giving these Churches what they need. At the recent All-Africa Lutheran Conference held at Marangu, a Zulu delegate is reported as having spoken as follows :

I cannot emphasize strongly enough that future African ministers should be trained on the spot. Americanized and Europeanized African pastors will not do much for Africa. I speak from experience.

[1] Bishop Lesslie Newbigin in *International Review of Missions*, April 1956, p. 228.

I knew a man who received a scholarship and went abroad for tw
years. After he came home he pushed down almost everything. H
is not even willing to marry a Zulu girl. We plead that future pastor
should be trained on the spot where they will have to fight the
battles rather than sending Africans and Malagasy people outsic
of Africa. We would ask that arrangements be made that we ca
get American and European professors to come and do somethin
here in Africa to really train soldiers on the battle front.[1]

The third point, about the place of fellowship in training,
the most important of all. " The leader " so easily appears, an
perhaps thinks of himself, as Moses going up alone into th
mountain into the darkness where God is. How different fro
the true man of God, who remembers that the Holy Spirit is give
to God's people without discrimination, and that on occasion th
message of the Lord may come to the prophet through the mout
of an ass !

The intellectual standard of younger Church leadership has rise
with extraordinary rapidity during this century. It is not certai
that this rise has been accompanied by a corresponding growth int
spiritual maturity.

It is important to bear this in mind, since the problem of th
handing over of control in the younger Churches to members o
those Churches is more complicated than may at first sight appea
It is true that missionaries in the past have often been far too slo
to believe in the possibilities of the working of the Holy Spirit i
Christians of recent conversion ; they have failed to recognize tha
the bearing of responsibility is the only way in which a man ca
learn to bear responsibility ; they have been unwilling to take risk
All this is true, but it is only one side of the truth. Missionar
history is strewn with the disasters that have followed upon a pre
mature or unwise handing over of responsibility to those who wer
spiritually unprepared to carry it.

In one area very well known to me, the decision was made eight
years ago to withdraw all missionaries except those working in in
stitutions, and to hand over all the local work of the Church to th
indigenous clergy. That Church is still struggling with the evil

---

[1] *Marangu* (Lutheran World Federation, Geneva, 1956), p. 64. It is fair
add that three other African speakers, while in part agreeing with the Rev. S
Mbatha, also spoke in favour of sending Africans to Europe and America.

that crept in during the ten years before a measure of missionary control was restored. It was right to hand over more responsibility to the indigenous clergy ; it was blindness not to have seen that this step should have been accompanied by an increase, and not by a reduction, in the number of missionaries. The clergy needed more help, not less, than they had been receiving, though of a rather different kind ; and, though one man can dictatorially control an area, four or five may be needed to stand in the background and support those on whom so heavy a spiritual responsibility has been newly thrown.

In many cases the acute conflict is not between missionary and national, but between the interests of the educated city congregation and those of the simple Christians of the villages. The missionary who has lived all his life in the villages is likely, in spite of the difference of race, to be much nearer to the village people than city lawyers and doctors of their own race. In another area well known to me power in the Church came to be vested in a committee largely composed of educated city laymen. One of the first acts of this committee was to resolve that no one should be taken as a candidate for the ministry unless he was already a graduate in arts. As a result a large village area of Christians of the depressed classes was left without any ordained indigenous ministry, since it could not itself produce candidates of the required standard, and city-bred graduates proved unadaptable to the work of the village.

The most important thing to-day is the spiritual, rather than the intellectual, quality of those indigenous Christians who are called to bear responsibility in and for the younger Churches. And how is it possible to produce spiritual quality ? In truth it cannot be produced ; it is always the gift of God ; yet it is possible to see that certain types and conditions of training hinder spiritual growth, and others are at least favourable to it. Nothing is so much occupying the attention of the younger Churches as the type of training needed by both ordained ministers and lay folk to fit them for their future tasks. As this is one of the points at which it seems likely that the younger Churches will for a time be prepared to accept help from the older, we may here consider in what manner, and to what extent, the Western missionary can still hope to be of service in helping to complete the unfinished task within the younger Churches.

Canon Max Warren has recently written that " the word ' missionary ' needs to be understood but it must not be discarded ".[1] I would like to agree with him, but I must admit to grave doubts as to whether he is right.

Very few people in Europe or America have as yet any sense of the depth and violence of the reaction of the coloured peoples of the world against the West. For more than four centuries the initiative has been in the hands of the West, and this has resulted in deep Western penetration of all the countries of the earth, sometimes violent, sometimes insidious, but always disruptive of the old patterns of life and thought. Westerners have little idea of the depth of the wounds cut in the minds of sensitive peoples by the feeling of political, cultural and economic dependence or inferiority. Now we are at the stage of a massive reaction, a reaction not always lovely in its manifestations, but deeply charged with feeling, and one of the major factors in the world situation to-day. Political independence is only the beginning of independent action ; many of the newly liberated countries would be heartily thankful to be independent of both the Russian and the American ways of life, economically, intellectually and in every other way as well. They are prepared to accept economic help from friends and allies, but only on the clearly understood principle that such aid must be " without strings " ; and all such aid is most carefully watched to ensure that it does not become the spearhead for a new form of economic imperialism. Under all the outward appearances of friendliness, there is all the time the deep, hidden, perhaps half-conscious, almost always unspoken, dislike of Western man, and suspicion of his purposes, of his integrity and of all his ways.

It is impossible that the Churches, living in such an atmosphere, should be unaffected by it. These Churches also are enjoying the sense of liberation. (Chinese Christians have stated that only after the expulsion of all foreign missionaries was it " possible for us to be ourselves " ; and that this " being ourselves " has meant for them a real liberation into new realms of spiritual experience and Christian responsibility.) Such Churches are fanatically attached to their independence and are not in any mood to tolerate any infringement of it. " We live in a day when the foreigner bringing gifts, whatever the gifts may be, is suspected, feared and often

[1] Max Warren : *The Christian Imperative* (S.C.M. Press, 1955), p. 121.

resented. There will be no understanding of the missionary task of our generation, unless this sombre fact is fully appreciated in all its significance." [1] Many of the Africans who have come under the influence of the Revival in East Africa have stated that the first sin they had to face and from which they needed to be cleansed was hatred of the white man ; the converse being true of most of the missionaries affected by the same influence.

It is in this context that we have to try to understand the associations of the word " mission " and " missionary " in younger Church minds to-day.

It is self-evident to Christians in the West that the Churches of " Christian lands " have a mission to the world, a mission to evangelize their less fortunate brethren. The call presents itself in terms of compassion (which is very far from being the same as sentimentality), of obligation, and of service. It is hardly too much to say that, from the younger Church end, mission is understood almost exclusively in terms of aggression. " What are you doing in our country ? Who gave you the right to be here ? Did we invite you ? " If the older Church in this imaginary dialogue responds, " But your country needs the Gospel, doesn't it ? " the reply would be, " But what evidence have we that you are the right and proper people to bring it to us ? " So far is the nature of mission from being self-evident in Africa and Asia that the Western Church finds itself challenged to state adequate reasons in support of its arrogant supposition that it is called to and qualified for " mission ". This curious divergence of psychological approach underlies all the discussions of the Willingen Missionary Conference of 1952, and perhaps accounts for their inconclusive character.

Something of the same kind has happened to the term " missionary ". The ordinary churchman at home thinks of the missionary as a man or woman who has made considerable sacrifices for the sake of an ideal. The hardships of missionary life have been rather too much romanticized, and are very different from what the stay-at-homes imagine them to be, but they are real enough ; there is a steady and exacting price to be paid for the privilege of being a missionary, and the fact that it is in most cases joyfully paid does not alter the fact that it is a price. To the younger churchman, on the contrary, the missionary may appear as the incarnation

[1] Max Warren : *C.M.S. Newsletter*, April 1956.

of Western superiority and arrogance, whose very presence is a
threat to the independence and spontaneity of the growing Church,
and who is likely to use economic power as a means for getting
his own way, when his way is in conflict with that of the local
leaders.

In several of the countries over which the tide of Japanese invasion
swept, all the missionaries were deported or interned. Japanese
domination was not altogether agreeable ; but, in the absence of
the missionaries, the Church tasted an independence which was
sweet, not to say intoxicating. After the war some of these Churches
for a time refused to have any missionaries at all ; even those which
are now willing to receive them are determined that missionaries
must never be allowed to return on the old terms, and that the
strictest precautions must be taken against their ever recovering a
position from which they might come to dominate the Church.
Two young theologians are now serving in the Theological Faculty
of the Nommensen University of the Batak Church in Sumatra.
The Church has made it quite clear that it wishes this service to be
regarded as falling within the cadre of " Inter-Church Aid ", and
that helpers from the West will be welcomed as " fraternal workers "
or as " the international team ", but not as " missionaries ".

What's in a name ? Is a missionary any less a missionary for
being called a " fraternal worker ? " To argue this way would
betoken triviality of mind. Names are important because of all the
associations that are inseparable from them. The Church of Sweden
has retained the name " High Mass " for the celebration of its
liturgy, as it has every right to do ; but many readers of this book
would receive a considerable shock if High Mass was announced
for next Sunday on the notice-board outside the church which they
attend ! It is a matter of grave perplexity to the younger Churches
that the full spiritual equality which has joyfully been accorded to
them by all their brethren in the West is still prejudiced by evident
inequality in other respects. It takes great grace on their part to
recognize that they have responsibilities that they cannot yet meet
from their own resources ; and, if a change of terminology (with
which a change of psychology is inevitably associated) makes it easier
for them to accept the help of which they clearly stand in need, the
change should gladly be made by all those who desire to help them.
Even the term " younger Churches " seems destined to go the way

f " native " and other good words which are no longer acceptable.
have used it in this book, in a historical and not in any pejorative
ense, because I cannot think of any other term ; but I am well
ware that many in the " younger Churches " would prefer that it
hould no longer be used. And now the Presbyterian Church in
ie United States has gone ahead of other Churches in deciding
iat its missionaries in " the foreign field " shall in future be known
s " fraternal workers ".

" Inter-Church Aid " is a term devised by the World Council
f Churches to cover a multiplicity of services which richer and
:ronger Churches are able to render to those which are in need.
t was adopted deliberately in order to make clear that within the
hurches there can be no one-way traffic. Those who are privileged
) render material service recognize that they have been enriched by
piritual blessings brought to them through those whom they have
erved. Younger Church leaders serve in a great many capacities
a the ecumenical movement ; their insights and ministrations are
elcomed with increasing appreciation in the West. We may find
iat the term " Inter-Church Aid " is not of universal validity, since
iere are so many areas in the world in which the Church does not
xist at all ; but it has proved its value by stressing precisely those
ictors of equality and mutual service that are all-important to those
hose sensitiveness on the subject of their acceptance as equals is
) deep and justifiable.

" Fraternal workers " is a term delightful in its vagueness ; it
an be used to cover almost anything. It has come to be used of
oung people who are lent by their own Church for a short period
) a Church in another country to do some special job in fellowship
ith that Church. It can cover also responsibilities undertaken for
longer period and by older people. What is important is that the
fraternal worker " is usually asked for by the receiving Church,
nd his continuance in office depends on the judgment of that
'hurch as to the usefulness of his work. The younger Churches
re insistent that this should be the status of the missionary, by
'hatever name he is called. The danger which lurks in the term
fraternal worker " is that it is wholly indefinite with regard to the
elationship between the worker and the Church. Is he to be
egarded as becoming a member of the Church which he serves ?
)r is he so transitory a phenomenon that the question of Church

relationship is of less than primary importance ? And is the ter:
suitable in the case of those who are prepared to give a lifetime
service to a Church other than their own ? These are questio:
which it must be left to the future to decide.

Let us return to the vocation of the " missionary ", using tl
term without prejudice, within the younger Churches at the prese:
time.[1] It is clear that many younger Churches are more ready th:
they were ten years ago to welcome the presence in their midst
colleagues from the West. What do they want them for ?

The emphasis over the last forty years has been on technic:
qualifications. This can be defended ; the younger Churches a
most likely to ask for help in areas in which they are not yet then
selves producing leaders with sufficiently high technical qualific:
tions. In some countries, such as India, a new missionary is mu
more likely to obtain the visa necessary for entrance into the countr
if the Church which calls him can point in justification to some speci
qualification or skill which he can offer in the service of the Churcl
and for which no national is immediately available. And inde
the missionary enterprise is now so complex that it is hard to thi:
of any technical skill for which a place cannot be found. To gi
one single instance ; countless leaders, indigenous and missionar
are daily being driven crazy by having to handle financial problen
which are beyond their competence and financial details which a
beyond their strength. Keeping accounts may not sound like mi:
sionary work in the ordinary sense of the word. But to a bisho
accustomed to keeping his accounts in the manner described b
Archbishop Temple as his own—adding them up upwards and the
adding them up downwards, and splitting the difference—an ab
diocesan accountant is about the best gift that heaven can supply
Apparently the twelve apostles would have agreed. But such tecl
nical qualifications alone are not sufficient justification for tl
presence of the missionary in a younger Church to-day. His prop
usefulness lies elsewhere.

In the first place, he is called to be a saint. So are all Christian
but there are also special vocations. In the area I know bes
hundreds of missionaries have worked. Only two have passed int

[1] For convenience I continue to use the terms " mission " and " missionary "
since there is no general agreement on the use of alternative terms, or even c
the question of whether the adoption of alternative terms is desirable.

ιe traditional memory of the Church. Each had rendered splendid ervice in many ways ; but each is remembered because he was a aint. Of late years missionaries have been so burdened with ad-ιinistration and the exercise of authority that they have appeared ιther as tired and disheartened men and women than as triumphant arriors of the Cross. The modern missionary, just because he has ot to bear the care of all the Churches, is spiritually in a stronger tuation. Unless he stands out, amidst the low level of devotion hich is all too common in the Church that he serves, by a con-ρicuous and recognizable likeness to Christ, perhaps he would have one better to stay at home. This is a formidable demand ; but hy should we not speak the truth ?

Secondly, he must be, to use the old phrase, a soul-winner. Vith impressive unanimity the younger Churches are beginning to oice this opinion. A missionary is an expensive creature. Whatever is technical abilities, he is not worth his pay, unless the very heart nd centre of all his work is to bring men and women to the point f personal surrender to Jesus Christ.

Thirdly, whether ordained or lay, man or woman, he must be a astor. He must have time for the individual. He must take time ɔ know the idiosyncrasies of his people, their customs, their ways f looking at things, their temptations. He must learn to bring an ducated Christian judgment to bear on all the problems of a kaleido-copically changing situation. Just because he stands a little back rom the immediate whirl of circumstances, his judgment may well e more independent and more trenchant than that of his local olleagues. If, as is quite likely, he finds himself in the position of ιastor to those who themselves will be pastors of pastors, his situa-ion, though it may be restricted from the point of view of numbers, s beyond measure strategic.

Fourthly, he must qualify himself to be, when needed and lesired, the friend and confidant of younger Church leaders. Most ιf such leaders live a very lonely life. Privacy is less known than n the West. Most careful discretion has at all times to be observed. f such a leader has no friend to whom he can unburden himself vithout reserve, his life is hard indeed. And sometimes it is the oreigner who, just because of his greater distance from the im-ιediacies of the problem, can be " your considerate stone ". Some ears before his death the great Bishop Azariah wrote to me, " You

are the only person now living who addresses me as Azariah ".
The greatest day in the life of D. E. Hoste, later Director-General
of the China Inland Mission, came when, after ten years of highly
non-monotonous colleagueship, the famous Confucian scholar
convert, Pastor Hsi, turned to him and said, " Dear Brother Hoste
what should I do without you ? "

If the missionary is to achieve any of these things, clearly he
must identify himself, as far as the Church itself permits it, with
the Church that he has come to serve. The younger Churches are
prepared to recognize the value of short-term ministries ; but in
creasingly their wisest leaders are coming to feel the need of those
who will stay until they really belong. It goes without saying that
a missionary who goes to work with an organized and developed
younger Church must accept joyfully and wholeheartedly the
authority of that Church and the leadership of its responsible heads.
He must readily accept whatever position in the Church they feel
it right to assign to him. This was common doctrine more than
thirty years ago, when I was a student ; the practical application
of the principle may lead to difficulties, but I have never heard of
any missionary candidate who questioned the validity of the principle

Nationalism has brought back the national language to honour,
and the fraternal worker will be expected to acquire a knowledge
of the local tongue. Gone are the days when I fought a lonely battle
on this subject, and when younger churchmen sedulously discouraged
the newly arrived missionary from learning a language which he
would always speak badly, and would hardly ever have occasion to
use. Mission boards and local mission authorities seem hardly to
have caught up with this change. Their attitude is still perhaps a
little too much indicated in the reply of a young missionary, who to
the question how he was getting on with the language, answered,
" The authorities are putting no *unnecessary* hindrance in the way
of my learning the language ". They will catch up. And this
change is immensely for the better. There is no shorter road to
the understanding of the psychology of a people than the mastery
of its language.

---

[1] It must be remembered that Azariah was the bishop's baptismal name, and
not a surname ; and in India even a wife does not address her husband by name.
More usually, to the amusement of our Free Church colleagues, we addressed one
another by the names of our dioceses

As to other methods of self-identification with the life of the
Church, much must be left to individual discretion and vocation.
Some missionaries have carried this to the point of seeking natural-
isation as citizens of the country in which they work. Others have
gone far in the effort to strip themselves of their essential foreignness. The question arises whether such an attitude does not really
belong to a period that is now passing away. Dr. Eddy Asirvatham
has recently written :

> India expects every genuine missionary to be a world citizen.
> To a large extent he must be raceless and nationless even as Jesus
> was. This condition is requisite if the missionary is to identify
> himself with the lowly, the humble and the despised of the earth.[1]

Is not Dr. Asirvatham here speaking in terms both of the liberal
theology and of the missionary situation of thirty years ago ? The
very last epithet that could be applied to Jesus in the days of His
incarnation are " raceless " and " nationless ". He was a Jew to
His finger-tips, in His outlook, in His obedience to the Law, in
His use of the Old Testament Scriptures. He refused to be a
" world citizen ", and to lose the point and urgency of His ministry
in the diffuseness of an appeal to the Gentile world. This Jewish
loyalty of His is part of that scandal of particularity, which could
be resolved only by the Resurrection. But we are not yet risen.
We are very much creatures of flesh and blood ; may it not be that
our very foreignness is one of the good gifts that we have to give to
the younger Churches ? It seems to me that Canon Warren is
much nearer to the reality when he writes :

> The foreigner who can speak out of the experience of his own
> people's life and history and show how the influence of Christ has
> modified laws, moulded custom, inspired culture, is a living witness
> to the fact that what has happened in one place can happen else-
> where. . . . No Church can afford to be without the inspiration of a
> foreigner's obedience to the missionary imperative, just as no Church
> can itself be fully obedient to that imperative, without being com-
> mitted to a foreign mission.[2]

The stage at which the foreigner is either terrifying or offensive

---

[1] Eddy Asirvatham : *Christianity in the Indian Crucible* (Calcutta Y.M.C.A.).
Quoted in *International Review of Missions*, April 1956, p. 219.
[2] Max Warren : *The Christian Imperative*, pp. 125–6.

belongs to the infancy or to the adolescence of the missionary enterprise. Where adult age and experience have been attained, foreignness is interesting and illuminating. It may be doubted whether
Dr. Billy Graham would have had quite the same success in Britain,
if he had not been an American. Any British preacher who has had
the privilege of ministering in the United States knows that, in
spite of anti-British prejudice in certain quarters in the States, he
starts with something on the credit side. But this stage has not been
perfectly reached in countries where memories of " imperialism "
are still somewhat recent ; not all younger Church leaders are wise,
not all younger churchmen are free from prejudice against the West.
The fraternal worker, even if his services have been asked for by
the Church which he goes to serve, cannot count on finding himself
at once in a friendly atmosphere.

The missionary of our day, whatever the purity of his intentions
and the humility of his approach to Christians and non-Christians
of another race, must prepare himself for the probability, almost the
certainty, that he will be called upon to suffer. Let Max Warren
once again be our spokesman :

> One thing only seems to be certain, a thing that no missionary
> should regret, and that is the fact that the role of the suffering
> servant will be his in a degree and after a fashion to which most
> of his predecessors were strangers. . . . The missionary follows,
> to-day, very closely in the footsteps of the Son of Man, " who came
> not to be administered unto but to minister ", and for all that He
> brought, was yet despised and rejected of men.[1]

There are some areas in which the Church is still at an early
stage of development, and causes of conflict, if they exist, are still
latent and have not come out into the open. There are a few areas,
still very few, in which the local Church and its leadership have
reached such a level of adult poise that the foreigner is welcomed
in the most natural way in the world, without adulation and without
suspicion. In far more cases the new arrival will find himself in an
atmosphere of adolescent uncertainty, in which the predominant
feeling is that the younger Church would do without him, if it could,
and is prepared to take it out of him for the primal sin of the necessity
of his own existence.

Only in very rare cases will he find a younger Church leader

[1] C.M.S. Newsletter, April 1956.

who will make it his responsibility to see that the newcomer is made to feel at home, is guided into the intricacies of an unfamiliar Church situation, and is fitted into the place from which he will best be able to render service to the Church. He will find that his actions are liable to the wildest misinterpretation, and may be attributed to motives that could never conceivably have entered his head. If, for the sake of efficiency in an unfavourable climate, it is necessary that he should draw a rather higher salary than some of his in-digenous colleagues, this may be the source of endless and bitter rivalries. If he shows signs of initiative, this may be at once attri-buted to hidden stirrings of imperialism, and a desire to restore the now outworn domination of the missionary. It may well be that for a long period he will find himself assigned to work in which there is far less scope for the exercise of his gifts than in the position which he occupied before leaving his homeland. He may find that little use is made of the expert knowledge through which his most constructive contributions could be made. And one shall say unto him, What are these wounds between thine arms ? Then he shall answer, Those with which I was wounded in the house of my friends.

Missionary candidates should be plainly warned of these things. If they are alarmed by them, they had better stay at home. Missionary service can be entered into only in terms of an unconditional and unquestioning loyalty. It can only be carried through in the steady determination to accept all that comes, without perturbation and without fear, to rejoice in hardness, and to believe that all things, without any exception whatsoever, can be turned to the glory of God.

CHAPTER 7

DYNAMIC WITNESS

OUR last chapter was concerned with the growth and development of the Christian life within a younger Church. We must now turn to the wider question of the younger Church as the instrument in God's hand for Christian witness beyond its own borders.

For a whole generation the non-Roman Christian world was challenged by the phrase, " the Evangelization of the World in this Generation ". It was under the inspiration of this challenge that the first great World Missionary Conference was convened at Edinburgh in 1910.

Many people would smile at that phrase to-day, as though it were merely the outcome of boyish zest and confidence in American " know-how ". After sixty generations of Christians have laboured in the spread of the Gospel across the world, shall we in our day accomplish their work, and achieve the conversion of the world in a single generation ? Now John R. Mott and his friends who popularized this phrase were very far indeed from being irresponsible hot-heads ; they knew exactly what they meant by the now much criticized phrase, and, as a brief study of the literature of seventy years ago will make plain, were prepared to give a reasoned defence of it.[1]

In the first place, they never confused evangelization and conversion. They were fully aware of the difficulty of converting a single Muslim or a single Jew. Their plans were not inspired by any foolhardy optimism. They simply saw that it was the duty of the whole Church to make the whole Gospel available to the whole world, now and not in some indefinitely incalculable future.

Secondly, they took seriously the progress that had been made, and the opportunities for future progress that seemed to be presented by a changed world situation. In a century of missionary work the ground had been broken and the tools had been prepared.

---

[1] The primary sources are the six volumes of the addresses and papers of John R. Mott, New York, 1950.

Most of the great languages of the world had been learned by Christians, and, where necessary, reduced to writing. Bible translations had been made in hundreds of languages. Geographical discovery had uncovered most of the secrets of the unknown world. The mysteries of the Nile and of the Congo were no longer mysteries. If the North and South Poles had not yet been discovered, that was of no great interest to missionary strategists who were less interested in penguins than Anatole France's mythical priest! Travel was becoming safe and rapid. A beginning had been made with the conquest of tropical diseases. And the extension of Western influence had produced widespread peace and calm in areas where tribal war had previously been endemic. Even disturbances such as the great persecution in Uganda in 1886 had resulted not in the destruction of the Church, but in its enormous and rapid increase.[1]

Thirdly, they took serious note of the way in which missionary interest was taking hold of hitherto untouched sections of the Church and in particular of the universities. Even at a much earlier date Oxford and Cambridge had made a great contribution to the missionary cause. But very few of the early missionaries had had a university education. This was (and to some extent still is) especially true in countries such as Germany and Holland, where many missionary candidates came from humble homes, and received in a missionary institution a training which by comparison with British standards was extraordinarily thorough, but still left them in a position of inferiority in relation to the Church and its university-trained ministry. But now at last the Student Christian Movements had touched the universities. Men and women of the highest ability were coming forward in astonishing numbers, ready to go anywhere and to do anything for the sake of Christ.

Fourthly, Mott and his friends caught the note of urgency. Each generation of Christians must accept responsibility for those non-Christians who are their contemporaries. We may be sure that the cause of Christ will triumph in the end. But my concern is with that man in Korea or Borneo who is living to-day. What God will in the end do with him if he dies without ever having heard of Christ, I do not know, and it is no concern of mine. What I do know is that Christ died for him; and, if Christ matters at all to

---

[1] We are still writing of the end of the nineteenth century; the far greater disasters of the twentieth were at that time still in the future.

me, I cannot evade the obligation to do the very utmost in my power
to see that the message is brought home to him. Whether he will
accept it or not cannot be foreseen ; on him rests the responsibility
of choice. But clearly he can neither accept nor reject a message
which he has never heard.

Let Mott be heard in his own defence. This is how, at a time
when the slogan " the Evangelization of the World in this Generation " had already attracted a good deal of adverse comment, he
defined its scope and defended it against criticism :

> (The Watchcry) does not mean the conversion of the world, for
> the acceptance of Christ rests with the hearer and not with the
> speaker. It does not mean the Christianization or the civilization
> of the world—important as both of these are. Nor must it be con-
> strued to mean an imperfect preaching of the Gospel. . . . Our Move-
> ment stands pre-eminently for the emphasis of the belief that by a
> great enlargement of the agencies employed by the missionary
> societies to-day, the Gospel can and should be brought within the
> reach of every creature within this generation. . . . It is of constant
> application to successive generations as long as the world remains
> unevangelized. Each generation of Christians must obviously evan-
> gelize its own generation of the unevangelized inhabitants of the
> world, if they are to be evangelized at all.[1]

Mott protested ceaselessly against the idea that what he and his
colleagues were recommending was a hurried passing from place to
place and tribe to tribe, sowing hastily the seed of a Gospel that it
was most unlikely that the hearers would be able to understand :

> I say " thoroughness " because our Commission does not stand
> for superficiality. We believe that there could be no greater danger
> than the spread of an imperfect type of Christianity due to ill-
> considered plans and to a hasty or superficial work of proclaiming,
> making plain and enforcing the truth. We therefore lay emphasis
> on thoroughness as well as promptness.[2]

And to the charge that this new concept of missionary work
relied solely on the multiplication of human forces, Mott could
reply eloquently :

> Above all there are the superhuman resources ; the dynamic power
> of the Gospel of Christ ; the unrealized possibilities of intercession ;

---

[1] John R. Mott in *The Student Volunteer*, Jan. 1895 ; reprinted in *Addresses
and Papers*, Vol. I, p. 305.
[2] *Ibid.* : *Addresses and Papers*, Vol. V, p. 41.

the triumphant power of holy lives and lives unreservedly yielded to the sway of the risen Christ ; and the presence of Christ Himself in His Church by His Spirit, the One who is able to subdue all things unto Himself. Thus, as the followers of Christ look outward on the great areas of the world, and then turn to survey the resources of Christendom, and to gaze by faith upon their superhuman resources, can they question the possibility to-day of making Christ known to all people ? [1]

Under the inspiration of Mott and of those who had learned from him the Edinburgh Conference of 1910 passed a resolution in favour of plans being made for the immediate occupation of " the unoccupied fields ". But the results were not proportionate to the hopes and expectations of those who had launched the idea. Edinburgh 1910 was indeed the beginning of an epoch—the epoch of reflection and of ecumenical co-operation ; at the same time it was the end of an epoch—the epoch of the glad and confident expansion of the Christian missionary enterprise under the inspiration of a rediscovery of the Gospel.

Already sharp criticism of " expansionism " had been heard at the time of the Conference. The man who was recognized as the deepest missionary thinker of the times, Professor Gustav Warneck of Halle, had written to Dr. Mott :

> Nothing is achieved by mere doctrinaire watchwords, indeed they do much harm ; we must have congregations that are spiritually and morally matured, and, moreover, native pastors who are spiritually and morally matured ; then only do we have sound foundations for self-administration. In the distribution of the missionary forces, the paramount question is not, where is there still an unoccupied field, but where at the present moment is the strengthening of the missionary force most urgently required ? It is upon this principle that every strategist disposes his forces. Where the greatest battle is to be fought, there the greatest force must be concentrated. . . . We have no superfluity of workers. If we scatter them because of a predilection for the watchword " occupation of the whole world in this generation," and push on into countries which are at present either difficult of access or not yet ripe for missions, we can easily miss the most hopeful opportunities, or we may lose hundreds of thousands to Mohammedanism, whilst perhaps winning some few Christians in a country like Tibet. [2]

---

[1] *World Missionary Conference* 1910, Vol. I, p. 11.
[2] *Ibid*, pp. 434-5.

These are weighty words. The case against St. Paul's reckless idea of advance into Macedonia could not have been better put by the most conservative among the elders of Troas. On the whole, the Germans then and ever since have been on the side of Warneck against Mott ; they have not fully accepted the distinction between evangelization and conversion, which is perhaps clearer in English than in German.

But there were graver reasons than the criticisms of a few scholars to account for the failure of the Edinburgh Conference to let loose a new world Christian movement. Those who met at Edinburgh could not have foreseen that only four years later the nations of Europe would engage in the first of those suicidal civil wars, which have made a mockery of the idea of Christendom, and have reduced to zero the credit of the so-called Christian nations of the world. The war of 1914 itself was perhaps only a symptom of something deeper.

The West was beginning to lose confidence in itself and in its civilization. More sympathetic study had revealed the greatness of the ancient civilizations and the arts of India and China. The comparative study of religion, with its discoveries of the noble and uplifting elements in the great religions and of vestiges of the divine even in the most primitive savagery, had rendered antiquated the earlier and comprehensive condemnation of all non-Christian religion as mere idolatry. At the same time, the counter-attack of the non-Christian religions was taking on a new and subtler form. Now the attack was directed not against the preaching of the Gospel, but against what was called proselytism—the use of unfair and material means to win over the poor and distressed, the exercise of excessive pressure on the young, the heartless break-up of families resulting from the conversion of one or two of their members. Earlier missionaries had not perhaps been quite so heartless and unscrupulous as they were represented ; but there had been enough in their methods that was questionable to make their successors highly sensitive on the subject of proselytism.

So the question of what the missionary went abroad to do was raised afresh, and in rather disturbing forms. This was the period of the American Laymen's Commission of Enquiry, with its liberal attitude to all questions of religion. It seemed to many that no more could be done than to commend Christianity as *one* of the great religions of mankind. Missionary candidates could be told that their object was to help the adherents of other religions to rediscover the great truths in their own religious traditions ; or, even more bluntly, to help Hindus to be better Hindus and Muslims to be better Muslims. The emphasis came to rest almost wholly on service and education, and not on the preaching of the Gospel with a view to definite conversion. The effects of all these things were visible in the statistics of missionary recruiting, and the expression of them was the Jerusalem Missionary Conference of 1928.

One of the mythologies on which we have been brought up is that each great World Christian Conference marks an advance on the one that has gone before. This is not necessarily so. A case could be made out for regarding the Jerusalem meeting in 1928 as the nadir of the modern missionary movement. This was the moment at which liberal theology exercised its most fatal influence on missionary thinking, the lowest valley out of which the missionary movement has ever since been trying to make its way. Even Dr. Wilhelm Andersen, who is rather inclined to hold the " upward ladder " view of conferences, is fairly clear as to the dangers that threatened the whole missionary movement in 1928 :

> No longer, as at Edinburgh, was the right of the Christian Churches to carry on missionary operations in the non-Christian world taken as something in itself self-evident. " The question whether we have in all circumstances the right to meet the non-Christian religious systems with the claim that we, and we alone, possess the truth, is one that must be settled not *a priori* but in the light of a penetrating study of the actual facts of the situation." Behind this formulation one can trace the influences of the " comparative religion " school of thought. Is Christian faith, perhaps, only one particular form of the mystical experience of the divine which is the common groundwork of all religions ? Should not Jesus, Buddha, Confucius, Mohammed and the rest be considered simply as different branches on the single tree of the religious experience of mankind ? Are the differences between the various religions perhaps only relative differences between a more perfect or a less perfect stage of evolution ? [1]

No great Christian conference, carried out in the spirit of prayer and expectation, can be entirely barren of results. Jerusalem 1928

[1] Wilhelm Andersen : *Towards a Theology of Mission* (S.C.M. Press, 1955), p. 22.

made its contribution in a fuller understanding and expression of the significance of the younger Churches, and in a clearer recognition that the Gospel is a Gospel for the whole man, in his social and economic setting as well as in his spiritual relationships. And the genius of William Temple for making men of one mind in a house helped the Conference to accept unanimously the Conference Message which he himself had drafted : " Our message is Jesus Christ ; we dare not give less, and we cannot give more ".[1] But evangelism was no longer in the centre of the picture, and no more was heard of " the Evangelization of the World in this Generation ".

But, if the great Churches and missions which met at Edinburgh and Jerusalem had become hesitant in their vision and uncertain in their vocation, there were others who felt no such hesitation or uncertainty.

The expansion of Roman Catholic missions during this century is a great epic. That Church has had its sleepy periods, and many of its congregations are doubtless as apathetic in missionary matters, if such a thing is possible, as their Protestant opposite numbers. But its principles have never varied ; the authority given to Peter, and through Peter to the Bishop of Rome, is a universal authority, exercised on all the faithful, and to be extended to all the unfaithful as they are brought within the fellowship of the Church. Tropical Africa is at the moment the spear-point of Roman Catholic advance. There seems no doubt of the intention of that Church to make the whole of tropical Africa a Roman Catholic continent, with its centre in the Belgian Congo, within the lifetime of some now living. In many areas Roman Catholic missionaries outnumber Protestant by ten to one. Not all are of the highest calibre, and to some extent the balance is restored by the far greater number of ordained Africans in the non-Roman Churches. Still, the progress is massive and unrelenting, and, of course, carried on without the least regard to the claims or feelings of the non-Roman Churches.

At the other extreme of the Christian spectrum are " the sects ", the bodies of extreme evangelical opinion and extremely democratic organization. These, too, show no signs of hesitancy or uncertainty ;

[1] Temple's feat in writing this Message, single-handed and unaided, lying on his somewhat extensive stomach on the floor of an ill-lighted and draughty room, is the greatest example of ecumenical virtuosity yet on record.

hey know that it is the Lord's will that the Gospel should be
preached throughout the world to-day, and they set themselves quite
simply and obediently to see that it is done. I am not speaking here
of the reckless and ill-planned ventures of the mere enthusiasts.
Missionary history is strewn with enterprises which in their heroism
and their folly resemble the attempt to climb Everest single-handed
by one man whose frozen body was found half-way up the mountain
by a later expedition. Nor am I thinking of such bodies as the
Seventh Day Adventists, admirable alike in their generosity and their
missionary zeal, whose habit it is, unfortunately, to settle where
others are at work, and all too often to create dissension and division
in the Christian congregation gathered by the labours of other
men. I have in mind such bodies as the Worldwide Evangelization
Crusade, which study the map to see where no one else has gone
and then set out to go there. In the last thirty years such bodies
have sent out into remote parts of the world—Central Asia, Spanish
Guinea, upland Siam and so forth—thousands of zealous missionaries, of simple faith and limited theological education, but willing
to bear any sacrifice and hardship for the sake of Christ. Most of
the pioneer missionary work in the world to-day is being done either
by Roman Catholics or by members of these groups.

This rapid survey impels us to recognize the immense importance
of the Whitby Missionary Conference of 1947. Whitby reached out
again beyond Tambaram and Jerusalem to the great Edinburgh
vision of 1910, but went beyond even Jerusalem in its recognition
of the younger Churches as the primary factor and the principal
agent in the evangelization of the world. This was the first international meeting of Christian leaders on a large scale after the tragedy
of the second world war. It was clear at once that the lessons of
the earlier missionary conferences had been well learned. The full
spiritual equality of the younger Churches, which had been the new
factor at the Tambaram Conference of 1938, was now no longer
a discovery ; it was simply taken for granted as one of the postulates
of thought. And, on the basis of that accepted principle, the representatives of the older Churches turned to their colleagues of the
younger Churches, and said bluntly, " Your full independence
and equality have been recognized, and are now no longer a
subject of controversy. The initiative rests with you. Tell us what
your plans are for the total evangelization of the countries you

represent, and what help you still need from us for carrying ou
the work ".

It was at once evident that the younger Church leaders had no
been thinking at all in such terms as these, and most of them wer
not ready with their answers. Not all were prepared to go as fa
as the Korean delegate who remarked, " There are 40,000 unevangel
ized villages in Korea. If you like to send us 40,000 missionaries
we shall be prepared to receive them all." But the idea began t
germinate, and the recovered emphasis on the total task of th
Church, on the total evangelization of the world, comes out on
almost every page of the Whitby report.

It appears in the general statement of the Conference, " Christia
Witness in a Revolutionary World " :

> The Gospel is to be preached to all men. Can it be so preache
> in our generation ? To preach to men is not the same as to conver
> them. God alone can command success, and it is always open t
> men to resist His will. Yet, when we consider the present extensio
> of the Church, and the divine and human resources available, w
> dare to believe it possible that, before the present generation ha
> passed away, the Gospel should be preached to almost all the in
> habitants of the world in such a way as to make clear to them th
> issue of faith or disbelief in Jesus Christ. If this is possible, it i
> the task of the Church to see that it is done.[1]

It comes out again in the famous statement on " Partnership in
Obedience " :

> On older and younger Churches alike, the demand of the hour i
> the establishment, at the earliest possible date, of pioneer work i
> all those parts of the world in which the Gospel has not been preache
> and where the Church has not yet taken root.[2]

Yet once again in the same statement :

> The younger Churches are preparing themselves to face the im
> mense task of evangelizing the great non-Christian population
> around them. . . . If this appeal is to be presented convincingly t

---

[1] *Renewal and Advance*, p. 215.

[2] *Renewal and Advance*, p. 175. It is to be noted that Whitby spoke, not o
Partnership, but of Partnership-in-Obedience ; it was not in the least intereste
in human arrangements for closer fellowship, which might be dissoluble at wil
but only in a common submission to the will of God such as can result only i
a divine and permanent fellowship among men.

the older Churches, it must come neither as a spiritual vision divorced
from earthly realities nor as a sentimental appeal without an intellectual foundation. . . . It must be set forth on the basis of carefully
considered programmes of advance and on radical re-thinking of
priorities.[1]

And yet once again in the general statement :

> From the older Churches the younger Churches are asking for
> literally thousands of men and women as missionary helpers : to go
> into immense areas where the name of Christ has never been heard
> and where there is no hindrance to the preaching of the Gospel but
> the lack of a messenger ; to take immediate advantage of opportuni-
> ties in lands where it seems likely that the Gospel will not have free
> entry for more than another ten or fifteen years.[2]

It is one of the tragedies of the modern missionary movement
that the message of the Whitby Conference has not yet been heard
or heeded by the Churches. For this there are a number of reasons.
In 1947 the Churches were already engaged in the preparations for
the first Assembly of the World Council of Churches at Amsterdam
in 1948. It is not surprising that the flute-like voice of Whitby was
lost amid the diapason pronouncements that Amsterdam launched
upon the world. A little later, the attention of the missionary world
was deflected to the Willingen Conference of 1952, which was to
deal with important but not immediately urgent issues, and the
inconclusive declarations of which did not present any stirring
challenge to the Churches.

Those who assembled at Whitby have been criticized for moving
in an atmosphere of unjustified euphoria, for imagining that the worst
days of the missionary enterprise were already past, when as history
has shown us they were in reality just about to begin. There is no
foundation whatever for this criticism. Delegates at Whitby were
fully aware of the menacing situation in which they met. For
instance, the Koreans knew already (though apparently the American
State Department did not) what was going to happen in their country
two years later. The Indians took into account the hindrances to
Christian work that might result from the declaration of India's
independence that was to take place less than two months after the
meeting of the Conference. But all these things were reckoned

[1] *Renewal and Advance*, pp. 181-2.   [2] *Ibid.*, p. 216.

with as spurs to a sense of urgency, and not in the spirit of defeatism :

> But above all earthly circumstances stands unchanged the command of Christ to preach the Gospel to every creature. . . . The situation is one of extreme urgency. The time is one of unexampled but almost certainly fleeting opportunity. Each year's delay may mean the closing of doors which may not be opened again till this generation has passed away.[1]

The immediate collapse of Chiang Kai Shek and the victory of Communism in China could not at that time have been foreseen ; but the Conference showed extraordinary prescience in its definition of the major threats to Christian advance,

> in certain countries under the influence or control of militant Communism, resurgent Islam or political Roman Catholicism. Recent policies in Egypt tend to limit the spiritual liberty of the Christian minority. The political activity of Roman Catholicism in Spain, in Italy, in Latin America and in other countries seeks to deny to Protestants certain freedoms . . . which are vital to the life of a civilized country. . . . Communism, as we have had experience of it in many lands, denies the spiritual principles for which the Church of Jesus Christ stands, and, where it is in power, constitutes a major threat to the existence and progress of the Church.[2]

These are not words of unthinking optimism ! It is never possible to turn back the clock of history. The world to which Whitby spoke was that of 1947, and not that of 1957. Yet Whitby did memorable and lasting service in posing blankly and uncompromisingly the question, " What is the Church for ? " Since Jerusalem 1928, the Church had been increasingly the centre of the missionary programme. We have already heard Dr. Hoekendijk's warning that a Church-centred outlook may lead to a static policy, the very contrary of that expanding vigour which ought to be the mark of the Church's life. We have seen how easily, and how disastrously, the Church can come to be regarded as an end in itself. Had not this inner petrifaction to a large extent set in in the life of the younger Churches in the period before the Whitby Conference ? If this was so, was this result due to the general application of theories which took insufficient account of the nature of the Church, as this is revealed to us in the Bible ?

[1] *Renewal and Advance*, p. 174.　　　　[2] *Ibid.*, p. 210.

About a century ago the idea was launched of " self-governing, self-propagating and self-supporting " Churches in the mission field. The intentions of those who formulated the theory were excellent ; the idea caught on, and has become a guiding principle of much missionary endeavour. Yet from the start there were several considerations that ought perhaps to have given the theorists pause. Self-expression is the aim of the artist. Self-realization is the aim of the pagan religions. But in the New Testament we are bidden to deny ourselves ; and this is a law for Churches as well as for individuals. The intrusion of the idea of " self " into the life of the Church is at the least perilous, and may be much worse than that.

It is in relation to the idea of self-support that we may first become aware of the dangers. What is a self-supporting local Church ? In some areas the answer given to this question was that a self-supporting Church was a local Church which provided the salary of its minister. Such a Church could choose and appoint its own minister ; for " mission Churches " the minister would be appointed by the mission. The result was that some Churches in these areas chose ill-qualified ministers, who were prepared to accept the lowest possible rate of salary, though very much better qualified ministers were available if the Churches had been willing still to accept outside help towards their maintenance. It has constantly been found that the first result of such a misapplication of the idea of self-support has been the sudden ending of all evangelistic effort and expenditure, and the abandonment to an indefinite future of the idea of the evangelization of all peoples.

It will be evident that in such a situation the difficulty has arisen through the close association of two things which do not necessarily belong together—self-support and independence. It is by no means clear that, in order to be independent, a Church must necessarily be self-supporting ; in fact there are famous Protestant Churches in Roman Catholic countries in Europe which are largely dependent on foreign help for the maintenance of their work ; yet no one in his senses would deny their claim to be independent Churches and to have full freedom in the management of their own affairs. No doubt there were plausible reasons for this association. It was hoped that, by dangling before the Churches the hope of independence, it would be possible to encourage them to contribute more liberally

to their own support ; and in part this aim was certainly achieved
But the drawbacks were far greater than the advantages. Ther
are various ways of achieving self-support ; the easiest are thos
which involve limiting the responsibilities of the Church and th
commitments in which it feels itself engaged. " The Church " cam
to be thought of in terms of the existing Church, and not as tha
body into which all the peoples of the world are to be gathere
together.

This was most conspicuously so in areas where the Church wa
small and poor, but had been endowed by its Western friends wit
institutions far larger and more splendid than it could ever hope t
maintain from its own funds. Where the disastrous dichotom
between " mission " and " Church " had already been established
it was all too easy to suppose that pastoral work was the responsibilit
of " the Church ", and institutional work that of " the mission '
So the Church settled down to the care of its own handful of be
lievers, and took little interest in the affairs of institutions for whic
it did not pay, and in the control of which it had no say ; and thos
who worked in institutions largely devoted to the education of non
Christians, or to the medical care of a large non-Christian popula
tion, were not greatly interested in the affairs of a Church, in whic
in a number of cases they were not even members. It was onl
gradually that it came to be realized how harmful this division wa:
and that Churches could take a very considerable share in th
direction of the work of institutions for the maintenance of whic.
they were as yet unable to raise the necessary funds.

The situation was even worse where " pastoral work " wa
assigned as the field of " the Church ", and " evangelistic work '
as the field of " the mission ". Then indeed the dichotomy pene
trated to the very joints and marrow of the Church. For what i
the Church, if it is not evangelistic, and if it can farm out its re
sponsibility for the proclamation of the Gospel to a body which i
only marginally a part of itself ? Where this separation had take:
place, the results in the life of the Church were doubly disastrous
If converts came in, they were the converts of " the mission ", an·
did not readily find a home in " the Church ", which had had n·
responsibility for their conversion. And the Church settled dow:
to a purely introverted existence, devoted to fostering the well
being, spiritual and material, of its adherents, and sometimes witl

rather anxious concern that the number of those eligible to
claim a share of the loaves and fishes should not be unreasonably
increased.

We now realize afresh the point of Dr. Hoekendijk's rather
passionate and one-sided argument. If that is what " the Church "
has come to mean, then, of course, it is impossible for it to engage
in any vigorous apostolate ; it has lost the very essence of its being,
and we may wait till doomsday before such a Church will rise up
to undertake the evangelization of the world. Recent years have
seen a great improvement in the relationships between " mission "
and " Church ". Much work that was previously regarded as the
responsibility of the mission has been handed over to the Church,
and many strains and tensions have been eased. But all such reme-
dies are no more than palliatives, unless the basic problem has been
faced and a right solution found. The point at which things began
to go wrong was a false understanding of the nature of the Church
and its functions, and a false interpretation of the meaning of the
term " self-support ". Our solution will not be valid unless we go
back and ask again the fundamental question as to the nature of
the Church, and as to the sense in which the word " self-supporting ",
if we are to keep it at all, can suitably be used.

To the first question we will reply that, in this connection, the
Church is to be understood as that body of faithful Christians which
accepts responsibility for preaching the Gospel to every creature in
the area which may reasonably be regarded as having been committed by God to its charge.

To the second question, when is a Church genuinely self-supporting, the only possible answer is that it is so when without outside
help it can undertake the total evangelization of the whole of the
area in which it is located, and the building up of the Church within
that area to fulness of life, ministry and witness. This and nothing
else is the task of the Church. It is in relation to this total task that
its resources must be calculated and its strategies determined. When
the nature of the Church is understood in this sense, and its task
interpreted on this scale, a great many problems fall at once into
the background. The separation of Church and mission is no longer
possible, since both are linked together in a common task. Many
things which previously seemed useful and attractive may have to
be abandoned, as having no relevance to the task as seen in its

majestic and challenging grandeur. We may well discover that there is no Church in the world that can claim in this sense to be either self-supporting or independent—we all have need of one another and must stand together in facing a task which is seen to transcend all geographical boundaries, and in each area to present challenges which the Church in that area is unable alone to meet.

It is sad that the international secular agencies seem to have gone so much farther than the Churches in understanding what is involved in the mobilization of all the resources of humanity for the welfare of the whole of humanity. The World Health Organization devotes itself to certain specific objectives in areas of special need. It sends out international teams of specialists. These co-operate with the inhabitants and the experts of the country in which the campaign is to be carried out. The expenses are met from the common fund, to which all the member states contribute according to their ability. Acceptance of help from such an international body is not regarded as a sign of national or racial inferiority; it is the expression of solidarity in the general cause of humanity, of sharing in a common task. Admittedly the task of spreading health and combating disease is far easier than the Christian task of fighting against the devil, the world and the flesh. But he would be a bold man who would maintain that the leaders of the younger Churches everywhere feel towards their missionary colleagues as the doctors of the economically weaker nations feel toward the visitors from W.H.O. We should not be too proud to learn from others not professedly Christian. If the Churches have forgotten how to think in terms of the whole Gospel for the whole world, they might do worse than to consider the example of these secular organizations, which do take the whole world as their parish, and are inspired by a secular concept of " wholeness ".

The strength of these international organizations is that all the nations which belong to them meet on the basis of equality, and all together survey the common needs of a world in distress. Thus the incidence of yaws or malaria in a particular region is considered as part of a general world problem, in the handling of which all are equally concerned. It is this sense of togetherness that excludes the feeling of inferiority on the part of some, and the resentment which the sense of inferiority always kindles. The Christian international organizations have made some progress in the same

irection ; and the gradual development of the sense of responsibility of all for each and of each for all marks the beginning of
new ecumenical outlook on the missionary problem.

How attractive this outlook is to young people to-day is interest-
ngly shown in the report of the Quadrennial Conference of the
Student Volunteer Movement in the U.S.A., the subject of which
was " The Ecumenical Mission of the Church ".

> Mission can no longer be regarded as a one-way process with a
> sending and receiving agency. It must be a common responsibility
> and concern among the Churches throughout the world. Further-
> more, mission can no longer be limited to some parts of the world.
> It is equally important and urgent in the territory of the " older
> Churches " as it is in the countries of the " younger Churches."
> The mission of the Church is universal or, to quote from one of
> the preparatory books for the Conference, it is " the whole Church
> bringing the whole Gospel to the whole world." [1]

This is an excellent statement. There is, however, a danger
that in this concept of wholeness (which is less new than some of
those who proclaim it to-day imagine) the significance and relative
urgency of the different parts may not stand out as clearly as they
should.

When the Student Volunteer Movement came into existence
seventy years ago, there was tremendous emphasis on the needs of
the non-Christian world ; it was taken for granted that missionary
service overseas was the highest form of Christian service, and that
any Christian student who was consecrated, physically fit, and not
otherwise committed, would probably before long find himself on
the way to " the foreign field ". In recent years there has been a
strong and perhaps partly justifiable reaction against this singling
out of one form of Christian service as more meritorious than others.
In some quarters the reaction has gone so far that advocacy of
missionary service hardly rises above a whisper, and is couched in
such terms as to suggest that missionary service overseas is rather
a crime to be condoned than a virtue to be encouraged.

I have heard an industrial chaplain say that in his opinion missionary service overseas was a form of escapism, to be indulged
in by those who were not prepared to face the harder and more

[1] Thomas Wieser in *The Ecumenical Review*, Vol. VIII, No. 3, April 1956,
pp. 327-8.

U.T.—6

immediately relevant tasks that awaited them in the "post-Christian world of our industrial cities.

I have heard a solemn discussion, in a conference on missionary questions, of whether there was any significance in a Christian " crossing a geographical frontier ", this being modern jargon for accepting a missionary call. It may at once be admitted that there is no significance whatever in crossing a geographical frontier. But a missionary, whether he be European or American or African, who is called to pioneer work in an African tribe which has never in any way been touched by the Gospel, has at once to cross as well the linguistic, cultural, psychological and religious frontiers ; and that may be judged to be at least a significant adventure.

I have heard it asserted that we must not attach any significance to the numerical factor, or to the idea that the number of nominal Christians in a country like Britain could prove that it was really more Christian than any other. With this point of view I have great sympathy. Numbers can be extremely misleading. And yet they cannot be altogether disregarded. Medical provision in a country which has one qualified doctor per 10,000 of the population is not as adequate as that in a country which has one doctor for every thousand of the population—a simple truth which no member of the World Health Organization is likely to deny. It just is not the case that the provision for Christian witness in the State of Rewa in Central India, with an area equal to that of Holland and a population of two million, and scarcely any regular and organized witness for Christ, is as adequate as that in Protestant Switzerland with a smaller area and a similar population. It is just the fact that four years ago the Church of Geneva arranged to visit within fifteen days every single family in the Canton that was not known to be Roman Catholic. This effort could be repeated every year, if it was thought to be desirable, and thus the Gospel in some form brought near to " every creature " in the area. The same plan could easily be adopted in Bradford or Plymouth, if the Church approved of this method of evangelism. It cannot be done in Karachi or Baghdad. Unless we are prepared to face such facts as these and to take them seriously, " the whole Church bringing the whole Gospel to the whole world " is just a mockery, or worse still, an evasion, the sign of our refusal in our day to face the challenge of " the evangelization of the world in this generation ".

One of the most interesting changes apparent in the attitude of
the younger Churches since Whitby 1947 has been their reconsideration of the possible place of the Western missionary within their
ranks. In a previous chapter we considered the work that a missionary might hope to do within the framework of a younger Church.
Once such a Church begins to see its responsibilities for the whole
of the population of its area, the relationship between its resources
and its tasks begins to take on a very different aspect. It becomes
clear that the help of the missionary may be needed not just in
one department or another of the Church's life, but in the whole
of its outreach as an evangelizing body. Let us quote again
from the inspired utterance of the younger Church leaders at
Whitby :

> The younger Churches . . . wish to make it clear that they
> desire to have the help of missionaries from the older Churches, not
> only in their institutional but also in their evangelistic and pioneer
> work.[1]

And, while firmly insisting on their independence, they assure the
future missionary of the reality of the colleagueship into which he
will be called :

> As the missionary becomes fully a member of the Church which
> he serves, he becomes, equally with his brethren who are also members of that Church, eligible for any position of labour, responsibility
> or dignity to which he may be called by the voice of the Church.[2]

This attitude towards the foreigner proclaimed by the leaders
at Whitby may seem to be in sharp contrast to the painful realities
of the situation as described in the last chapter. It is true that
younger Churches, like older, can be very far behind the vision of
their leaders. But the existence and the intensity of this contrast
depend very much on the extent to which the younger Church has
recovered the vision of the evangelistic task. In a Church which is
fired with missionary passion, the distinction between indigenous
and foreign no longer seems to matter very much. The one concern
is the finishing of the Unfinished Task ; and since there is so much
more to be done than can possibly be accomplished by all the available forces combined, the foreigner who is willing to throw himself

---

[1] *Renewal and Advance*, p. 181.   [2] *Ibid.*, p. 177.

unconditionally into the fray can count on being welcomed as a friend and brother from the start.

Amid much that was inconclusive in the findings of the Willingen Conference of 1952, the one thing that stood out clearly was the rediscovery of the missionary nature of the Church itself :

> There is one thing which cannot be doubted—missionary activity belongs to the *esse*, to the nature, to the existence of the Church. Church and mission form an indissoluble unity. Both alike are founded on the same self-impartation of the triune God. Hartenstein interprets the finding of Willingen in the following terms : " The being of the Church consists in its participation in God's plan of salvation, in His mission for the redemption of the world. The missionary enterprise reveals the deepest meaning of the Church as that Body which is sent by God, as the new humanity, as the firstfruits of redemption. It is impossible to speak rightly of the Church without speaking of its mission to the world. The Church exists in its missionary activity." [1]

One of the most remarkable developments of recent years has been the acceptance of this principle by the younger Churches, and a wider recognition of the truth that a Church can be at the same time a receiving and a giving Church—that a Church need not wait for the moment at which it becomes fully " self-supporting " before launching out on missionary work of its own.[2] Several Churches which are still receiving a measure of support from the West have started to take a hand in work outside their own borders. The Church of South India has sent missionaries to Papua. Indian Lutherans are working in the service of the Batak Church in Sumatra. The Churches of the Philippines are undertaking work in Thailand. An Indian Christian of the ancient Syrian Church in Travancore has been rendering outstanding service among students in Indonesia. And, of course, the Churches of the Pacific islands have their long record of heroic and sacrificial missionary service in their island world. In the nature of the case these ventures cannot be very large or expensive. They indicate a new grasp, on the part of the younger Churches, of the principle of wholeness and interdependence. And there is no doubt that this venturing out into farther

[1] Wilhelm Andersen : *Towards a Theology of Mission*, p. 54.
[2] The principle is not new. It was clearly stated by Bishop Azariah at the time of the formation of the Indian Missionary Society of Tinnevelly in 1903.

places has stimulated the evangelistic zeal of these Churches in relation to their responsibilities nearer at hand.[1]

It has been said over and over again that the initiative now lies in the hands of the younger Churches. Their full spiritual equality has been recognized, and it has been acknowledged that they must play the larger part in the evangelization of their own countries. But what is to happen, if a younger Church fails to rise to the height of its responsibilities, and to take the initiative in setting evangelistic work in motion ? We speak of " the younger Churches " as a unity. In point of fact, however, there is an immensely wide range of disparity among them—in age, in maturity, in capacity of leadership, in spiritual vigour. Some small younger Churches are, in theory, " the Church " of a very wide area, which they may have neither the strength nor the inclination to evangelize. They may feel disinclined to invite missionaries from other lands to undertake that which is beyond their strength. Indeed, where ancient resentments are still smouldering, younger Church leaders sometimes give the impression that they would rather that their fellow-countrymen died as heathen than that they should be brought to the knowledge of Christ by Christians from the West. If such a situation is reached, there is nothing for it but for the older Churches to rebel. A dictatorship of the younger Churches is no better than a dictatarship of the missionary societies. " Partnership " is not a humon alliance for mutual convenience, it is *partnership in obedience* to the command of Christ to preach the Gospel to every creature. If this obedience is lacking on the one side or the other, the partnership would seem to lack a valid foundation. The world situation is changing so rapidly that opportunities are being lost every day. If an older Church seems to hear a clear call to evangelize, it may be necessary that it should go forward, leaving the younger Church to follow when it is sufficiently awake itself to hear the call.

A striking example of this paradoxical and apparently retrograde development is to be found in Sierra Leone. As the name of its capital, Freetown, recalls, Sierra Leone was founded as a home for the slaves freed by the British gun-boats up and down the west

[1] The Churches of South-East Asia have adopted the term " ecumenical mission " for this particular form of inter-Church aid and mutual service—a rather confusing usage, in view of other tasks which the hard-worked term " ecumenical " has to fulfil.

coast of Africa. Folk from many tribes were brought together. Uprooted from their own tribes and their natural African background, they developed a peculiar and artificial society, that of the Creoles, speaking English in public life, and the "Krio" patois among themselves. This community, living in the coastal or "colony" area of Sierre Leone, was one of the first and most successful mission fields ; before long all the Creoles were Christians. "The Creoles had education ; they clung tenaciously to a mid-Victorian type of Western culture ; they held high appointments in almost every walk of life, and, what was more, they had the Gospel. Unfortunately they quickly developed a spirit of patronizing superiority toward the indigenous tribesmen who formed, and still form, the great majority of the population of Sierra Leone."[1] The last sentence of this quotation indicates where the trouble begins.

Sierra Leone suffered from one of those premature and ill-considered attempts to create an independent Church, to which we have already referred. As early as 1860 the Church Missionary Society brought into existence the Native Church Council, placing responsibility for the congregations in the hands of the African clergy, and reducing the missionary staff almost to vanishing point. The theory, of course, was that the Christians of the Colony area would gradually spread out into the interior and bring the Gospel to their African brethren. What happened, as ought to have been foreseen, was exactly the opposite. In the early days there had been some fairly promising evangelistic work in the interior, but gradually this withered away to practically nothing. The Creoles proved to be in many cases even more remote from the tribesmen than the missionaries had been. Those who were sent up-country to do missionary work mostly ended up by being, in fact, chaplains to the small Creole settlements in the inland towns. "Evangelistic work has not been making much headway, and many of these Churches now consist of a mere handful of Creole settlers and a sprinkling of tribesmen converts."[2]

[1] S. A. J. Pratt : "Spiritual Conflicts in a Changing African Society" in *The Ecumenical Review*, Vol. VIII, No. 2, Jan. 1956, p. 155. The whole of this penetrating article by a leading Sierra Leonean Christian should be read.

[2] *Ibid.*, p. 161. The same situation has prevailed in Liberia : "The Americo-Liberians were Christians, and they have held to their faith. They have built their churches and prepared their own ministers. But they made no attempt to evangelize the original inhabitants. All that has been done in this respect is the result of mission endeavour." *Marangu*, p. 156.

What had happened to the Anglicans happened also to the Methodists ; the Church and the missionaries had got locked up in the Colony in a wholly unprogressive and unproductive situation.

At length a group of English Methodist missionaries could stand it no longer, and determined to break the deadlock. The Mende Mission of the Methodist Church came into being. A pioneer mission entirely staffed by Europeans in so ancient a mission field is indeed a strange spectacle. Yet, given the existing situation, it is hard to see what else could have been done, if the tribes of the interior were ever to be evangelized. At first progress was slow ; but now, as an enthusiastic Methodist friend remarked to me, " It's like a forest fire." In time to come the co-ordination of this new and vigorous Church with the old and static Church of the Colony will present the most delicate problems of ecclesiastical statesmanship.

This is not a normal situation. But it is a reminder that the free operation of the Spirit of God can never be constricted within the limits of the theoretical formulation of missionary and ecumenical bodies. If groups of workers from Western Churches at times find it necessary to break out beyond the limits of the vision of a younger Church, it is to be hoped that they will not be forgetful of all the lessons that have been learned in two centuries. The foreigner must always regard himself as a passing phenomenon. From the very first day he must lay the foundations not of a mission but of a local Church. Throughout he must plan for a Church which can take its place within the framework of the already existing Churches. He must resist the temptation to self-righteousness. If he has been accorded a vision which for the moment has been denied to the neighbouring younger Church, he may act on that vision only in the spirit which makes it legitimate for Christians to provoke one another to love and to good works.

CHAPTER 8

THE DYNAMIC MINORITY

IT is clear that in the second half of the twentieth century life is going to be a great deal more difficult for the younger Churches in almost every area than it has been in the last hundred and fifty years.

Revolutions can only rarely be carried through without violence. As the coloured races of the world have almost without exception decided to enter on the path of revolution, it is to be expected that violence will be endemic over what may be a long period of settling down. Whatever the evils of " colonialism ", it did at least guarantee over large parts of the earth's surface such tranquillity as they had never known before. For instance, up till 1948 South India had enjoyed a century and a half of peace, disturbed only by occasional communal riots and by the outbreaks of violence which were from time to time the undesired accompaniments of Mr. Gandhi's non-violent campaigns. How different is the scene on which the younger Churches look out to-day !

Korea has been torn in half by a bitter and devastating war ; the present uneasy peace does not conceal from anyone in South Korea the intentions of the North to resume the invasion as soon as circumstances are favourable. China has settled down more or less peacefully under the Communist régime ; but the People's Republic and the government of Chiang Kai Shek glower at one another over the not too wide waters that separate Formosa from the mainland. Vietnam, like Korea, has been divided into two states, which co-exist only in a state of very precarious peace. Malaya has suffered under an emergency of eight years' duration, and the end is not yet. The government of Burma, wrestling with Communists, with Karen and Arakanese separatists and with mysterious forces of Chinese nationalists, has never been able to establish its authority over all the territory that it is supposed to govern. Indonesia's declaration of independence was followed by the naval and military invasion of Ambon, the largely Christian people of which had no wish to accept the unitary, non-federal constitution

r Indonesia which was favoured by the Javanese. The dreadful
assacres in India in 1947 mercifully burned themselves out within
few weeks. But India's assumption of independence was quickly
llowed by the armed invasion of the Nizam's dominions. The
mpaign was short, few lives were lost ; the Nizam's government
as bad and died unlamented. But to the outside observer Mr.
ehru's action was uncomfortably like Hitler's invasion of Austria.
he Kashmir issue continues to bedevil relations between India
id Pakistan, and has several times brought the two countries to
e brink of war. Pakistan is as convinced that its claims are morally
ipeccable as India is that its claims are legally unassailable ; and
ch country is offended that the West fails to recognize the perfect
ghteousness of its position. Pakistan at last has managed to make
self a constitution ; but tension between East and West Pakistan
id political irresponsibility continue to make it doubtful whether
e country can survive. Ceylon, the one country in Asia where
:mocracy appeared to be really working, has now endangered its
vn future by adopting a policy of making Sinhalese the national
nguage, and runs the risk of throwing the considerable Tamil
inority into a state of permanent indignation and non-co-operation.

The situation in the Middle East is as inflammable as any that
is ever existed anywhere in the world at any time. The independ-
ice of the Sudan precipitated a rebellion among the southern tribes,
it surprisingly, since not by any means all the three million pagans
id Christians of the South are convinced of the advantages of their
ibjection to the six million Muslims of the North. The dreadful
[au Mau emergency seems at last to be receding ; but what will
leave behind it ? Unless means are found for a real healing of
e soul of an African people, what is driven underground may be
en more poisonous than that which came to the surface in the
[au Mau rising. The policy of the South African Government,
hatever may be thought of its immediate effects on the life of the
nion, continues to darken the relations between the black man and
e white through the whole continent of Africa. Events in Colombia
id Argentina suggest that the problems of a Protestant minority
a Roman Catholic country are not markedly different to-day from
hat they were in the sixteenth century.

The general picture is not cheerful. Of course it is important
it to exaggerate. Humanity takes its crises much less tragically

than politicians imagine. The peasant continues to plough and to sow, while the legions thunder by. Men and women marry and bring forth children on the brink of Armageddon. Sometimes crises pass away, and there is always the underlying hope of a better time coming. Further, it must be noted that times of security are not always those which are most favourable to the progress of the Gospel. It may well appear fifty years from now that the experience of the Chinese Churches under Communist domination has produced more spiritual benefit than spiritual loss, and some Chinese Christian leaders would maintain that this is already evident.

Nevertheless, it is as well that the younger Churches should seriously take stock of their situation, and should plan their strategies in the light of a reasonably calculated expectation of what their future may be.

First, they must take account of the possibility that they may suddenly and for a long period be cut off from one another and from their friends in the West. The loss of spiritual and intellectual fellowship is far more serious than the loss of the financial aid which has in the past accompanied it. On the whole the Churches in Mesopotamia and the Middle East were not seriously persecuted by the Muslim invaders a thousand years ago. It was mainly their isolation from the great centres of Christian life and thought further west, and the intellectual impoverishment following on that isolation, which reduced them to the shadowy existence that is theirs to-day.

Secondly, it is unlikely that in our lifetime the younger Churches will feel altogether comfortable in the setting of the independence of their respective countries. Nationalism and the resurgence of the ancient religions are separate streams. But in a number of countries they have flowed together, and produced currents and whirlpools amid which the Christian will not always find it easy to navigate his craft.

India is a " secular republic " and religious liberty is written into its constitution. But there are not lacking elements which would wish to change all that, and to make Hinduism the dominant influence in the state. " The Mahasabha is perhaps the most influential Hindu communal organization to-day. It stands for the preservation of Hindu orthodoxy and the establishment of a Hindu State in India, in which the interests of Hinduism are to determine

he political and social programmes." [1]   Even more extreme is the
Rashtriya Swayam Sevak Sangh, the leader of which expressed himself in April 1956 in the following terms :

> Now that we are free from foreign rule and that steps are being
> taken to achieve economic freedom, let us endeavour to fight against
> our religious slavery. . . . Hindusthan, the Hindu race with its Hindu
> religion, Hindu culture and Hindu language (the natural family of
> Sanskrit and her off-springs) complete the Nation concept. . . . The
> non-Hindu people in Hindusthan may stay in the country wholly
> subordinated to the Hindu Nation, claiming nothing, deserving no
> privileges, far less preferential treatment, not even citizenship rights. [2]

In March 1956 Pakistan declared itself an Islamic Republic,
and decided that the head of the State must be a Muslim.   How
Islam is to be reconciled with democracy and with modern ideas is
an as yet unsolved problem.   A few years ago a serious attempt
was made to ensure that all law in Pakistan should follow the lines
of the Shari'a, the traditional Muslim law, and to set up a kind of
inquisitorial tribunal to determine the conformity of all legislation
with this standard.   This would ultimately have put all power in
the State into the hands of the extremely conservative *Ulemas*, and
would have made a Church-State of Pakistan.   For the moment
this attempt has been frustrated, but it is by no means certain that
it will not be revived ; and in any case, an Islamic state is one in
which it is difficult for adherents of any other religion to feel perfectly
at home.

The close connection of Buddhism with nationalism is already
a major factor in the politics of South-East Asia.   In Ceylon constant
attempts are being made to equate full loyalty to Ceylon with the
profession of Buddhism.   In Burma, the identification of religion
with nationalism is even more pronounced : ". To be a true and loyal
Burman is equated in the minds of many with being a Buddhist. . . .
Everything Buddhist is looked upon as being truly Burmese . . .
leaders are not tired of pointing out the so-called denationalizing
effects of Christianity, and they cite the revolt of the Karens as
proof. . . . The British government is being blamed for the decline
of Buddhism in the country." [3]

[1] *Christianity and the Asian Revolution*, p. 136.
[2] *N.C.C. Review*, June–July 1956, pp. 263–4.
[3] *Christianity and the Asian Revolution*, pp. 243–4.

In Africa the situation is less clear, since Africa, except in the Muslim areas, had no highly developed and theologically self-conscious religion to oppose either to Christianity or to the advance of secularism. But there are already evident trends in favour of a rediscovery of " Africanism ", of the elements that were of value in the old African culture. This is perhaps a parallel in the political sphere to the experience of those " splinter-Churches ", which broke away from the missionary-established Churches in the desire to be more genuinely African. Where this will lead it is impossible at present to say : it is likely that in the future " Africanism " with some kind of a religious tone will be a growing force.

Now all this means that Christians in these countries are likely to find themselves in the position of a nonconformist minority.

It may well be maintained that in this their situation is not different from that of their brethren in the West. We now know well that there is no such thing as a Christian nation, that committed Christians are a minority, and that at any moment they may be called to endure the obloquy of criticizing or opposing the policies of their country. But there are differences. The situation of Christians in Burma and that of Christians in Britain are not identical. The coronation of the Queen was far more than a political or imperial spectacle ; it indicated the desire of a great many people that Britain should continue to regard itself as at least in some sense a Christian nation, and that it should not officially accept as part of its national life anything which is irreconcilable with Christian principles. President Eisenhower's gesture in calling the crowd assembled before the Capitol for his inauguration to join him in prayer was widely hailed as an appropriate action on the part of the Chief Executive of a nation that still desires in some sense to regard itself as a nation under God ; and, to the vast majority of those in America who care about such things at all, this means " under the God who is revealed in Jesus Christ ".[1] In 1956 the President commented on his own action in the following terms :

> It seemed to me a perfectly natural thing to do. I was seeking some way to impress upon the audience at that moment that all of us realized a new chief executive would be inaugurated over a nation that was founded on a religious faith. Our founding documents so

---

[1] The Jews are an important minority in the United States but a minority of only about 5 per cent as compared with Christians.

state in explaining our government and what we intended to do. . . . To pray seemed to me a perfectly natural thing to do as a method of showing that I also believe.[1]

In such a nation any Christian group may for a time be non-conformist in relation to some of the policies or practices of the nation, but Christians as such are not a permanently nonconformist group. It is otherwise in most of the new nations of Asia and Africa. Each of the great ancient religions is totalitarian in its habits and its claims ; it determines not only the religious outlook and beliefs of its adherents, but also every detail of their daily life, personal and social. If nationalism and religion become identified, then religious nonconformity can very easily come to be regarded as equivalent to political unreliability. This has so recently been the case in our own country that we cannot be surprised if the same phenomenon is found elsewhere. Until 1828 the nonconformists of England were regarded as so politically undependable that, by the Test and Corporation Acts, they were virtually excluded from all share in the government and administration of the country in which they lived. Christians in Asia and Africa are not under any such legal or political disabilities ; yet the suspicion of disloyalty or unreliability is a very uncomfortable thing ; and, as long as it exists in any degree, it must to some extent condition the kind of witness to their faith which Christians are called to bear in their respective countries to-day.

Evangelism or Christian witness must be understood in a far larger sense than has been customary in the past. Of course evangelism in the old sense of direct personal witness to individuals and groups must go on ; the Church must bear witness to the Gospel or die. But there are to-day wide realms, other than that of direct proclamation of the Gospel, in which a total Christian witness has to be brought to bear on total national situations.

In the first place, the concern of Christians for the principle of religious freedom and equality is obvious. It was largely through the efforts of Christians that a generous recognition of the right of adherents of all religions to practise, preach and propagate their faith was included in the Indian constitution. It is already apparent that such declarations can be understood in different senses by different people, and that only the greatest watchfulness on the

[1] Quoted in *Faith at Work*, April 1956, p. 17.

part of Christians can guard against the frittering away of the rights which are legally guaranteed to minorities.

Here the self-interest of Christians naturally plays a part. There are much more interesting areas in which truly national and altruistic service can be rendered.

The Christian is called, by his very being and experience, to be an interpreter between two worlds. Few of the leaders of the Eastern nations are genuinely and naturally at home in the Western world. All too many of them are not really at home in either world. An indoctrination with Western culture in early years may have left them restless and dissatisfied in the sphere of their own traditional culture ; yet in the world of Western culture they move with hesitant and uncertain steps. This is to some extent true even of men like Pandit Nehru and Professor Radhakrishnan, whose knowledge of Western life and thought is profound. They have learned it from outside, because they have not shared the inner experiences on which the life of the West has been built up. Shamefully un-Christian as we have become, it is yet true that the tongue we speak is the tongue of the Authorized Version of the Bible, of Milton and of Bunyan, and that something of Christian principle and Christian experience remains in the fibre of almost every one of us. Only a Christian can understand what this experience is ; everyone else, however deeply read and instructed, views it from outside as an observer or an analyst, and therefore in part misunderstands, in part distorts it. Very different is the situation of the Christian leaders in these countries. Again and again Christians of the most diverse origins are astonished at the plenitude of fellowship at which they can arrive just because all their basic principles and values are the same. This ease of understanding opens to the Christian in the lands of the younger Churches an immense field of service. After all, Asia and Africa have got to live together with Europe and America (not to mention Russia). Where is the daysman who can lay his hands upon them both ? The answer is not far to seek it is the Christian of the younger Churches who is the citizen of both worlds, and who, if he will take the trouble to qualify himself in both directions, can serve as the interpreter between those who otherwise find it hard to meet.

In another field also, that of political life, the Christian is called to be an interpreter.

All the newly independent nations, and some of the older ones, claim to have established democracy in their countries. Further-more, almost without exception they have chosen to model them-selves on the highly complex and specialized forms of British democracy.[1] This is a new and perplexing thing. Democracy is by far the most difficult form of government to make work, and so far it has been moderately successful only on the basis of a strong and active Christian tradition.

Of the European countries which have tried democracy Spain and Portugal have apparently indefinitely abandoned it. In Italy it clings on precariously, threatened by the totalitarian forces of clericalism on the one hand, and by Communism on the other. Indeed it looks rather as though democracy required not only a Christian foundation, but a Protestant Christian foundation ; and that, of Protestant countries, it works best in those whose national life has been deeply penetrated by the principles of John Calvin. And, oddly enough, it seems to work best of all in those countries which have retained monarchy, the Crown being in such countries the symbol of the stability and continuity needed to correct the violent fluctuations of feeling and policy which are liable to endanger the life of democratic states. All this being so, the introduction of a developed form of Western democracy into countries which are not monarchical, and not Calvinist, and which have no Christian tradition at all on which democracy can be based, is a highly venturesome project.

What, then, are the Christian principles underlying democracy, in so far as we have been able to work them out in our own experience ?

First, there is the sense of the infinite value of every man, the right of every man to live his life in the enjoyment of such essential liberties as do not in their exercise involve infringement of the liberties of others. But this derives, not from the view that all men are intrinsically equal, but from the conviction that all men are of significance in the eyes of God, and that the value and importance of each cannot be judged without reference to this unalterable relationship of each to God.

[1] Living in Switzerland, I cannot but be astonished that the peoples of these multi-lingual, multi-racial countries have paid so little attention to the Swiss method of dealing with these intractable problems. I believe that if in 1941–43 Mr. Gandhi and Mr. Nehru had been prepared to consider something like the Swiss Constitution for India, the separation of India and Pakistan could have been avoided.

Secondly, the recognition that the voice of wisdom may often come from the ordinary man and not from the expert. Historically this derives from those Independent groups in Britain which took seriously the biblical idea that the Holy Spirit is given to all believers, and not only to the clergy.

Thirdly, the conviction that government can only be by free discussion, in which all points of view can be expressed and heard. This is the direct opposite of all totalitarian concepts of government. Clearly this can work only if all parties are agreed in this conviction. In cases where totalitarian parties plan to use the privilege of liberty for the overthrow of liberty, even the most liberal and democratic of states may be obliged to impose restrictions, which on its own principles it is bound to deplore.

Fourthly, the determination that the rights of minorities must be scrupulously respected and maintained. This does not, of course, mean that minorities must be allowed to do whatever they like, or that the scruples of a small minority should hold up a reform which is recognized as being for the general good. Yet the principle is in accord with the Pauline rule that the strong ought to bear the infirmities of the weak ; it involves a total denial of the false doctrine of the infallibility and omnicompetence of every majority of 51 per cent.

Fifthly, it must be understood that each party which secures a majority of one will not immediately reverse all the actions of its predecessors. This means that democracy can work only within the framework of an agreement to respect the constitution, written and unwritten ; and that is possible only if there is a deep and underlying agreement as to the nature of the good life for man. The Communist has a wholly different idea of the good life for man from that which has been current in the Christian world ; therefore inevitably it is his open and declared aim to make all democratic systems unworkable. Where a democratic government is faced with the aggression of a party that will, if it can, make use of the liberty it enjoys to seize power and will thenceforth use power to deny all liberty to others, the defence of liberty for all may involve certain restrictions on the liberty of some.

If all this is true, what chance of survival has democracy in countries where there is no Christian basis on which it can be built ? Hinduism is built on the social inequality of caste. Untouchability has been abolished by law. But one of the things that we have learned from the Communists is that political equality expressed in legal enactments can lead only to " formal democracy ", unless it is accompanied by at least a measure of equality in social privilege and economic opportunity.[1] Islam has from the start been based on the principle that in an Islamic state there cannot be equality between Muslims and non-Muslims, and that the best the latter can hope for is to be accepted as tolerated second-class citizens. Can Islam so reconstruct itself as to abandon this age-long principle, and yet remain recognizably itself ? One solution that would commend itself to many statesmen in the new countries would be the establishment of the purely secular state. But is this a genuine solution ? Is this not to surrender power wholly to Leviathan ? Democracy, autonomous and uncontrolled by any principle higher than its own interests, can be as cruel and irresponsible as any other form of government that has ever been devised.

Here is the challenge to the Christians of Asia and Africa. They are the only people who really understand the spiritual foundations on which democracy rests, and the principles through the acceptance of which alone it can be made to work. Can they make these principles effective in the life even of nations which do not as a whole accept the Christian way ?

On the whole the response of Christians to the political challenge in these countries is encouraging. It is remarkable that at the moment of writing three ministers in the cabinet of Indonesia are Christian. The President of South Vietnam is a Roman Catholic. Since India's independence, the Minister for Health for the whole of India has been that remarkable Christian lady, the Rajkumari Amrit Kaur. But it is not enough that Christians should be active in politics ; they must know why they are there. They must understand the true nature of government, the meaning of democracy, the limitations on the authority of any State, the moral principles without the observance of which any state is sowing the seeds of its own destruction. And what Christians have understood they must be able to commend to others who are not Christian.

[1] The Indian Government itself has recognized that " Any number of enactments by themselves will not transform the situation unless there is a genuine changing of heart on the part of every . . . citizen ".
Quoted in *Newsweek*, 24th September 1956, p. 26.

Here is the problem. How can principles, which in their essence depend on the Gospel of Jesus Christ, be commended to those who do not accept that Gospel ? To say " Not at all " would be a cynical abandonment of the responsibility for the Christian witness at a vitally important point of modern life. To suppose that the answer is " Entirely " is the illusion which is the weakness of much of the work of Christian optimists. But there is an intermediate point. The art of government is the art of the possible. It is the duty of Christians clearly and tirelessly to bear witness to the moral principles on which all government must be based, even when the hearers cannot be expected to admit the relation between these principles and the Christian revelation, or to carry into effect measures which the general conscience of their nation is not as yet ready to accept.

The central issue is that of power. Is a state really all-powerful within its own sphere ? If the answer is " Yes ", democracy has been abandoned, and the broad road is open to totalitarianism. If the answer is " No ", the question at once arises as to the nature of the limitations. The principle of democracy is that the will of the people should prevail. In what circumstances can we affirm that the will of the people should not and must not prevail ?

This problem has been so admirably stated by Dr. Kitson Clark that it seems to me impossible to improve on his words :

> You cannot be content simply to say that the will of the people must prevail. You must add to that the rider that it must be the will of the people, who must realize that there are certain things the people ought not to do, even when a majority of the people wishes very much to do them ; it must be the will of the people expressed in a certain way, engendered in certain conditions which must allow the free expression of opinions, even of opinions which may seem absurd and repugnant to the ordinary man. In fact the will of the people may be allowed to prevail with safety only if the people realize that they are not the final and sovereign power in the universe.[1]

A few pages later, referring to Blackstone and Halifax, Dr. Kitson Clark continues :

> That is, in the conception of both, behind the activities of the human legislator, there was conceived to be a system of rules which

---

[1] G. R. Kitson Clark : *The English Inheritance* (S.C.M. Press, 1950), p. 21. This admirable book seems to be far less widely known than it deserves.

it was his duty to observe, rules which sprang from the nature of an ordered universe and in the last resort from the will of Almighty God who had created and ordered that universe.[1]

But how is this to be brought home to those who do not accept the Christian presuppositions ? It is just the fact that we do not all agree as to the nature of the good life for man. The slow and uncertain progress made in the definition of human rights raises doubts as to whether human rights can hang together, or hang at all, unless there is something outside them on which to hang them. For that something the Christian knows the short and simple monosyllable " God ".

Here is the problem of the Christian in a non-Christian state. It is his business unwearyingly to bear witness to the truth that politics is a spiritual affair, that it deals with realities other than food and warmth and taxes, and that it has reactions such as cannot be expressed in human codes. How far the Christian can bring this home to non-Christian legislators must remain uncertain. What is certain is that he will not be able to do it at all, unless he has thought deeply on the nature of political reality. The Christian attitude in politics must be one of slightly disillusioned realism, since he accepts the reality of human sinfulness and knows that no human order can correspond to the order of God. At the same time it is essential that he should be convinced that some forms of human order are much nearer than others to the will of God, and that he should believe that even the partial realization of the divine order is an ideal towards which every Christian is bound in conscience to strive.

The next field of evangelism, in the broad sense of the term, is that of social activity and social reform.

Here it has to be admitted that the attitude of many Christians of the younger Churches is still hesitant and uncertain. As far as purely charitable activity is concerned, the missions and Churches have a magnificent record. In almost every country in the world they have been the pioneers in women's education, in hospitals for women and children, in schools for the blind and the deaf, and in the care of lepers. But there is a distinction to be drawn between this sense of responsibility for action in relation to existing evils or suffering, and that educated social conscience which questions the whole existing order of society and demands that it be reconstructed

[1] G. R. Kitson Clark: *The English Inheritance* (S.C.M. Press, 1950), p. 35.

nearer to the ideal of social justice. It is in this latter area that not all Christians see their way clear.

Some would maintain that this is the field of governments, themselves an institution appointed by God, in which the Church has no business to interfere. Canon Warren has quoted the views of an African pastor, present at Marangu, who " has obviously accepted the strict Lutheran doctrine of submission to the civil power in everything except where sin is demanded. And for him passive obedience was not just a regretful acquiescence. His attitude was far more positive than that. He clearly held the view that as touching the affairs of this world the State had a virtually absolute claim on the Christian man's allegiance." [1]

Others, while not holding so clearly defined a view, would maintain that the task of the Church is simply to call men out from the world, to bring them into subjection to Jesus Christ, and to prepare them for eternal life. This was the pietistic belief of many missionaries in the past. Many younger churchmen have learned this view from their Western friends. In part, this may be a rationalization of the sense of impotence; as Christians are so few, what can they do against all the massive powers of the government ? But in part it is a seriously and conscientiously held view as to the nature of the Church. Purged of its narrowness, it is a view that must always be maintained, if the Church is not to sink to the level of a society devoted to the multiplication of loaves and fishes.

But even the Christian of pietist conviction cannot contract out of his nation. He cannot evade his share of responsibility for its life; and there is open to him at the present time a field, in which, if he is willing, he can render yeoman service by the sheer integrity of his life and conduct. Corruption in public and commercial life is a recurrent menace to states and societies. It is little more than two centuries since Sir Robert Walpole maintained in Britain that every man has his price. In a single generation France and the United States have been shaken by scandals of the largest dimensions. Serious as these things are in states with well-established governments, they are even more serious in the newly independent

[1] *C.M.S. Newsletter*, February 1956, pp. 5–6. But note also the comment of Dr. Franklin Clark Fry, Chairman of the Central Committee of the World Council of Churches : " Sometimes being quiet is as bad as being a rascal. There have been Lutheran Churches which kept quiet at the wrong time, and so assisted the rascals."

countries, where the hold of governments on situations is still some-what precarious and sound traditions have yet to be established. On the whole, self-government has worked far better in the new nations than unfriendly critics in the West had predicted. New teams of largely untried statesmen have shown courage and resourcefulness in dealing with the immense problems involved in working over the whole administration of their countries from a colonial to an in-dependent pattern. Yet there have not been lacking disquieting signs of moral instability such as is incompatible with firm and ordered democratic government. For instance, recent events in the Gold Coast have made evident the prevalence of standards of morality rather different from those acceptable in countries with a longer Christian tradition. In India, it is the government itself which has complained that progress in some of the great engineering and constructional works, on which future social and economic progress depends, has been slower than it ought to have been as a result of the lack of honest and competent administration at every level of the operations. This is where the Christian ought to be able to shine. Happily honesty is not the monopoly of Christians ; but it ought to be a characteristic by which every Christian is everywhere known. This is a form of evangelism far outside the limits of the formal churches, which may in course of time prove more effective than a large number of sermons.

But, valuable as such witness is, it is still not enough. All over the lands of the younger Churches great social changes are on the way. It is essential that Christians should be aware of them, should think ahead of governments, and should exercise an independent judgment on the way things are going. Most of the governments in the new nations are committed to the ideal of the Welfare State. In carrying out their programmes they are prepared to accept a good deal of socialism, and the nationalization of a considerable part of the nation's industrial life. On the whole the Christian may incline to the view that in the end this is the policy that should be followed, though he may wonder at times whether governments have thought through all the problems that are likely to grow out of, for example, a widespread redistribution of land and a change in the system of land-tenure. But the intelligent Christian may be quicker than some others to detect the dangers implicit in hurried measures of social change.

The peril of the social reformer is that he tends to be a theorist, and to think of mankind in the mass. Men and women become pawns to be moved about, it is to be hoped with their good will, in this direction or that, as the evolution of the social ideal may demand. Life tends to lose its personal quality and to become mechanized in mind and organization as well as in physical process. This can be a major disaster to a population which is only gradually emerging from the restrictions and limitations on personal life that are characteristic of the tribe. The cynical judgment of an American on the life of his country was that " we have passed from barbarism to decadence without the intervening stage of civilization ". If certain trends continue in some of the newly independent countries, in thirty years' time people may be saying ruefully, " We have passed from the primitive collectivism of the tribe to the organized collectivism of the beehive state without passing through the intervening stage of a genuinely personal existence ".

It is this danger that lies behind Mr. M. M. Thomas' passionate affirmation of the Church as the only place in India in which a genuinely personal life is possible. He writes :

> The missionary movement and the small congregations of the Christian Church founded in different parts of Asia . . . are in their essence the one personal reality in all Asia. Proclaiming the Gospel, and confronting every man with a responsible decision to repent and enter the historical community of the redeemed, the Church in Asia stands as the one community of persons. . . . If the missionary movement and the Church in Asia continue to proclaim the transcendent Word of God and to be a community of Grace in tension with the political, economic and social orders of Asia to-day and to-morrow, it will be the greatest contribution they can make to Asian society.[1]

Tribal existence has its power and its charm. Every individual has and knows his place in society. Individual choice and decision is not entirely suppressed, but for the most part personal decision, even in so intimate a matter as marriage, is not called for, and conformity is the greatest of the virtues. This tribal society is everywhere breaking down, and we cannot preserve it, if we would. What is to take its place ? The mere anarchism in which individualism runs loose ? The rigid regimentation of the totalitarian state, in which again, except for the privileged few, conformity is the

[1] *The Christian in the World Struggle* (Geneva, 1951), pp. 78–9.

greatest virtue ? Or the free life of the Church, in which men are held together by loyalty, in which individual decision and responsibility are fostered, but individualism is held in check by a fellowship which is greater than the individual and all his concerns ?

Mr. Thomas is right in laying stress on the significance not so much of the Christian individual as of the congregation. Every Christian congregation knows that it is part of a fellowship that runs far out of sight, an international fellowship almost co-extensive with the earth, based not on kinship or race or clan but simply on a common relationship to God, renewed from generation to generation as the young enter personally into that fellowship which comes from God alone and is never a merely human gift. It is this external, and eternal, point of reference which enables the Christian group to transcend itself, to be lifted above the flux of time and the flow of contemporary trends, and so to exercise an objective judgment and criticism on the policies of states. The Churches ought not to interfere in anything that is legitimately the business of the State ; but they have been called to be the watchdogs of the State. It is their business to bark, to raise the cry of alarm, at any moment at which states seem in danger of infringing or diminishing those values of personal existence which they have been called into being to preserve.[1]

We come back, finally, to what inevitably and always is the central task of the Church. It is not simply the Church ; it is the Christian Church. It is confronted by great non-Christian systems, and whether it will or no it is perpetually engaged in the conflict of ideas. What determines the life of men and nations is ultimately their faith. Faith in Jesus Christ is different from any other kind of faith, religious, communist or secular. The war in the world of ideas goes on ceaselessly and without truce ; and, since the Christian believes that ultimately the truth in Jesus Christ must prevail over every falsehood and every lesser truth, he is pledged to a particular stand and an inescapable responsibility in that warfare.

[1] Cf. also Max Warren : *The Christian Mission* (S.C.M. Press, 1951), p. 52. " Who else will persevere in love, who else will keep this fundamentally humanizing factor in the foreground, if the Christian Mission fails ? And who but Christians will be able to save a misguided humanism with its defective understanding of man, and its ignoring of God, from giving to the education of man for the new society a direction which can only end in disaster ? "

We have already referred to the way in which, in almost all the lands of the younger Churches, the ancient forms of religion are finding a new ally in nationalism. It would be a grave mistake, however, to suppose that what we are faced with is merely the self-interested use by nationalistic forces of these old systems of belief. Each of the ancient religions seems to be undergoing a spiritual revival, in the attempt to prove to itself and others that it has an adequate answer to the problems of the modern world, and that it can serve as a spiritual basis for the life of men and nations in that world.

The Hindu revival is particularly interesting. Hinduism has in the past been considered a religion of fixed destiny and of acquiescence in it. A man's fate is written on his forehead, and, since it is impossible that he should change it, the best that he can do is to bear it without complaint, in the hope that dutifulness in this life may secure for him a better station in another incarnation. It is characteristic of the Hindu outlook that India has never produced its own tradition of historical writing. History belongs to the sphere of the transitory and the unreal, from which, according to the ancient prayer of the Upanishad, it must be the desire of every man to be delivered. But nothing could be more unlike this view than the vigorous, thrusting attitude of young modern India. The Hindu of to-day is convinced that there are real tasks to be accomplished, a country to be transformed, a destiny to be created. He is sure that his country has a great role to play among the nations of the world, and that historical responsibility is much more than a high-sounding phrase. Can Hinduism provide a spiritual interpretation of this new attitude, and the impulse to high moral endeavour which the situation demands ? Modern Hindus are convinced that it can.

The most interesting and brilliant figure in this Hindu recon-struction is Dr. S. Radhakrishnan, at present Vice-President of the Indian Republic. Radhakrishnan holds that the ultimate reality is essentially unknowable, and that therefore no religion can claim to have the full and final truth. This makes it possible to find a certain, though perhaps unequal, value in all faiths, and to call upon all together to join in a search for reality which will lead to a fuller and more perfect apprehension than has ever yet been achieved. In such a synthesis and co-operation, Hinduism with its emphasis on the mystical, and its affirmation that the true nature of man is not o be understood only in terms of this life, would naturally have a very significant part to play.

The ancient Hindu concept of *Māyā*, vanity, has often been nterpreted in terms of mere illusion and nothingness, or as the denial of any significant reality to this world of time and space. This Radhakrishnan will not accept. *Māyā*, in his view, implies that " this world of experience is a mixture of truth and illusion, a complex of the eternal and temporal, positing an element of indeterminism in the world process which demands choice in human conduct, thus making life in the here and now worth living ".[1] Again, Hinduism, rightly understood, does not teach men to flee from activity in the world ; it teaches detachment, freedom from desire for results or reward for work, as this principle is set forth in the *Bhagavad Gītā*. Hinduism, like other religious systems, is certainly in need of reform ; but this should take place by a rediscovery of its own spiritual resources, especially as these are set forth in the great Upanishads.

Hinduism, apart from certain extensions in South-East Asia,[2] is primarily the religion of India ; and, since the normal way of becoming a Hindu is to be born one, it has not ordinarily been a missionary religion. Very different is the history of Buddhism. This great system, of philosophy and conduct rather than of religion in the strict sense of the term, has had the strange fate of dying out completely in India, the country of its origin, and of having become through its missionary efforts the dominant religion of Ceylon, Burma, Tibet and Thailand, and one of the great spiritual forces in the life of China, Korea and Japan. In the long course of its history wide differences have grown up between the southern (Theravada) Buddhism, which has kept close to the original ideal of individual renunciation, and the northern (Mahayana) Buddhism with its elaborate doctrine of incarnation, and its incorporation of many religious elements that are not found in the teaching of the Buddha himself. The characteristics of the contemporary revival of Buddhism are the recovery of its missionary sense, and the drawing together of the two widely separated wings.

---

[1] *Christianity and the Asian Revolution*, p. 132. The whole of the chapter " Resurgent Hinduism," pp. 123–37, deserves careful study.

[2] Notably in Bali, where the basis of culture is still Hindu, in contrast to the prevailing Muslim culture of the greater part of Indonesia.

Just at the time that these lines are being written the sixth
World Council of Buddhism is due to come to an end. The Council
was convened in Rangoon in May 1954. For two years thousands
of monks and scholars from all over the Buddhist world have been
meeting in the Pagoda of World Peace near Rangoon, to work out
the message of Buddhism for the modern world. As the title of the
meeting-place makes clear, the central emphasis of the message is
likely to be on Buddhism as the only hope for the peace of the world.
We look out on the sorry spectacle of a warring and divided world.
To the Buddhist this is a conclusive and damning indictment of the
Christian faith. For more than a thousand years Christianity has
been dominant in Europe; for four hundred years it has been
dominant in Asia; and what has it made of the world? It has
failed to curb those passions and ambitions of men and nations that
are the cause of international wars and internal strife. It has failed,
according to the Buddhist, because of the error that lies at the heart
of all its teaching. Peace can come only through the extinction of
desire. Christians are taught to desire eternal life, and this very
desire binds them to that world of change and corruption within
which no peace is to be found. The heart of Christian doctrine is
love; love itself is a form of desire, and therefore Christians cannot
be set free from passion which is the root of all evil. In Buddhism,
in the adoption of the noble Eightfold Path alone [1] can there be any
hope for the peace of the world.

It cannot be said that the Buddhists have as yet made notable
progress in working out the application of the Master's teaching to
the problems of the modern world. The traditional ideal of Buddhism is the monk, who has abandoned everything, and who, though
he may contribute to the spiritual redemption of mankind, has no
longer any direct concern with its social redemption. There is a
gap between this ideal and the practical message that the world of
to-day seems to demand. But for the moment awakened Buddhism
feels that its primary concern is to renew the missionary activity of
ancient days, and to make the Master's teaching widely known
throughout the world. For many years Buddhists have been willing

[1] The Eightfold Path of (1) Right knowledge.   (2) Right Intention.
(3) Right Speech.   (4) Right Conduct.
(5) Right Livelihood.   (6) Right Effort.
(7) Right Mindfulness.   (8) Right Concentration.

o learn from Christians ; the Young Men's Buddhist Association in Ceylon is not a creation of yesterday. The development of missionary activity on a large scale in the West is a more recent phenomenon. A Buddhist Society exists in London, and has attracted a large number of able and highly educated people. Buddhist activity in America is on a larger scale, and there too has not failed to attract adherents, though there is not as yet anything that can be called a widespread Buddhist movement. But, in these days of the hydrogen bomb, when men are so avid for any gospel of peace, it is likely that many who have failed to find an answer to their question in Christianity as presented by the Churches will be prepared to give consideration to this other doctrine, clothed as it is in the venerable antiquity of the mysterious East.

The first aspect of resurgent Islam that presents itself to the Western observer is the renewal of political power. Islam has always been a great brotherhood and a conquering religion, but for four centuries its political influence had been on the wane. Among the most important consequences of the first world war was the constitution of a group of independent Islamic states across some of the greatest trade-routes in the world, and, as we now know, in close relation to the world's chief sources for the supply of oil. Recent events have added Pakistan and Indonesia to the free Islamic nations of the world.[1] Perhaps the chief underlying cause of the present terrible crisis in the Middle East has been the evident determination of Egypt and Saudi Arabia to exclude the West from exercising any influence on the affairs of the Middle East.

We should not, however, imagine that the renewal of life in Islamic countries is merely political ; here, too, there is a serious attempt to discover means by which Islam can be made a living gospel for nations in the modern world. The difficulties are very different from those faced by Hindus. If Hinduism suffers from having too little in the way of definite doctrine, Islam suffers by having too much. Mohammed was a legislator. In the Koran he laid down definite and unchangeable prescriptions, having all the force of the divine word, for almost every aspect of his people's life.

---

[1] It is to be noted that Indonesia is not officially an Islamic state in the same sense as Pakistan, and that the word " Islam " is not found in its constitution. Nevertheless there is an increasing tendency for politicians and statesmen to identify the interests of Indonesia with those of Islam.

Christianity is infinitely adaptable just because Jesus gave to His
followers the example of a life, and hardly any definite commands
or prescriptions for the details of daily life. Mohammed gave commands, which undoubtedly raised the level of civilization among
the Arabs of the seventh century, and yet have tended to fix his
religion and the countries that have adopted it at a certain level
which is not that of civilization in the modern world. Even when
we have cleared away all the distortions and prejudices which in
centuries of conflict have clouded the Christian apprehension of
Islam, it is hard to see how any honest interpreter of the Koran
can maintain, for instance, that it accords to womanhood a status
such as is compatible with the Christian ideal.

Orthodox Muslims would not accept a single word of these
strictures as well founded. And even those who are less orthodox
sometimes seem unaware of the inner contradictions in which they
are in danger of landing themselves. This comes out plainly in
the history of the efforts which Pakistan has made to provide itself
with a constitution. The original Constituent Assembly (since
dissolved, after failure to reach the conclusion of its work) laid
down, among the principles on which the Islamic state was to be
constructed :

> Wherein the principles of democracy, freedom, equality, tolerance,
> and social justice as enunciated by Islam, shall be fully observed ;
> Wherein the Muslims shall be enabled to order their lives in the
> individual and collective spheres in accord with the teachings and
> requirements of Islam as set out in the Holy Quran and the Shari'a.[1]

Now it is easy to use high-sounding terms ; but obviously everything depends on the content which is put into them. It is clear
that in the first section quoted above the words are derived from the
liberal and Western education that the writers had received, whereas
the second section is dependent on their Muslim past. Are the two
ultimately reconcilable ? For, in fact, the Koran does not proclaim
equality in any sense in which that term is used in the West ; it
does not permit equality between Muslims, who alone can be fully
citizens of an Islamic state, and those of other religions, who cannot
hope for more than tolerance on a basis of limited privilege. How
is the contradiction to be avoided ?

[1] *Report of the Basic Principles Committee* (Karachi, 1952), p. 1.

It is fascinating to watch the development of modern movements in Islam, in which there is an honest attempt to keep the great principles of the religion and at the same time to make it viable in the modern world. In an at present rather confused world of thought four main lines of development may perhaps be distinguished.[1]

First, there is the return to the Koran itself, as distinct from the innumerable traditions which in the course of history have become attached to the name of the Prophet, some of which may be genuine, others of which reflect rather the vicissitudes of Islamic thought in the centuries through which it has passed. It is not difficult to see here a parallel to the cry, " Back to the Bible ", and the revival of " biblical theology " in the Christian world.

The second stream is that of the modern and liberalized lives of the Prophet himself. In these it is not difficult to recognize the influence of the Gospel picture of Jesus Christ, or at least of the criticisms of the character and career of Mohammed which have been made by Western scholars. Harsh traits are a little modified ; difficult episodes are explained away or rendered more acceptable ; and, by a number of subtle changes in the delineation, the Prophet of seventh-century Arabia is transformed into the ideal and the example of modern democratic man. The crop of liberal lives of Jesus presents itself immediately as a parallel.

Thirdly, there is more radical criticism of historical Islam itself and a willingness to subject it to a very thorough reconstruction. This has reached its most notable expression in the writings of two highly distinguished Indians (or Pakistanis, as we should now say)— Sayyid Amir 'Ali, the author of *The Spirit of Islam*, and the poet Sir Mohammed Iqbal (1876–1938). These writers claim the right to accept anything that presents itself as valid in Western thought and scientific discovery, and a corresponding freedom in the re-interpretation of Islam in the light of these new ideas. Sayyid Amir 'Ali goes so far as to argue that polygamy is really forbidden by the Koran ; since, although Mohammed permitted a man to have four wives at any one time, he laid it down that, unless a man could

---

[1] It is difficult to get reliable information about these movements. By far the best book on the subject known to me is H. A. R. Gibb's *Modern Trends in Islam* (Chicago, 1947), but this is already somewhat out of date. A good short account is in A. Guillaume : *Islam* (Pelican Books, London, 1954), pp. 154–91.

treat them all with perfect equality, he must not marry more tha
one ; " As absolute justice in matters of feeling is impossible th
Koranic prescription amounted in reality to a prohibition ".[1] On
has the feeling that, if the interpretations of these high-minded an
courageous writers were accepted, as little would be left of Isla
as was left of Christianity in the hands of Loisy and the Roma
Catholic modernists.

Fourthly, there is a serious attempt to relate the Shari'a, th
traditional Muslim law, to the conditions of modern life, to mitiga
the harsher prescriptions of the law, and above all to bring the statu
of women under Muslim law nearer to that which has prove
acceptable in other civilized societies.

Since all these changes are in living process to-day, it is evide
that the Christian who speaks of " Islam " must do so with gre
caution ; otherwise he may find that he is fifty years out of dat
except in so far as the strongly conservative tendencies of the religiou
teachers in almost all Muslim lands make it possible still to spea
in terms of the traditional Islamic orthodoxy.

The intellectual and religious situation would be complex enoug
in Asia and Africa, even if new ferments of Communism had n
been added to all the other elements in the witch's brew. But th
too must be accepted now as a permanent factor in the situatio
Various enquiries have showed that comparatively few missionarie
had thought it necessary to acquaint themselves with theoretic
Marxism, and that Church leaders as a whole were to a large exter
unaware of the extent to which Communist ideas had penetrate
their flocks. Steps have now been taken to include the study o
Communism in missionary preparation and in theological course
in the various countries of the younger Churches ; and it must no
be taken for granted that this is an indispensable part of the Christian
armoury.

For there is much in Communism to attract young people in a
the newly independent lands, and still more in the countries tha
are still under colonial rule. The peoples of these countries ar
poor, and believe that it is their destiny to become rich. An aur
of heroism surrounds the name of Russia as the one country whic
has succeeded in transforming a nation of poor peasants into a grea
industrial and military power. Of course much of this depends o

---

[1] Quoted by A. Guillaume, *op. cit.*, p. 157.

one of those innumerable mythologies that bedevil our strangely credulous age. It is assumed that nothing had been done to develop Russia before 1917, and the very considerable achievements of the Tsarist age are forgotten. It is forgotten that the early Bolsheviks so successfully destroyed what they had inherited from the Tsars that it was not until 1937 that Russia reached again the standard of living to which it had attained in 1917. Russia has played her cards well. She has persistently posed as the foe of colonialism and the friend of oppressed peoples. Communist propagandists are experts in fomenting every kind of discontent, whether it be that of colonial peoples panting for greater freedom, or young people of the newly independent countries impatient that their governments seem to have slowed down the pace of the revolution to a thoroughly bourgeois crawl. Many in those countries who have never taken the trouble to study Marxist theory (and those who have been thoroughly indoctrinated are probably far more numerous than most Christians imagine) are inclined to believe that the future is in the hands of Communism ; and, whatever else they fail to adopt, they are likely to take over the Communists' rejection of all existing forms of religion.

What is to be the attitude of the younger Church Christian to these vigorous philosophies and religions by which he is surrounded ? One of the common phrases heard in missionary circles to-day is that the non-Christian religions are to be approached with respect. This is an admirable sentiment, but it can be interpreted in far too superficial a sense. It is quite true that direct attack on any one of these religions is likely to lead to vigorous counter-attack. In Muslim countries any criticism of Islam, and in particular anything that can be interpreted as disrespect to the memory of the Prophet, is likely to get the Christian into difficulties with the law. But these are trivialities. We must go far deeper into the matter, if we are to know what our attitude to these other religious systems ought to be to-day.

For these are living systems. What makes them live ? What constitutes their hold over millions of our fellow-creatures ? Here is a dark and mysterious problem for the Christian. The appeal of Jesus Christ, the simplicity, the sublimity, the adequacy of the Christian faith are so self-evident to us that we find it hard to understand how anyone to whom they have been adequately explained can continue to reject them. Yet so it is. A large number of those with whom we have to deal to-day have not lived in heathen darkness; they have studied the Gospels, they have acquainted themselves with the doctrines of the Christian faith, and they have rejected it. Why is this ? Why did Mr. Gandhi so often say, in the later years of his life, that he found in the *Bhagavad Gitā* deeper spiritual values than he found in the Gospels ? Why do so many men of the highest intelligence and integrity devote themselves to the service of religions which we regard as inadequate and out of date ? We may attribute a great deal to sheer conservatism, to the influence of the national movements and their new alliance with the ancient religions ; we may allow something for the purely worldly motives of fear of disapproval, of the loss of friends or influence. We must recognize the power of sheer sinfulness in human affairs, as we must recognize it in our own hearts. But, when all this has been said, it remains true that our friends of these other religious faiths treasure them, defend them, live by them, find spiritual values in them ; and that centuries of faithful Christian witness in these countries has hardly even begun to shake the towers and fortresses of these ancient non-Christian systems.

To say that all this is a mystery is not very helpful. Let us be honest, and say that a large part of the trouble is that we do not know well enough how the minds of the adherents of these religions work to-day. Almost every theological student in the younger Churches has had some training in the classical forms of the religions of his country. This may be even more of a hindrance than a help in coming to grips with the contemporary evangelistic problem. The evangelist to-day has the task of working himself into the mind of those other religions in their contemporary, and that in many cases means fluid and elusive, forms. If he wishes to preach to the Buddhists with any chance of being heard, he must read the books that Buddhists read to-day—not the rather flamboyant manifestos that often pass current in the West as introductions to the esoteric mysteries of the East, but the books that Buddhists really turn to when they feel the need of comfort and illumination. He must listen to their teachers with respect and sympathy. He must think his way into the idiom of their thought. This is no new doctrine. A missionary of considerably earlier date, who had made himself master of the art of lyrical preaching beloved by the Indians, used o sit for a long time before preaching murmuring to himself ; and, when asked what he was doing, explained that he was repeating the *Bhagavad Gītā* to himself, to get into the mood and atmosphere n which he could proclaim the Christian Gospel to Hindus. That was the right spirit. But is it to-day the *Bhagavad Gītā* that we need ? That is precisely the question to which for the most part we do not know the answer.

Herein lies the immense importance of the schools for the study of the ancient religions, which are a characteristic feature of the modern missionary enterprise. The Henry Martyn School of Islamics has for a good many years done yeoman service, both in study, and in making the results of study available to Christians in many fields of service. A society or school for the study of Hinduism s of more recent growth. That for the study of Buddhism has hardly got beyond the stage of planning. There is a danger that such institutions may get lost in the endless labyrinths of the classical literature of those ancient faiths, and so lose their modern relevance. The ancient literatures cannot be neglected, if only because, as we have seen, in each of the great religions there is a movement in favour of return to its own most ancient and purest sources. But the urgent need is for a deeper understanding of what non-Christians are thinking and saying to-day. If these schools can interpret that to us, they will be putting into the hands of the modern Christian evangelist the tools without which he cannot be adequately equipped to bear witness to every man in his own tongue wherein he was born.

If we are so lucky as to reach this deeper understanding, what do we do next ?

We must not let sympathy, or respect, or personal friendship, blind us. Christ is a destroyer as well as a fulfiller. In Him every partial and measured truth will find its full and perfect radiance, but only by passing through the experience of death and resurrection. Christianity is not identical with other faiths. If Jesus is the truth, and His Gospel is the message for all men, then the Word of God as it comes to us through Him is unique, and there is literally no other name under heaven given among men whereby we may be saved. On that we have no right to compromise ; and, in any case, how could anyone who loves our Lord wish to compromise ? But let us not deceive ourselves ; this faith will sooner or later lead us into head-on and inevitable conflict. Many wise people believe that, in the past, controversies between Christian and non-Christian have been about peripheral things—idolatry, polygamy and the rest ; and that the real battle for the soul of men and nations is now just about to begin.

It is already clear that others besides Christians are beginning to be aware of the possibility, indeed of the reality, of conflict. This comes out in an extraordinarily acute and penetrating analysis of the religious situation in India to-day by the outstanding Indian Christian thinker, Dr. P. D. Devanandan :

> Perhaps the most shattering experience to many of us in recent times is the strange and sudden alienation of many of our Hindu friends whom we had looked up to as sympathetic and understanding people, whose religious living we held in esteem, though we could not agree with their credal beliefs. They have expressed severe criticism of our missionary work. They are opposed to it on two scores. One is that Christian evangelism in India is an " anti-Indian activity ". . . . The other school of opposition is led by thoughtful neo-Hindus who denounce the work of Christian evangel-ism on the score that it is contrary to a fundamental axiom of the Hindu belief that all religions finally lead to the same goal, and should therefore be viewed with neutral " tolerance." Such tolerance is fiercely intolerant of what is described as " proselytism," the " giving up " of one religion in order to " go over " into another religion.[1]

It is clear that the controversy over " proselytism " has moved on to new ground. A few years ago the attack was directed against the use of what was regarded as unfair pressure, economic and social, and the appeal to unworthy motives to increase the number of " converts ". Now any attempt to persuade anyone to become a Christian, inwardly and outwardly, is condemned as unnecessary and wrong. The Hindu is prepared to admit the possibility of " conversion ", in the sense of the acceptance of certain new ideas derived from a source outside his own religion ; the idea that such acceptance should lead a man to desert the religion in which he was born is anathema to him. But what is anathema to the Hindu is

---

[1] Paul D. Devanandan : " The Religious and Spiritual Climate of India To-day " in *The Ecumenical Review*, Vol. VIII, No. 3., April 1956, pp. 307–24. The whole of this article deserves the most careful study.

a plain necessity to the Christian. To quote again from Dr. Devanandan :

> When the Hindu talks about a Hindu becoming a Christian by faith he is thinking of accepting certain desirable elements of the Christian creed, torn out of their setting in the total creed. . . . Whereas from the Hindu point of view such acceptance of foreign religious elements to the original core of the Hindu creed is possible, it is not so to the Christian. . . . It would not be possible, for instance, for a Hindu, if he continues to be a Hindu, to accept the claims of the absolute Lordship of Jesus Christ in his personal life, for that would be to bring everything else under the judgment of Jesus Christ as Lord and Saviour. It would not be possible again to continue to be a Hindu and accept the Christian teaching about the Church, which again is a fundamental of the Christian creed. Therefore when a Hindu claims that it is possible for a Hindu to accept the Christian faith and continue to be a Hindu he means accepting not the Christian faith as the Christian understands it, but the Christian faith as the Hindu would have it to be.

This is the challenge which Christian and non-Christian alike have to face. If it means that the climate for evangelism is less favourable than in recent years we had been led to suppose, it is as well to be informed of the realities of the situation, and to recognize that in this respect we are really no worse off than in the past— the natural man has never taken kindly to the demands of the Gospel.

Such, then, is our situation ; for what Dr. Devanandan has written of India can, with only slight retranslation, be made relevant to many areas in the non-Christian world. Have we any idea as to how, in this situation, the realities of the Gospel are to brought home to the non-Christian ? As regards details, the answer must be No. But certain general considerations are already beginning to present themselves as probably valid.

We are being driven to face again the problem of sin, and the nature of redemption from sin. Christianity alone among the great religions faces fearlessly the reality of evil, and recognizes that the remedy must be adequate to the deadliness of the disease. Hinduism tends, like Gnosticism of old, to think that evil is synonymous with ignorance and that knowledge is the way to deliverance. Communism identifies evil with bad social and economic conditions, and, believing in the essential goodness of man, expects the millennium to come when the social revolution has set man free to develop according to the true laws of his being. Islam, for the ordinary Muslim, is so much a matter of outward observance and duty that it is easy for the deeper corruptions of the heart, and with them the deeper problems of forgiveness, to pass unobserved. Buddhism, by dissolving the reality and continuity of the personality to which moral responsibility can attach, dissolves also the idea of sin. To each of these great systems the Christian doctrine of salvation comes as a challenge to reconsider its own foundations.

But how is the challenge to be made effective ? What is the Christian weapon in the inevitable conflict to which we are committed ? The answer is clear. The person of Jesus Christ is our only weapon. We begin to see the points at which the person of Jesus Christ, rightly understood, challenges every system which does not yield full and complete allegiance to Him.

" I am the truth." If Jesus is right in making that claim, then the highest possible experience of truth is in personal encounter. To meet with Jesus is to meet a personal and living God, and to attempt to go beyond this is not to rise higher but to fall back into the lower world of idea and imagination. This is what the Hindu finds hard to accept. Dr. Radhakrishnan puts those religions which hold to a personal God in the second rank of his classification of religions, the first rank being reserved for those which hold that the Ultimate and Supreme Being is impersonal, since personality involves such limitation as is inconsistent with the very idea of the Supreme Being. Clearly this issue is not going to be decided purely by intellectual argument ; perhaps it is only in the experience of living fellowship with the Risen Christ that the answer can be found.

In the approach to the Muslim, more important than anything else is the steady presentation of the figure of Jesus as He is seen in the Gospels. Let the Muslim make his own comparison with Mohammed. It is not for the Christian to insist on the comparison, or to vaunt the superiority of Jesus. If the Muslim himself begins to be influenced by the ethical standards of Jesus, he may find himself gradually led on to a change in his religious convictions. This is, in fact, the recorded experience of almost all converts from Islam. Their attention was first attracted by some action on the part of a Christian that seemed to imply ethical standards other than those with which the Muslim is familiar. From this they were led on to onsider with care the character of Jesus, as the expression and the inspiration of these ethical standards. The question of redemption and reconciliation arose only after allegiance had already been yielded to Jesus as Friend and Master.

For the Buddhist, it would seem that the great discovery must be that of the nature of *Agape*, love as it is seen in Jesus and as it is demanded of His followers. The Buddhist thinks of love generally as no more than one form of desire, and therefore as one of the things that the Enlightened Man must put away from him. The Christian must maintain that desire in itself is not evil, and is given to be transformed into the means of fellowship and of mutual service. But, if the Buddhist can be led to understand the nature of *Agape* as sheer self-giving without demand, he may begin to see that his doctrine of desire and the suppression of desire is too simple, and does not cover all the realities that are present in the revelation of Jesus Christ.

In discussion with the Communist everything would seem to turn on the question of the Resurrection. With many of the Communist ideals of social change and social justice we may find ourselves profoundly in sympathy. The difference is on the issues of perspective. Communist theory can be accepted as true and complete only on the materialist assumption that time and those things which exist in time are the only realities. But, if Jesus is risen from the dead and has brought life and immortality to light through the Gospel, then the Communist perspective is false ; and the falseness of the perspective distorts even those parts of his doctrine which might otherwise be true. We are reminded of the profound saying of Coleridge : " Not without celestial observations can even terrestrial charts be accurately constructed "—a remark in which is contained in germ the Christian affirmation against every form of materialism and of humanism which leaves out God.

Such may be the bare bones of the Christian approach to the non-Christian systems of to-day. But who is to clothe these bare bones in flesh and sinew, and so to breathe upon them that they come alive, that arid principle becomes a living proclamation of the Gospel ?

It has to be admitted that at the present time the younger Churches are ill-supplied with interpreters. The great majority of our Christian leaders were the children of Christian parents and were brought up in a Christian atmosphere. This means that they

know the non-Christian systems from without, and have had to
learn their traditions and philosophies almost as a foreigner has to
learn them. Few of these leaders, with their many responsibilitie
in the Church, have had time, or the sense of vocation, to maste
the intricacies of non-Christian thought. The same applies to mis
sionaries. For the last two generations almost all missionaries have
been missionaries to Christians, swamped with the innumerabl
tasks they have had to perform within the Church, and in training
the leaders who should in time replace the missionary. A change i
on the way ; it is coming to be realized that a better understanding
of the climate of thought in the non-Christian world is a necessar
part of the training both of missionary and of national leader. Bu
it will take time for this change to have its full effect. And still w
suffer under the grave disadvantage that we come to these system
and to their life as strangers and from outside.

It has often been remarked that the great thinkers of the Earl
Church were men who had come to the Christian faith as adul
converts after making a career in the non-Christian world. Amon
the Greeks we may mention Justin Martyr, who found faith i
Christ as the term of a long pilgrimage in the philosophic world o
his day. Among the Latins, Tertullian, Cyprian, Ambrose an
Augustine had all pursued with success a secular career, Tertullia
and Cyprian as lawyers, Ambrose as a government servant, Augustin
as a teacher of rhetoric. These men brought with them into th
Church a full knowledge and experience of the pagan world an
all its ways. It was their aim to interpret the faith to the men o
their day. The vigour of their writing and the generous range o
their speculations justifies the saying that the Church survive
because the Christians not merely out-lived and out-died, but als
out-thought, their contemporaries.

Is it impossible that God should give us such converts to-day
The two men who in this century have left a mark on the India
Church as poets, Narayan Vaman Tilak and H. A. Krishna Pilla
both grew up in orthodox high-caste Hindu surroundings, and ha
strong anti-Christian prejudices to overcome. It was both the rich
ness of their Hindu culture and the strength of their attachment t
the Hindu tradition that, after conversion, gave them such powe
as Christian witnesses. We need many such to-day to reinforce th
ranks of the existing Christian scholars—men and women who hav

lived the full life of those other faiths and known them through and through, and can interpret them both to us and to their fellow-countrymen, in the light of that Christ whom they have found to be the end of the imperfect striving of all men after truth, and the peace in which all men can rest.

CHAPTER 9

WHICH WAY DO WE GO?

*B*UT *when these things begin to come to pass, look up, and lift up your heads ; because your redemption draweth nigh.*[1] That should always be the attitude of the Christian in time of trouble. It is still true that man's extremity is God's opportunity.

We have tried to be honest about the situation by which the Church is faced to-day. It is full of difficulties. The Church is divided by bamboo and iron curtains. In some countries it is faced by persecution, in others by the limitation of freedom to evangelize. As always its spiritual resources seem hopelessly inadequate to the task that God has laid upon it. All this is true. But there is a regrettable tendency in some Church circles to-day to sit down and moan about our difficulties. We shall regard these as particularly great only if we forget the history of the past, and the problems by which our predecessors were faced. Carey and his friends held on for thirty years in the tiny Danish settlement of Serampore, because freedom to preach the Gospel in British territory was not fully granted until 1833. Morrison completed his Chinese New Testament and Dictionary, at a time when the interior of China was completely closed to the foreigner, and missionaries held on only with some difficulty on the fringes. Older people will still remember the shiver of horror which went through the Christian world at the first assassination of Protestant missionaries in China in 1895, and the far worse shock, as news came through of the death of hundreds of missionaries and thousands of Chinese Christians in the Boxer troubles at the turn of the century. Our predecessors had their problems and we have ours. Our business, as theirs, is not to moan, but like practical men and women to sit down and say, " What are the possibilities to-day ? In this situation, where do we go from here ? "

The first thing which is evident is that all our thinking to-day must be ecumenical. In the political field we are painfully aware

[1] Luke 21 : 28.

that we live in one world. An event in some distant part of the
world may set our house aflame. Economic dislocation in another
country may send our economy reeling. We have not quite so
clearly realized this in the affairs of the Church. But such great
events as the Evanston Assembly of the World Council of Churches
in 1954 have brought home to innumerable people the interdependence of the Churches, and the real unity of life and purpose which
underlies their many divisions.

Unhappily the division of the ecumenical movement itself
into halves renders genuinely ecumenical thinking extremely difficult. Everyone knows that the modern ecumenical movement, as
represented in the World Council of Churches, grew out of the
missionary movement. Its first great manifestation was the first
World Missionary Conference, Edinburgh 1910, to which we have
so often referred. But the World Council of Churches and the
International Missionary Council are still separate organizations ;
it has not yet proved possible to co-ordinate the inner life of the
Churches with their missionary outreach, though each of these
world-wide bodies exists " in association with " the other, and progress towards their ultimate unification has of late been much more
promising than many friends of both halves of the movement had
ventured to hope for.

Much Church history lies behind this division. It is the tragic
fact that the Churches which issued from the Reformation have
on the whole not been in the least interested in the evangelization
of the world. The Protestant Churches were two centuries behind
the Roman Catholic in the beginning of their missionary work in
Africa and the East. Even then " missions " were not on the whole
the work of the Churches but of special groups and societies, for
which the Church took no responsibility, and which in many cases
it regarded with a certain amount of disfavour. This situation has
continued until our own day, especially in Germany, in Holland,
and in Switzerland. Even in England, where the connection of the
missionary societies of the Church of England with their Church
has been far closer than in the other countries just named, missionary
work has been far more the interest of certain special groups than
the outreach of the Church as a whole. In consequence, when
missionary councils joined to form the International Missionary
Council, it did not follow that they would in every case have their

Churches behind them. And when the Churches joined to form the World Council of Churches, it was by no means certain that they would carry into that world organization the necessary passion for the evangelization of the world.

Schizophrenia is an uncomfortable abnormality which ought not to be allowed to continue any longer than is absolutely necessary. It is to be hoped that the two great international organizations will ultimately find their way to unity, and that thus a genuinely ecumenical outlook will be made possible for the Churches. But this cannot be brought about simply by diplomacy. It is not just a case of amalgamating two organizations which happen to have grown up on rather different lines. The changes that need to take place are far more radical than that, and, in my opinion, cannot be described in any terms other than those of conversion.

There is first the conversion of the Churches.

There are certain Churches, such as the Methodist Church in Britain and the Presbyterian Church in the United States of America, which are in the happy position that their " missionary society " is simply the Church in missionary action ; the distinction between mission and Church does not exist in the " sending country ", though even some of these admirable bodies have lamentably brought it into existence in " the field ". Nevertheless, there are very few Churches in the world, Catholic, Protestant or Orthodox, older or younger, which it would be safe to describe as missionary-hearted. This is not simply a question of the number of missionary sermons preached, or the number of dollars raised for the missionary budget. It goes far deeper than that. A Church is missionary-hearted only if it lives daily and hourly in the conviction that world-wide witness is that very thing for which the Church exists, and by its engagement in which it manifests the reality of its being. A Church is a missionary Church only if every single part of its life and its organization is related to this central principle. And a Church which is not a missionary Church has only slender claims to the name of Church, however orthodox its doctrine and however impeccable the apostolic succession of its ministry.

The Churches give themselves away in their grudging attitude towards missionary vocation, if it happens to hit young people who are regarded as specially promising. Once again, to quote the Whitby findings :

It has to be recognized with regret that many Churches have never yet taken seriously the obligation to make the Gospel known throughout the world, and accept grudgingly, if at all, the duty to help the younger Churches by making available for service overseas the ablest men and women in their own ranks. There are still cases in which leaders in the Church discourage rather than promote recruitment among those best suited for missionary service. These things ought not to be.[1]

Those hard words were not written hastily or without due consideration ; they were based on extensive acquaintance with the facts. Some years ago I compared notes with three colleagues by some years my juniors, all of them men of great distinction whose names are known throughout the world ; we found that the experience of all of us had been the same, in that we had undertaken service overseas only in the face of the strongest discouragement from the authorities of our respective Churches. It may be that the situation has changed for the better in the last thirty years, but I have little reason to think that it has so changed.

The Roman Catholic Church has the great advantage that it does not have to ask its servants where they would like to go. Most Christians of other Churches would feel that the drawbacks attendant on this kind of discipline outweigh its advantages. But freedom cannot be exercised without responsibility ; and it is the sense of responsibility for the evangelization of the world that often seems so sadly lacking in the non-Roman Catholic Churches. It is essential that the freedom of the individual should not be circumscribed by undue pressure. But there are few theological colleges and seminaries, in older or younger Churches, in which it can be taken for granted that every single man will have seriously considered the possibility of service overseas, and will accept an appointment nearer home only if considerations of health or family responsibility make it clear that he cannot accept the call to service where the need is greatest.

The Churches need to be converted on the subject of division and unity. It is a commonplace that the aim of the ecumenical movement is the unity and renewal of the Church. It is equally a commonplace that the call for Church union is coming most strongly from the lands of the younger Churches. It is certainly not the case

[1] *Renewal and Advance*, p. 175.

that Church union is among the primary interests of Churches in the Western world.

For this there are many reasons, not least among them the extraordinary difficulty of the enterprise of Church union. But, in consequence, there is grave anxiety among friends of the ecumenical movement, lest it lose, or may already have lost, its impetus in the direction of unity. A great part of the work of the World Council of Churches is carried on in the field of what before 1948 was called " Life and Work ". The measure of co-operation obtained in these fields undoubtedly appears to many sincere Christians to be the measure of the unity that we need or can stand at the present time, and there is apparent a certain lack of interest in going farther. Is there not a danger that the division of " Faith and Order ", the express concern of which is the unity of the Church, may be swallowed up or hidden under other and superficially more pressing concerns ? The note of alarm has recently been sounded by an acute Roman Catholic observer. He points out that, whereas the aim of the union of the two movements in 1948 was to bring the special interests of each to bear on all the concerns of the other, there is a real danger that the practically minded, who are likely to be the majority in any large concern, may come to regard the theological studies tending towards unity of faith as a luxury more troublesome than useful, and may feel under no obligation to take seriously the results of these studies. The leaders of the World Council have always emphatically denied that there was any danger of the submergence of " Faith and Order " ; but perhaps they have underestimated the dangers involved in the marriage of " Faith and Order " to its slightly older and stronger partner " Life and Work ".[1]

It is not the business of the World Council of Churches to press for any particular form of union, or to issue instructions to the Churches. It is its business incessantly and clearly to recall to the Churches the meaning of " the proclamation of the whole Gospel to the whole world by the whole Church ". It is in the light of that supreme obligation that many of our present divisions seem unreasonable and irrelevant. It is not that we are called to unity, for our own sake, by the almost desperate situation of the Church

[1] See *Vers l'Unité Chrétienne*, No. 82, April 1956, pp. 2–3 ; issued by the Dominicans of Istina, Boulogne-sur-Seine, France.

in the world ; we are called to it for the sake of Christ, the fulfilment of whose good purpose for His world is constantly being
frustrated by the divisions in His Church.

Now to affirm this urgency of union is not to say that any or
every kind of union is in itself good. Unity is to be sought not for
the sake of unity, but " that the world may believe " ; and, if at
any point the choice is clearly between unity and truth, it is
truth that must unhesitatingly be followed. Yet " loyalty to truths
received " should not be used as the final argument against enter-
taining the possibility that in Christ there may be a fuller truth
than any of us has attained in separation.

Furthermore, it is not to be supposed that union can be attained
without sacrifice. It is as impossible to create a united Church,
retaining in every detail the form, the spirit and the traditions of
each of the uniting Churches, as it is to make an omelette of billiard
balls. It is as impossible for each of two uniting Churches to retain
its individual independence as it is for the two partners who enter
into a marriage. It seems that true freedom can be won only at the
price of the surrender of individual independence. The extreme
hesitancy that some Churches manifest in relation to direct negotia-
tions for Church union, in contrast to their willingness to enter into
endless and indefinite theological discussions of the same, may be
in fact an expression of their fear as to what would happen to old
and beloved traditions, if the decision to unite with others was once
irrevocably made.

But Church union is no longer a theory. In many countries it
is an accomplished fact. In Canada, in Japan, in South India,
united Churches of very different types have existed long enough
to be tested by the vicissitudes of time and to have given proof of
continuing vitality. None of these united Churches is perfect ; each
has shown signs at certain points of hurried workmanship. Yet each
has survived ; each desires to reach out into wider fellowships ; those
who have had experience of union affirm with no uncertain
tone that the gains are greater than the losses, and that there
can be no question of going back to the antecedent situation of
disunity.

In this connection the recent history of the Church of Christ
in Japan is specially interesting. That Church, the Nippon Kirisuto
Kyodan, came into existence in the war period under considerable

pressure from the government, and for a time included in itself the great majority of the non-Roman denominations in Japan. With the end of the war and the relaxation of external pressure many of the more confessionally distinctive groups, notably the Anglicans [1] and the Lutherans, and even some of the Presbyterians, withdrew from the Kyodan. This was not unnatural. In order to accommodate so large a number of groups, and living under the difficult conditions of unfriendly government control, the Kyodan had contented itself with a minimum statement of faith, such as was not likely to satisfy those who believe that formal credal statements are the very basis of the Church's life. Even within the groups (Methodist, Presbyterian and Congregationalist) which continued in the Kyodan after the war, there was no clear agreement as to what should be done ; Congregationalists tend to dislike credal statements, and believe that the best safeguard of the Church's life is loyalty to the Spirit of Jesus Christ ; others feel strongly that in a non-Christian country the lines of Christian faith and profession must be clearly and sharply drawn.

In view of the past history, it was a triumph of the spirit of Christian unity when in October 1954 the Eighth General Assembly of the Kyodan almost unanimously adopted the Confession of Faith prepared by its Executive Board. The Confession is a brief document, which, after four clauses dealing with the authority of Scripture, the nature of the triune God, redemption through Christ, and the nature and task of the Church, ends up with the Apostles' Creed, thus taking its stand alongside the historic confessions of the Christian Churches through the ages.

As interesting as the Confession itself are the comments of Japanese leaders upon it. The Moderator of the Church, Dr. Takeshi Muto, writes :

> In spite of all these counter-factors, being together and working together for fourteen years in the name of our Lord Jesus Christ irresistibly drew us together in matters of faith. Our sense of difference faded away, misunderstandings were cleared and the sense of unity was greatly strengthened. Such being the case, not a single member Church seceded from the Kyodan on account of the adoption of this Confession.

---

[1] Only a part of the Nippon Sei Kokwai, the Anglican Church in Japan, had joined the Kyodan.

Dr. Muto quotes from Professor Ken Ishihara, the Chairman of the drafting committee, as follows :

> It is, I think, a great significant event for the Kyodan that it has come to adopt the Confession of Faith fourteen years after its birth. It is significant, because the Kyodan has by now grown in unity so that it is confident that the time has come when it can stand up as one unitary Church confessing one common faith. It is significant because in declaring the Confession which is elaborated in such a definite form as cannot be easily modified, the Kyodan as a historical and responsible existent faces squarely the rest of the world. . . . In this objective presentation of our Confession we are showing to the world that we are no longer self-complacent subjectivists who are under the influence of mysticism.[1]

It would hardly be possible to find, in the whole literature of Christian union, a better description of the process of growing together that must continue for generation after the union has actually taken place. At the same time, it has to be recognized that every one of these unions presents a challenge to the Churches throughout the Christian world. The repercussions on the world-wide Anglican Communion of the union effected in South India are too well known to need detailed discussion. Some years ago, I referred to this union as " A Dangerous Experiment " ; [2] the violence of the partisanship, for and against the new Church, which has raged within the Anglican Churches, indicates that the term was not ill-chosen. But this is only one example of the kind of challenge that is certain to come in increasing volume from the younger Churches to the older and from one part of the world to another ; " It is not now a case of finding arguments in favour of union ; it is for you to find a reasoned and acceptable defence for remaining in separation ".

Church union cannot be hurried. Precipitate action is likely to lead only to a new fission. Those are right who maintain that the problem must be viewed in the light of the whole world situation and not only in relation to particular local needs or advantages. Yet it is clear that all the Churches everywhere are being called to take the problem far more seriously than ever before, and to recognize

[1] See *The Ecumenical Review*, Vol. VIII, No. 2, Jan. 1956, pp. 201–2.
[2] In *Christian Partnership* (S.C.M. Press, 1952).

that failure to act, when the Spirit moves, may be in fact positive disobedience to the will of the Lord.

Second only to the conversion of the Churches is the need for the conversion of the missionary societies and the mission boards.

These bodies have rendered wonderful service, and without them there would be no younger Churches to-day. Yet such bodies can become rigid, set in their ways, unresponsive to new needs, and sensitively jealous of any infringement of their own independence and sovereignty. Just because they are mainly located in the West, they tend to be imperfectly aware of the changed climate in the lands of the younger Churches, and in some measure unresponsive to the revolution that is going ahead in Church and State. These are days in which situations change so quickly that immediate decision and resolute action are needed. It is hard to imagine any organ of Christian action less fitted for immediate decision and resolute action than the several hundred mission boards scattered in all the Christian countries of the West.

It would be unfair not to recognize the great progress that has been made in the direction of responsible and co-operative action.

From a very early date there was a good deal of close co-operation between missionary leaders in the West, but this was not always clearly reflected in their activities in the field. Missionaries were so used to division at home that it hardly seemed odd to them that fifteen different missionary societies should be working in Madras. The first step towards better understanding was the establishment of the principle of comity—that missions would not steal one another's sheep, and that they would not establish work in areas where others had already staked out their claim. Agreement was never complete. And comity could not prevent one Church from following its members into the territory of another ; could an Anglican leave good Anglicans destitute in bare pastures presided over only by Baptist shepherds ? As Bishop Newbigin has pointed out, with the increasing mobility of Christians, the Churches were faced with the alternatives of either developing the complete Western denominational set-up in every city, or moving towards Church union. In South India they chose Church union.

The next stage was that of Missionary and Christian Councils in the East, and Conferences of Missionary Societies in the West.

It is astonishing to reflect that, with some few exceptions, all these instruments of co-operation date from the period after 1921. There had been earlier conferences and much good will ; but the establishment of permanent instruments of Christian co-operation is an achievement of this generation. What the missions did before these existed it is difficult now to imagine—they have rooted themselves so firmly in almost every country as a natural part of the Christian landscape.

Great joint enterprises, such as the Christian Medical College at Vellore in South India, have brought many missions together in fellowship, not always without dust and heat. The support of the " orphaned missions " during the war was a splendid example of such co-operation as has later flowered into Inter-Church Aid. The new villages, into which the government was gathering the population in Malaya, presented a remarkable challenge to the Christian forces. Many missionaries who had been recently expelled from China were available for service. The speed with which the challenge was taken up indicates a flexibility of missionary planning such as has not always been evident in the past.

After the second world war, when Japan again became open to missionary endeavour, the principal American mission boards with interests in Japan formed a co-operative committee, in order that aid to the Japanese Churches should be co-ordinated, and should come as the offering of a fellowship rather than as subsidies offered by individual Churches.

The Lutherans, more practical and intelligent than others, have gone ahead of all other denominations in forming a committee of the Lutheran World Federation for world mission. This has already shown its effectiveness in helping to make funds and personnel available in the places where they are most needed and could best be used, and in planning the first all-African Christian Conference to be held on African soil.

The Anglican Churches have now an Advisory Council on Missionary Strategy of the Lambeth Conference, which has been in existence since 1948, and has met once in the last eight years. Its influence on the missionary strategy of the Anglican Communion has so far been less than revolutionary, but, with the next meeting of the Lambeth Conference due in 1958, its influence is likely considerably to increase.

U.T.—7*

All these signs of a more ecumenical outlook are encouraging. But how much there still is to set on the other side—how much adherence to traditional methods, and how great an unwillingness to launch out into the unknown.

Some years ago a young friend of mine accepted a temporary appointment in a theological seminary in one of the most strategic centres of the whole Christian world. It happened that he belonged to a different family of Churches from that responsible for the seminary. His own Church, so far from rejoicing in this venture of devoted and sacrificial service, warned the young man that his action was highly irregular, and might jeopardize his chances of ordination on return to his own country.

In 1951, a new Anglican province of West Africa was formed. The diocese of Liberia did not enter into it, since all its connections are with the Protestant Episcopal Church of the United States, whereas the other five dioceses are the fruit of the work of British missionary societies.

And so on and so on. The fact is that, though we talk a good deal about " ecumenical missions ", we have hardly begun even to think of what is involved in the idea.

Let us recognize at once that the difficulties in the way of intimate co-operation are formidable. We are divided, and it is only when we come together that we feel the full force and curse of our divisions. In such united institutions as those referred to earlier in this chapter, the question of intercommunion cannot be shelved. Some Churches readily accept intercommunion ; some admit it with hesitation ; others, like the Syrian Orthodox Church of South India, do not permit it at all. Great charity is needed on both sides, if this issue, which comes up intermittently as the ecumenical scandal at world conferences but in a united institution has to be lived with day by day, is not to become a source of division and embitterment on both sides.

Most interdenominational missions have side-stepped this difficulty by organizing themselves regionally according to the difference of Church tradition and practice. This way out was discovered long ago by the prudence of Hudson Taylor of the China Inland Mission ; the Anglicans were all packed off to West China, where they could not get into much mischief, and could later be provided with a bishop and their own episcopal organization. The Sudan United

Mission in Nigeria works on similar lines. Let it be recognized that this represents only a rather diffused and etiolated ecumenism.

The heart of the difficulty, however, is the unwillingness of mission boards and other authorities to make any surrender of their own autonomy and sovereignty, and to recognize that the day of racial and denominational missions is nearing its end. Can anyone accustomed to read the signs of the times doubt that this is really so ? This is in no contradiction to the need, which has elsewhere been so often stressed, of a great and immediate increase in the number of whole-time missionaries abroad ; it is a question of the means and of the channels through which their services are to be made available to the younger Churches that need and ask for their help.

If a question is put frankly to the younger Churches, as to the means that are acceptable to them, there can be little doubt as to the answer that will be received. It is far easier for them to accept help which comes to them through an international organization than that which comes from a single country and through the channels of a single Church. This accounts for the popularity of the Inter-Church Aid idea.

Inter-Church Aid comes through the World Council of Churches, a world-wide body, *in which most of the Churches which receive help are themselves members*. The aid given is usually commendably free from denominational and other strings. How different this is from the pattern of missionary aid, as it has been given in the past, and as it continues into the present ! The younger Churches have never felt themselves to be *members* on equal terms of the missionary societies on which they have been dependent for financial and other aid.

Other factors in the situation to-day tell heavily in favour of a more ecumenical attitude. Missionaries from certain countries are unacceptable to certain Churches, because of past colonial connections and the prejudices that these have left behind. Some countries have missionary candidates for whom they have no immediate outlet, and inadequate funds to support them if an outlet were found. Other societies have an urgent need for missionaries and funds to support them, but cannot find suitable candidates in their own country. Only central planning can bring needs, men and money into a satisfactory relationship.

The strongest argument of all in favour of changed methods is the unparalleled urgency of the situation. Wise planners have always known that the time might be short. To-day this is more than ever evident. Within a few years younger Churches all over the world may be cut off from the help of their friends elsewhere. A few years are given during which the older Churches can help the younger in the provision of better theological training, of more adequate Christian literature, and of an indigenous leadership spiritually equipped to face the dangers of isolation in a hostile world. In many parts of Africa the penetration of Islam is once again becoming the dominant factor in the situation, and, unless the Christian forces can be greatly and immediately strengthened, the race will be lost to Islam. If ever there was a time for strategic thinking and planning, for the cutting of old red-tape, and for resolute and co-ordinated action, it is to-day.

If Churches and missions were to begin to take this challenge seriously, they would not even have to create new machinery. The machinery is already there. The International Missionary Council has more than thirty years' experience of world-wide survey, of pioneer research in many directions, and in the organization of world missionary conferences. It has no authority and no executive power. Mission boards are so touchy on the subject that it has only rarely ventured even to give advice, and even then has scarcely dared to raise its voice above a whisper. If the missions and the younger Churches really wished to work co-operatively, all that would be needed would be to strengthen the International Missionary Council and to give it a measure of authority. No other body is so well equipped to discern where the urgent opportunities of the day are to be found, to indicate what steps should be taken, and roughly what they would cost ; to suggest which Churches should be asked to supply the needed workers, and which should be invited to help with the necessary funds. An autocratic central body is unthinkable. But little is gained by giving such a central body advisory powers, if it is likely that its advice will in all circumstances be disregarded. And to give even a general undertaking to consider advice from above involves a limitation on the sovereign authority of missions and Churches.

From my acquaintance with mission boards and Churches, it seems to me most unlikely that they will take such steps as would make " ecumenical missions " on a large scale a possibility in any measurable future. It is much more likely that the non-Roman bodies will elect to continue in their present state of chaotic ineffectiveness, leaving to the Roman Catholic Church the advantages of central planning and of steady and methodical advance.

We pass on to the conversion of the congregation. It has become an accepted principle in ecumenical thinking that the instrument of evangelistic advance should be the Church and not the individual. In this connection the Church means principally the worshipping group. That group cannot be effective in evangelism unless it manifests a quality of life and fellowship superior to anything that is to be found in the world outside ; unless it is conscious of the world-wide fellowship to which it belongs ; and unless it really is convinced that it is the will of God that the Gospel should be preached to every creature.

Unhappily it is all too easy for the congregation to become inbred and sufficient unto itself, either because it has become too closely integrated with a nominally Christian society, or because it has lost the points of natural contact with the non-Christian society that surrounds it.

The former situation can easily arise in a wholly Christian village in India or on a Pacific island. The village is the congregation. Its festivals are the festivals of the Church, which have long since replaced those of heathen days. The school is the mission school, and the Church is the only purveyor of culture. Speech has become penetrated, and perhaps corrupted, by biblical turns of phrase unknown to the non-Christians. All are connected by the ties of relationship and common interest. There is no very obvious and immediate sphere of evangelistic activity, and Christian life can degenerate into the complacent and not very exacting sanctification of the *status quo*.

The contrary situation is that of the small Christian group in the city, eastern or western, where the majority of people are pre-Christian or post-Christian. The worshippers come from widely separated areas in the city. What holds them together is the Church. They have no other common social root, and no Christian activity other than those directly connected with the Church. They may be too weak to hope as a community to exercise any influence on municipal affairs. If opposition is strong, as in Muslim lands, they

may almost have lost hope of expansion through individual conversion. In such circumstances the merit of even continuing to
exist is so great that it may seem to be all that can be asked of the
group ; and its members feel that they have done well, if they have
done no more than to support and encourage one another in the
difficult task of holding on to the Christian faith.

These are extreme cases. But inbreeding and lack of interest
in the world outside are no monopoly of any one type or form of
Christian congregation ; they seem to be almost endemic in the
Christian world. What is to be done about it ? Where can conversion start ?

The best starting-point is a revolution in the worship of the
group. All true Christian worship is ecumenical, since it is the
ceaseless worship of the whole Church in heaven and earth, into
which for a few brief moments each worshipping group is privileged
to enter. This great idea can easily be lost or deformed. Protestant
worship is all too often directed to the edification of that particular
group, assembled for worship at that particular moment—as though
the Church ceased to exist between services, and had to be called
back into existence by a new " event ". " Catholic " worship can
all too easily degenerate into a mystical individualism, as expressed
in that abominable phrase " making my communion ", which is
still too often heard. Just how each group is to be brought back
into the reality of ecumenical worship is a problem for each de-
nomination and each minister ; but there are worse ways of starting
than a discriminating use and exposition of the Hymnal.

The second point of attack is information. Every now and then
the Church becomes news. Billy Graham and Dr. Schweitzer occa-
sionally make the headlines, and that is all to the good. But the
ordinary churchgoer knows surprisingly little of what is going on
in the world-wide Church. Of the thousands who have read of
the Mau Mau troubles in the press, how many have understood
anything of the heroism and suffering of faithful Christians in those
hard times, or have realized that their sufferings, with the sufferings
of Christ, have gone into the cup which is offered to us as the Cup
of blessing ?

The problem of Christian information is admittedly very difficult. How are people, whose ordinary horizons are narrow and
limited, to be brought into living touch with a world-wide Church ?

How is the news to be selected and how is it to be distributed ? The greater part of the religious press is inevitably sectarian, and fulfils a responsibility in relation rather to one communion than to the Oikoumene. Language adds other difficulties ; however regrettable, it is not altogether surprising that the names of Nommensen, the German pioneer among the Bataks of Sumatra, and of Skrefsrud, the Norwegian apostle of the Santals, are hardly known in Britain, even among those whose missionary interest is keen. There has certainly been improvement in recent years, with the wider use of the Ecumenical Press service and other such inter-confessional sources of information.[1] But the non-Roman Churches have a long way to go before they reach the high level of presentation and the effectiveness of distribution that are characteristic of the Roman Catholic Church, especially perhaps in France.

Worship, knowledge—and so we come finally, like St. Paul, to finance, the collection for the saints. Money is not everything, but it is a very useful thing ; and the world-wide expansion of the Church, now as always, is being held up by financial starvation. Few lay people seem to be aware of the seriousness of this factor, but a moment's reflection on the fall in the value of money would make the situation clear. Let us take one single illustration. The Church Missionary Society, by immense efforts, has managed to keep its income above the half-million mark. This means that it is able to do about two-fifths or less of the work which it was able to do a generation ago, when its income first reached that figure.[2] The class which in the past has mainly supported the overseas work of the Church is that which has been hardest hit by inflation and by the new burdens of taxation. The new rich are for the most part not interested, and new money is difficult to find.

All problems of missionary finance would be solved if every congregation, in older and younger Churches alike, decided that all the offerings in church on the first Sunday in the month should go to Christian work outside its own limits. Here I am not thinking only of missionary work in the ordinary sense of the term. I include the care of the sick and the aged, refugees, church building elsewhere,

[1] *The National Christian Council Review* (of India) is a good example of a periodical which makes judicious use of such ecumenical material.
[2] Income from all sources in 1913–14, £479,650 ; income from all sources in 1955, £533,371.

and all the innumerable purposes for which Christian money is required. I am sure that any congregation which set out to walk upon the waters in this way would be upheld. I am sure that the Lord would pour forth such a blessing that there would not be room enough to receive it (Malachi 3 : 10). My acquaintance with church-wardens and stewards and other lay officers of the Church does not lead me to suppose that this revolutionary proposal will be widely adopted, and I do not think that the storehouses and barns of the congregations are likely to be seriously overstrained.

So we come, lastly, to the conversion of the individual. Here I am not referring to the initial seed of faith in Christ, but to that later stage, when the individual should accept responsible steward-ship for the good gifts of God in relation to the Church and to the world. The rediscovery of the significance of the layman in the life of the Church is one of the major aspects of the ecumenical movement to-day. Even to summarize the extensive study projects which have been put in hand would occupy more space than we can spare, and we must limit our consideration to the single aspect of the Christian layman overseas.

" Every Christian a witness " is a sound New Testament prin-ciple. What is its application in modern times ?

In spite of the recession of " colonialism ", more citizens of the nominally Christian countries are residing in non-Christian coun-tries than ever before. It is believed that the number of British civilians in India is actually greater to-day than it was before Indian independence. Clearly this should be the great striking force of the Christian cause. All history lamentably shows that the nominal Christian who fails to live up to the standards of his religion is a greater hindrance than anything else could possibly be to the proclamation of the Christian faith.

Nothing in recent developments of Christian service is more interesting than such projects as " Overseas Service " in Britain [1] and similar efforts in Holland, the aim of which is to prepare those who are going to live abroad in purely secular capacities for adjust-ment to their new surroundings, and to bring home to them the

---

[1] It is impossible for reasons of space to give here details of this extraordinarily interesting and promising venture. A note to the Director, Dr. Harry Holland, Moor Park College, Farnham, Surrey, will probably be rewarded by literature giving the details for which there is not space here.

possibilities and responsibilities of Christian commitment in unfamiliar surroundings.   So far such efforts have been on a small
scale ;   their potential value is incalculable.   The paid Christian
worker is always to some extent the object of suspicion ;   the layman,
who has no professional interest in the Church, can bear Christian
witness in many places to which the professional Christian has no
access, and all the more effectively because the genuineness of his
testimony, spoken or unspoken, is more readily accepted.

This is no new idea.   A hundred years ago the great generation
of administrators and soldiers who had come under the influence of
the Evangelical revival bore uncompromising witness to their faith,
on the principle laid down by John Lawrence that " Christian things,
done in a Christian way, will never give offence " ;   and almost
compelled the missionary societies to advance and to take up work
in newly opened regions, when the societies would perhaps have
preferred to advance more cautiously.

There is another type of Christian witness not to be confused
with the general Christian faithfulness to which reference has just
been made.   A considerable number of young Christians would
like to serve Christ abroad, but hesitate to engage in whole-time
missionary service, because they do not see how their professional
qualifications would fit in with such service, or from an exaggerated
idea of the drawbacks of being a paid and labelled Christian, or
from a sense of special vocation to some other form of service.   For
such there seem to be unlimited openings in the international teams
of such bodies as the World Health Organization ;   in the building
of dams ;   in the great projects of reconstruction and resettlement.
We have already alluded to the need for reliable and incorruptible
administration in such projects.   No one who believes that the earth
is the Lord's and the fulness thereof can doubt that there is a truly
spiritual aspect to the harnessing of the forces that He has created
for the service of man, and that the Christian engaged in such
service can render a twofold witness—by the integrity of his life,
and by bringing to light that spiritual foundation of the work to
which the eyes of others may be blind.   Those who accept such
service as a Christian vocation must do so with their eyes open,
and must be prepared for a great deal of frustration.   On many
projects the foreigner does not stay long enough to make intimate
contact with the people of the land ;   on others he finds his lot cast

so much with other foreigners (also no doubt in need of Christian witness !) that his opportunities for acquaintance with " the natives " are few and far between. And he must accept from the start the painful fact that, in our neo-pagan society, any Christian, not merely the professional Christian, is so marked in the eyes of his fellows, that he will have almost as high a barrier to climb as the full-time chaplain or missionary. His advantage is that he is likely to spend most of his time in places where both chaplains and missionaries are unknown ; he is fooling himself if he imagines that his task as a Christian will be in any way easier than theirs.

All this non-professional Christian activity is most ardently to be encouraged. But it must not be imagined that it will do what it cannot do. I sometimes fear that we may be rationalizing our failures. Over the last thirty years most missionary societies have failed to find adequate recruits for missionary service. We have therefore tended to say that for the moment we do not require more missionaries, but that the needed work will be done by the non-professional Christian layman. This is not true. What the non-professionals can render is a splendid service, but it is not *the same service* as that of the whole-time missionary. A thousand non-professionals cannot do the work that can be done by a single missionary in a sphere which is his and is not theirs. What the situation calls for is a great many more whole-time and dedicated missionaries, who are prepared to give the whole of their lives to this special vocation.

Lest this may seem unduly restrictive, a word must be put in in favour of another vocation different from that of the permanent missionary. Arrangements are being increasingly made for exchanges, through which a leader in a younger Church serves for a year or more in the West,[1] and a Western leader serves for a limited period in a younger Church, usually in a theological seminary or some similar institution, where a Western language is currently used. Of the mutual enrichment provided by such exchanges there can be no possible doubt. But such temporary supplies do not meet the central need.

It is from the younger Churches themselves that the demand

[1] For instance, at the moment of writing Dr. P. D. Devanandan, from whom we have quoted a number of times, is serving as a professor on the staff of Union Theological Seminary, New York.

for more missionaries is now beginning to come. At a certain point in the attainment of independence, a younger Church is likely to feel that the foreigner is merely an encumbrance from the past, a hindrance to " our being ourselves ". With increasing wisdom, and particularly if the evangelistic task comes to be seen in all its amplitude, the attitude changes. The foreigner, who was formerly feared as a rival, comes to be welcomed as a colleague, and his contribution is valued as one expression of the genuinely ecumenical nature of the Church.

How, then, is the missionary challenge to be presented to the younger Christians in the West of to-day ?

The romantic appeal must be firmly rejected. Orchid-gatherers and uranium prospectors can outbid the Church at all times in this field. In any case, it was never a satisfactory motive ; and one hot season in the field, with the progressive discovery of the frailties of fellow-missionaries and of the imperfections of younger Churches, was always quite enough to dispel the idea that missionary work has anything to do with romance.

The work of a missionary to-day does not demand any special qualities of heroism. The recent murder of five American missionaries by Indians in Ecuador shows that the missionary may still be exposed to certain risks not shared by his colleagues in Clapham and Tooting, though by way of compensation he is much less likely to be run over by a bus. But this is exceptional. Most missionaries live in civilized surroundings. The drawbacks of climate and tropical disease have largely been conquered by modern scientific methods. Missionary salaries are low ; but the level of clerical stipends in the West is so shockingly inadequate that, where missionary societies are properly organized, the missionary is only slightly, if at all, at a disadvantage, as compared with his brethren who have elected to stay at home.

In spite of vigorous assertions to the contrary by those who have never themselves been missionaries, missionary service does involve sacrifices such as are not involved in any form of service in a man's own country, though these are a little difficult to put into words, and are not such as the missionary candidate imagines to himself in advance. Except for one who is specially gifted linguistically, work carried out in a foreign tongue continues for many years to be three times as exacting as any work carried out in one's own.

Loneliness, lack of companionship and of congenial exercise, can be real trials. But these are superficial things. The more deeply the missionary enters into the life of his adopted country, the more likely he is to find himself striving unto blood against the evil that lies hidden behind the non-Christian systems of religion. We have joyfully recognized all that is good in the non-Christian world. It is merely myopic to refuse to recognize the other side. Idolatry, witchcraft, the worship of evil spirits and the seeking of fellowship with them, are terrible and evil things. I do not think that any missionary who has lived really close to the village folk in India or Africa doubts the existence of this unseen, malignant, persistent and almost personal power of evil. There is plenty of evil to be fought against in the West, but there is a difference; somehow in the lands that have once been Christianized the Cross has prevailed against the evil spirits as it has not prevailed in the lands that are yet to be won.

But perhaps the hardest sacrifice of all for the missionary is the certainty that he will become an alien in his own country. The more perfect his identification with the life and the people of the land of his adoption, the less possible will it be for him ever to settle down again contentedly in the civilization in which he has grown up. Probably less than a third of those who start out on a missionary career are able to complete the full term of service. Of those who do, many retire in the land they have served. That has become their home, the air that they most naturally breathe. Of course in all this there is joy and contentment and enrichment; but it is idle to deny the loss that has to be accepted for the sake of the gain.

The missionary vocation can, then, still be presented in terms of sacrifice. It can also be presented in terms of urgent need. To realize this, it is not necessary to look further than the S.P.G. Report for 1955, *Tomorrow is Born Today*, which has just come to hand. The Anglican Archbishop of the West Indies reports : " We began the year in Guiana with two vacancies here and ended it with six. And this takes no account of any possible plan of extension." [1] " There are only three priests in the whole of Tobago now. Soon there may be only two. Not long ago there were six." [2] A quotation from the same report shows that these needs and shortages are not

[1] P. 24. [2] *Ibid.*, p. 29.

due to the failure of the Churches to develop indigenous leadership
and responsibility. A missionary in India reports : " When I first
came to Moradabad close on thirty years ago there were about a
dozen European workers all told. Now, since last May, I am the
only S.P.G. missionary left. This is as it should be and shows that
our Indian workers have been trained to take the responsibility and
that they realize that it is they who are to be leaders of the Indian
Church." [1] Similar quotations could be multiplied from the reports
of missionary societies and of independent Churches all over the
world. In many areas, if the indigenous workers could be strengthened by doubling the numbers of their foreign allies, it would still
be possible only to touch the fringe of the work that is waiting to
be done.

We are still, however, on the periphery of the missionary challenge. That remains, where Carey firmly planted it 170 years ago,
in the central concept of the Kingdom of Christ. Christ has a
Kingdom. That Kingdom is to be proclaimed to the uttermost
parts of the earth. It is not being proclaimed to the uttermost
parts of the earth. Therefore *Dieu a besoin des hommes*, God has
need of men. Acceptance of the missionary vocation should never,
any more than conversion, be an emotional experience. It is rather
the painful, and perhaps almost unwilling, acceptance of the last
term in a train of logical reasoning, which leads remorselessly to a
single conclusion. A human voice may set the process of thought
in motion. It is only the Holy Spirit who can lead it to its proper
conclusion.

We shall never present the idea of the world-wide Church and
its claims convincingly to the younger generation unless we can
ourselves recover the sense that this is a world and a time in which
great things are yet to be done, until we can say with Rupert Brooke,
" Now God be thanked who has matched us with His hour." It
is this sense that is on the whole so sadly lacking in the Churches ;
the miasma of dejection has spread far and wide. When we look
at the mountainous difficulties, it is not surprising that this is so.
If we look away to God and to the rock whence we were hewn, the
aspect of things is surprisingly different. What is the situation of
the Church to-day ? We look out on disobedient Churches and an
unfinished task. What of the past ? It can be summed up in two

[1] *Ibid.*, p. 15.

phrases. It is the history of disobedient Churches and of an unfinished task. And yet God has used even those disobedient Churches
to do great things, and has brought into being a universal Church.
Missionaries have on the whole been a feeble folk, not very wise,
not very holy, not very patient. They have broken most of the
commandments and fallen into every conceivable mistake. And yet
God has used their weakness to bring into existence a universal
Church. Missionary societies and Churches have run their affairs
in a way that would have reduced any ordinary business firm to
bankruptcy in a year. They have tolerated rivalry, overlapping,
waste and imprudence. And yet God has taken them up, with all
their follies, into His service for the creation of a universal Church.
Converts have been terribly disappointing. Some have lapsed,
others have grown arrogant and unusable, the majority have sunk
down all too quickly into spiritual mediocrity. And yet, with all
their failures, they have been God's front line for the winning of a
universal Church. And so it goes on.

Bad as we are, we may at least be thankful that there is no reason
to suppose that we are worse than our predecessors. Foolish as
we are, it is even possible that we have learned a little wisdom from
their folly. And there is no reason whatever to suppose that God is
incapable of doing to-day what He has done in the past, and going
forward, through our weakness, our blindness and our incompetence,
in His purpose of winning for Himself a universal Church.

It has been my privilege to be closely associated since 1948 with
the building of *Agape*, the now famous Christian youth centre in
the Italian Alps. To have lived through these years is to have become
accustomed to moving in the world of miracle. Ten years ago
Tullio Vinay looked up at a very ordinary steep Alpine slope, and
saw in vision a group of graceful and dignified buildings. A small
and weak Church, no money, an unknown man—and faith in the
promises of God. To-day the buildings are there—all built by
strength of arm and shoulder, with scarcely any mechanical con-
trivance—only we the builders know the weight of those stones—
and, in consequence, if you put your hand on a wall at *Agape*, I
think that you can literally feel the love that has gone into the building. That is grand. But over the years I have watched the sacramental meaning of *Agape* for some of those who came to build.
In the early years after the war, many came from broken countries

and with broken hearts. Like Nehemiah's builders, they felt that
" There is much rubbish ", the rubbish of a distracted society and
of a beleaguered civilization, and little hope that anything could be
built for the future. And then, in the physical labour of construc-
tion, they found again the assurance that something could be built.
Perhaps they had only very vague ideas of what they wished to build
in society or in the Church. Not all had found that Jesus is the one
foundation for all true building. But the " We shall build " of the
pioneers of *Agape* was seen to have a wider significance than that
with which it was originally spoken.

The title of the Willingen Report (1952) is *Missions under the
Cross*. Am I right in detecting in that title a certain note of dismay
and disillusionment, as though some strange thing had happened
to us ? Where have missions ever been except " under the Cross " ?
Where else could they be ? That is the only place in which the
Christian is ever safe. The Cross is the place of humiliation and of
judgment ; but it also is the place of refreshment, of enlightenment
and of power.

In the chapel of my old home in India there hangs a reproduction,
left by my predecessor, of Piero della Francesca's famous fresco of
the Resurrection. With his incomparable genius for giving eternity
to a moment, the artist has fixed forever the profound sleep of the
guards and the tranquil solemnity of the Risen Christ. On the left
of the picture all is still winter ; in the right the trees are already
bursting into leaf. Because Christ is risen, we are between those
two worlds. We look out on the dark billows of our world in tempest,
on its desperate disappointments, its anxious calculations, its delusive
hopes. We are already partakers of the new calm world of reconciliation and achievement. The Gospel we bring to the world is
the Gospel of hope because it is the Gospel of the Resurrection.
But that Gospel has power only because the Resurrection is the
Resurrection of the Crucified.

It is as the Crucified that Jesus draws the hearts of men to
Himself. The rendering of Psalm 96 : 10 given in some manuscripts
of the Septuagint is not original, but it is true : " Tell it out among
the heathen that the Lord hath reigned from the tree ". This is
the strangest of all transformations. God has taken that place of
horror and disaster and made it the place of peace. In our darkest
hours of despair, it is to the Cross that we turn to find consolation.

When we are tempted to doubt everything, it is the Cross that tells us plainly that God is love. Bowed down by the sense of failure, we turn to the Cross and receive the grace of forgiveness. When the way is not clear before us, and we hesitate about the vocation of a lifetime, it is the Crucified who says to us, " Follow me ".

INDEX

AFGHANISTAN, 31, 62
Africa—*see also* Church in Africa
" Africanism ", 172
All-Africa Lutheran Conference, 133
and Communism, 102, 190
and democracy, 177
and the Gospel, 30, 162
Islam in, 30, 102, 114, 169, 212
polygamy, 117
unrest in, 169
Agape (youth centre), 222, 223
Allen, Roland, 125, 126, 127, 128
America—*see also* Church in America
and colonialism, 85
and Welfare State, 81
Lutheran Churches, 57, 59
Presbyterian Church, 139, 202
Protestant Episcopal Church, 66, 210
Southern Baptists, 86, 93, 118
Student Volunteer Movement, 161
" the Frontier ", 56–7
American Laymen's Commission of
Enquiry, 150
Andersen, Wilhelm, *quoted*, 151, 164
Aquinas, Thomas, 16
Argentina, 169
Art in primitive society, 97
Arabia, 114
Asirvatham, Eddy, *quoted*, 143
Augustine, 96–7, 98, 198
Azariah, V. S., 36, 128, 129, 141, 142,
164

Bach, J. S., 105
Baptism, 37, 38, 44, 129, 130
Barth, Karl, 106
Basutoland, 118
Batak Church, 31, 115, 117, 138, 164,
215
Belgian Congo, 30, 114, 152
Bhagavad Gītā, 185, 192, 193
Bible
and history, 7
and nature of the Church, 156
and spiritual renewal, 109
exposition, 106–8
renewal of biblical theology, 27
story of the Bible, 49

Bible—*(contd.)*
" the people of a book ", 99–100
training leaders, 63
Black Death, 53, 74
Booth, William, 76
Boxer Rising, 200
Brooke, Rupert, *quoted*, 221
Buddhism, 120, 123, 171, 185, 186, 192,
193, 196, 197
resurgent, 185–7
World Council of Buddhism, 186
Young Men's Buddhist Association,
187
Bunyan, John, 174
Burma, 114, 168, 171, 172, 185
Bushnell, Horace, *quoted*, 39–40, 41
Butler Act, 106

Calvin, John, 18, 175
Cambridgeshire Syllabus of Religious
Instruction, 108
Carey, William, 200, 221
Celebes, 115
Celsus, 13
Ceylon, 24, 87, 169, 171, 185, 187
Chester Beatty papyrus, 50
Chiang Kai Shek, 156, 168
China, 8, 94, 126–7, 136, 150, 156, 168,
170, 185, 200. *See also* Church in
China
Church—*see also* Younger Churches
and Communism, 26, 79, 80, 156
and home, 38 *et seq.*
and Kingdom of God, 10–13, 20, 21,
24, 27, 33
and missionary calling, 23, 24, 32,
137, 152, 219
and non-Christian faiths, 190 *et seq.*
and population, 53 *et seq.*
and Sacraments, 19, 34, 37, 38, 64–5,
66, 126, 129–30
and State, 69 *et seq.*, 86, 95, 183
in Africa, 31, 47, 67, 89, 116, 117,
118, 130–1, 133, 152, 172
in America, 39, 40, 56–7, 59, 80, 86,
139, 202
in Canada, 54, 205
in China, 8, 94, 126, 136, 170

Church—(contd.)
  in Hungary, 79–80
  in India, 36, 55, 60–5, 91, 114,
    115–16, 119, 121–3, 128–9, 182,
    194, 205
  in Indonesia, 114, 115
  in Pacific, 164
  in Russia, 104
  in Sumatra, 31, 115, 117, 138, 164
  in Uganda, 31, 36, 89, 113, 147
  Chalcedon Council, 15
  " Churches of Believers ", 37
  Constantinople Council, 8
  in Feudal Age, 73, 74, 77
  in industrial areas, 55
  in rural areas, 54
  in the New Testament, 8 et seq., 17,
    27
  lay ministry, 65–8, 129, 216 et seq.
  Nicea Council, 8
  unity, 201 et seq.
  witness of Israel, 28, 32
  world-wide witness, 17, 20, 23, 32,
    91, 160, 161, 165, 191, 193, 202–3,
    221
Church of India, Burma and Ceylon,
  91
Church of South India, 62, 63, 92, 164
Church of Sweden, 138
Church Missionary Society, 166, 215
Clark, G. R. Kitson, quoted, 178–9
Colet, John, 53
Colombia, 169
Colonialism, 85 et seq., 168
Communism, 26, 78–9, 86, 102, 104,
    126, 127, 130, 156, 168, 170, 175,
    176, 190–1, 195, 197
Confirmation, 37–8, 130
Conversion, 37, 39 et seq., 42, 44, 45–6,
    50, 107, 123, 146, 194
Cook, G. H., quoted, 98
Coulson, C. A., 106
Creoles, 166

Dante, 97–9
Dead Sea Scrolls, 50
Democracy, 175–8
Devanandan, P. D., quoted, 194, 195
Diaspora, Christian, 31, 32, 59–60
  Jewish, 28, 29, 125
Dombois, Hans, quoted, 23

East Africa, 85, 95
Eastern Churches, 25, 26

Edinburgh Conference, 1910, 146 et
    seq., 201
Egypt, 156, 187
Eisenhower, President, quoted, 172
Eliot, T. S., 105
Eutyches, 14
Evangelical Revival, 100, 217
Evangelism, 103, 152, 162, 173, 179,
    181, 194, 195
Evangelization of the world in this
    generation, 146, 148, 152, 162
Evanston Assembly, 201
Existentialists, 101
" Expansionism ", 149

Federation of German Evangelical
    Churches, 91
Florovsky, George, 91
France—Protestantism, 59–60
French Revolution, 75
Fry, Christopher, 105
Fry, Franklin Clark, quoted, 180

Gandhi, 90, 168, 175, 192
Germany, 91, 104, 201
Gold Coast, 87, 88, 118, 181
Graham, Billy, 103, 144, 214
Green, John Richard, 99

Hardy, Thomas, 100
Heim, Karl, 106
Hinduism, 176, 185, 187, 194–6
  and Christian worship, 119–20
  Mahasabba, the, 170
  Rashtriya Swayam Sevak Sangh, the,
    171
  revival, 184–5
Hoekendijk, J. C., 22, 23, 156, 159,
    quoted, 21
Holy Communion, 34, 64, 65, 66, 99
Hoste, D. E., 142
Hromadka, J. L., quoted, 80
Hsi, Pastor, 142

India, passim. See also Hinduism and
    Church in India
  National Christian Council of India,
    90
Indonesia, 86, 114, 115, 123, 164, 168,
    169, 177, 185, 187
Industrial Revolution, 55–6
Inter-Church Aid, 138, 139, 209, 211
International Missionary Council, 93,
    201, 212

International Review of Missions, 21,
    124, 125, 133, 143
Iran, 124
Iraq, 114
Ireland, 38
Islam, 25, 26, 30, 35–6, 70, 114, 124,
    149, 170, 177, 187–8, 191, 196
    in Africa, 30, 102, 114, 169, 212
    in India, 113, 193
    in Indonesia, 114, 185, 187
    in Pakistan, 171, 187, 188

James, William, 40
Japan, 25, 113, 114, 128, 138, 185, 209
    Church of Christ (Kyodan), 205–7
Jerusalem Conference, 1928, 21, 151–2,
    153, 156
Jews, 28–9, 146, 172
    Diaspora, 28, 29, 125
Jones, Stanley, 20
Jordan, 114
Julian the Apostate, 13
Justin Martyr, 65, 198

Kashmir, 112, 169
Kingdom of God, 10–13, 20, 27, 33, 79
Kingsley, Charles, 76
Koran, 187–90
Korea, 130, 154, 155, 168, 185

Lambeth Conference, Advisory Council
    on Missionary Strategy, 209
Latourette, Kenneth, 8
Laubach, F., 116
Lewis, C. S., *quoted*, 46
Literacy campaigns, 116
Lord's Supper, *see* Holy Communion
Lutheran Churches, 57, 59, 69, 90, 92,
    122, 164, 180, 206
    Lutheran World Federation, 93, 209

Malaya, 168, 209
Manning, Bernard, *quoted*, 26, 107
Marangu, 133, 134, 166, 180
Marxism, 71, 72, 91, 92, 105, 110, 190,
    191
Mau Mau, 169, 214
Maurice, F. D., 76, 78
McGavran, D. A., 120–5
Mende Mission, 167
Miller, W. McE., 124
    quoted, 125
Micklem, Nathaniel, 37
Milton, John, 99, 174
Missionary vocation, 137 *et seq.*, 147
    et seq., 161–2, 163, 219–22

Mohammed Iqbal, 189
Monophysites, 13, 14
More, Thomas, 75
Morrison, Robert, 200
Mott, John R., 146–9
    quoted, 148–9
Muto, Takeshi, *quoted*, 206

Nairne, Alexander, 107
Nationalism, 89 *et seq.*, 130, 142, 170,
    171, 173, 184
Nehru, Pandit, 169, 174, 175
Nestorians, 14
Newbigin, Lesslie, 208
    quoted, 132
Nigeria, 89, 114
Nkrumah, Dr., 88

Overseas Service, 216

Pakistan, 113, 169, 171, 175, 187, 188
Pacific islands, 114, 164
Palestine, 28, 29
Papua, 164
Parker, T. M., *quoted*, 70
Paton, D. M., 126
People's Movements, 120–4
Philippines, 31, 113, 164
Pickett, J. W., 115
Pillai, H. A. K., 198
Pollard, William, 66
Population, 53 *et seq.*
Pratt, S. A. J., *quoted*, 166

Quadrennial S.V.M. Conference, 161
Quiller-Couch, Arthur, 107

Radhakrishnan, S., 174, 184, 185, 196
Rajkumari Amrit Kaur, 177
Raven, C. E., 106
Reformation, 16, 18, 75, 91, 201
Ritual murder, 118
Roman Catholic Church, 10, 38, 43,
    56, 92, 132, 213, 215
    missions, 121, 152, 153, 201, 203
Russia, 25, 35, 73, 80, 85, 86, 104, 136,
    174, 190–1

Salvation Army, 76
Saudi Arabia, 187
Sayyid Amir 'Ali, 189
Schweitzer, Albert, 214
Seventh Day Adventists, 153
Siam, 113

Sierra Leone, 165–7
Smethurst, Arthur F., 49, 106
Smyth, Charles, 99
Sudan, 169
Sudan United Mission, 210
Sumatra, 31, 115, 138, 164, 215
Swiss Federation of Protestant Churches, 92
Syrian Church, 119, 164, 210

Tambaram Conference, 1938, 20, 51, 153
Taylor, Hudson, 210
Tel-el-Amarna letters, 50
Temple, William, 140
    quoted, 45, 152
Thailand, 164, 185
The Messiah, 105
Thomas, A. D., 120
Thomas, M. M., quoted, 182
Tibet, 31, 185
Tilak, N. V., 198
Timor, 115
Togoland, 89
Travancore, 119
Turkish Empire, 35

Uganda, 31, 36, 53, 89, 113, 147
U.S.A.—see America.

Vellore Christian Medical College, 209
Vietnam, 168, 177

Walpole, Robert, 180
Warneck, Gustav, quoted, 149
Warren, Max, quoted, 136, 137, 143, 144, 180, 183

Welfare State, 81–3
    and thrift, 84
Wesley, John, 76, 99, 123
West Africa, 47, 86, 87, 95
West Indies, 220
Westcott, Bishop, 17
Whitby Conference, 1947, 20, 153–6, 163, 202
Wieser, Thomas, quoted, 161
Williams, H. A., quoted, 33
Willingen Conference, 1952, 23, 137, 155, 164
    Report, 223
Wolsey, Cardinal, 75
World Council of Churches, 58, 93, 132, 139, 180, 201, 202, 204, 211
    Evanston Assembly, 1954, 201
    First Assembly, 1948, 155
World Health Organization, 160, 162, 217
World-wide Evangelization Crusade, 153

Younger Churches
    and Church union, 203, 211
    and non-Christian faiths, 191 et seq.
    and political challenge, 177–81
    and self-support, 157–60, 164
    and social responsibility, 84, 179 et seq.
    and the missionary, 112, 122, 125, 129, 132, 135, 136 et seq., 150, 160, 163–5
    evangelistic zeal, 163–5
    " foreignness " and, 119, 120, 143–4
    leadership in, 132–5
    " people's movements ", 120–4